etter Homes and Gardens.

herb
gardening

W9-BLN-525

WILEY

John Wiley & Sons, Inc.

Better Homes and Gardens® Herb Gardening

Contributing Writer: Karen Weir-Jimerson
Contributing Project Editor: Kate Carter Frederick
Contributing Designers: Lori Gould, Sundie Ruppert
Editor, Garden Books: Denny Schrock
Editorial Assistant: Heather Knowles
Contributing Copy Editor: Fran Gardner
Contributing Proofreaders: Terri Fredrickson, Susan Lang
Contributing Indexer: Don Glassman
Photographer: Dean Schoeppner
Contributing Photographers: Norm Aubin, Marty Baldwin, Graham
    Jimerson, Pete Krumhardt, Scott Little, Kritsada Panichgul, David Purdy,
    Denny Schrock, Francis Sullivan

Meredith® Books
Editorial Director: Gregory H. Kayko
Editor in Chief, Garden: Doug Jimerson
Art Director: Tim Alexander
Managing Editor: Doug Kouma
Executive Director, Sales: Ken Zagor
Director, Operations: George A. Susral
Business Director: Janice Croat
Prepress Desktop Specialist: Brian C. Frank
Color Quality Analyst: Tony Hunt

John Wiley & Sons, Inc.
Publisher: Natalie Chapman
Associate Publisher: Jessica Goodman
Executive Editor: Anne Ficklen
Assistant Editors: Charleen Barila, Meaghan McDonnell
Production Director: Diana Cisek
Manufacturing Manager: Tom Hyland

This book is printed on acid-free paper.

Note to Reader: Due to differing conditions, tools, and individual skills,
Meredith Corporation assumes no responsibility for any damages, injuries
suffered, or losses incurred as a result of following the information
published in this book. Before beginning any project, review the
instructions carefully and, if any doubts or questions remain, consult local
experts or authorities. Because codes and regulations vary greatly, you
should always check with authorities to ensure that your project complies
with all applicable local codes and regulations. Always read and observe
all the safety precautions provided by manufacturers of any tools,
equipment, or supplies, and follow all accepted safety procedures.

Better Homes and Gardens® Magazine
Editor in Chief: Gayle Goodson Butler

Meredith National Media Group
President: Tom Harty
Executive Vice President: Doug Olson

Meredith Corporation
President and Chief Executive Officer: Stephen M. Lacy

Recipes tested by the Better Homes and Gardens® Test Kitchen®.

For general information on our other products and services or for
technical support, please contact our Customer Care Department within
the United States at (800) 762-2974, outside the United States at
(317) 572-3993, or fax (317) 572-4002.

Wiley also publishes its books in a variety of electronic formats. Some
content that appears in print may not be available in electronic books. For
more information about Wiley products, visit our web site at www.wiley.com.

Library of Congress Cataloging-in-Publication Data

LOC information available upon request
ISBN: 978-0470-91916-3
Printed in the United States of America

10 9 8 7 6 5 4 3 2 1

table of contents

the wonderful world of herbs

Herbs have been used for centuries to bring health, beauty, fragrance, and other benefits to homes and gardens.

p.6
AN INTRODUCTION TO HERBS
Easy to grow, herbs lend themselves to so many practical purposes they belong in any garden.

p.8
TYPES AND USES
Herbs have myriad uses, including culinary, medicinal, cosmetic, decorative, and aromatic. Learn how herbs can enhance your life.

p.10
NATIVE ROOTS
Herbs offer a passport to a world of flavors. Discover the plants' origins and how they are used in ethnic cuisines.

An introduction to herbs

Herbs have it all—interesting foliage, attractive flowers, and heady scents.

Herbs come in all shapes, sizes, colors, and flavors. They include plants that vary in form from towering trees and spreading shrubs to climbing vines and creeping plants. This diverse plant category has one thing in common: Herbs are the workhorses of the plant world. They play roles in the garden, kitchen, crafts room, and spa as well as having a long history of medicinal use.

Herbs are also easy to grow. Regardless of your climate and herbal interests, you'll find a wide range of species and varieties that complement your garden, excel in containers, and add edible beauty to your landscape. This book will help you discover the ancient and modern secrets of herbs. In the following pages, you'll find everything you need to grow and use these versatile plants.

Types of herbs

Plants are categorized by their life cycle, and herbs fill all three categories: annual, biennial, and perennial.

Annual herbs, such as basil and cilantro, sprout, bloom, produce seed, and die—all in one season. These fast-growing plants are perfect for containers and window boxes, as well as for edging landscapes or flower borders. The more you clip and harvest, the more annual herbs continue to produce—a very profitable arrangement for the gardener and the plant.

Biennial herbs live and grow for two years; the first year the plant produces foliage. It overwinters and comes back the second year to flower and fruit, after which it dies. Biennial herbs include parsley, angelica, and caraway.

Perennial herbs last the longest—some for many years. They are ideal additions to landscapes, garden beds, borders, and containers. Perennial herbs include hardy species, such as oregano and chives, that can survive winters in cold climates. Tender perennials include rosemary and lavender, which return year after year in temperate regions. In general, perennials get bigger and better every year, making them economical as well as low-maintenance planting choices.

Herb plant use

Herb plants are useful from top to bottom. For most species, the leafy green parts of the plant can be used in preparing food or making tea. Dill, rosemary, and thyme are a few examples of leafy herbs commonly used fresh or dried in cooking. Some plants, such as lavender, borage, and bee balm, produce edible or usable flowers. Herbs that produce edible seeds include coriander, caraway, and dill. Herb stems are also employed: Rosemary stems are useful as grilling sticks and sage stems release their fragrance when burned in the fireplace. Chicory and florence fennel are grown for their flavorful roots.

Gardening with herbs

Most herb gardeners appreciate the plants for their versatility. There are herbs to suit any garden, whatever its size and style. Many herbs are adaptable to a wide range of climates. Most herbs require a sunny location, but some species thrive in partial shade. While they come in a wide palette of leaf shapes and textures, most herbs are leafy plants (herbaceous), and they grow in a wide array of hues, from gray to green to blue. Many herbs offer colorful blooming displays, including the showy flowers of lavender, anise hyssop, and bee balm.

Above left: **Feverfew is a perennial herb that grows about 2 feet tall and produces large quantities of small white daisylike flowers with yellow centers.**

Above center: **Lavender is one of the most popular herbs. Used in aromatic sachets, the leaves and flowers keep clothes smelling fresh and also help deter insects.**

Above right: **Basil produces leaves that make flavorful pesto. Harvesting leaves from annual herbs such as this makes them produce more growth.**

Opposite: **A well-positioned herb garden allows you to snip and use herbs every day. A circular herb garden in a sunny spot outside a back door allows easy access.**

Herb types and uses

It was common practice in ancient times to use flowers, stems, leaves, and roots of plants to treat the body.

Most of us are introduced to herbs through food.

What would Italian food be without the flavor of oregano? Can you imagine French dishes sans tarragon or rosemary? And would Thai and Vietnamese dishes taste the same without lemongrass or holy basil? Herbs have had a long history of other uses too. Consider their multitude of talents:

Culinary: Flavor without calories

Ethnic cuisines and a revived interest in locally grown whole foods have introduced a wide variety of herbs to cooks and food fans alike. Fresh and dried herbs offer distinctive flavors that enhance foods in healthful ways. Herbs often top lists of healthy foods because they flavor food without adding empty calories, fat grams, or scads of sodium. That's why people who love natural flavors, as well as those on restricted diets, turn to herbs to add great taste to their food.

Raising herbs for culinary use allows gardeners and chefs to experience herbs at their peak of freshness and to experiment with seasonings that may not be readily available otherwise. Growing culinary herbs provides you with a source of delicacies as well as essentials that can be preserved for year-round staples. Many herb species include varieties that produce different flavors and aromas within the herb's spectrum. For example, thyme comes in many varieties with different flavors. Lemon thyme tastes and smells distinctively different from common thyme. Growing herbs in a kitchen garden or containers allows you to enjoy their freshness and flavors when keeping them within easy reach.

Dying: Natural color changes

For centuries herbs colored our world through yarn and fabric dyes. Natural dyes can be made from various herbs—and from different parts of the plants: leaves, flowers, stems, and roots. Yellow dye is made from chamomile and yarrow. Brown hues can be gotten from comfrey, fennel, and juniper berries. Green dye can be made from rosemary and hyssop. Russets and reds, harder to produce, come from st. johnswort and dandelion root. The most difficult dye colors to create—blue and purple—can be made from hibiscus and violet flowers.

Crafting: Flowers and foliage

Fresh herbs make edible floral arrangements; just set them in the center of a table and clip off tasty leaves and flowers. Dried herbs can be fashioned into wreaths and swags. Sachets blended with the fragrant charms of lavender, scented geranium, and rosemary add fragrance to drawers and closets while keeping insects as bay. Crafters of soaps, lotions, and skin- or hair-care concoctions use herbal essential oils.

Aromatherapy: Reaping the scents

Herbalists use herbal scents in a form of alternative medicine called aromatherapy. Essential oils or pure essences extracted from herbs are used to alter a person's moods, help alleviate physical symptoms, and provide healthful side effects. Essential oils are made from herbs using different methods including steam distillation. There are many practical uses for these essences: in the environment, such as room sprays or sachets for clothing; for inhalation, such as steeping herbs in hot water, then breathing the steam to help alleviate chest congestion; and for direct application, such as herbs used in bath salts, compresses, and massage oils.

The scent of herbs also has repelling qualities. Plants containing phenols, naphthalene, pyrethrum, and citronella are natural insect repellents, keeping flying and crawling pests away from people and possessions. It's no surprise that these same chemical components are part of the pest repellents used today, whether replicated synthetically or derived naturally. Our ancestors used wormwood to deter moths and flies; rue to control Japanese beetles; and tansy to repel moths and ants.

Medicinal: Natural remedies

Herb gardens have long been nature's pharmacy. Ancient physicians turned to native plants to remedy illness and improve health. For every illness, there was an herbal remedy: Insomnia was treated with chamomile; migraine headache sufferers were prescribed feverfew; asthma was assuaged with mullein; and a dose of basil helped nausea subside. Plant parts were brewed into teas and ingested internally, and mashed into poultices that were applied externally. No doubt, this trial-and-error method of treatment resulted in a wide range of effects.

But herbal medicine wasn't a precise science, and some of the herbs that were historically used have now been proven ineffective, baseless, toxic, or even deadly.

TEST GARDEN TIP

Herbs' wild past

In the ancient world, wild-grown herbs were gathered on hillsides and in meadows. Later they were tamed into herb gardens and employed as outdoor spice and medicine cabinets. Flash forward to today: Herbs still play an important role in modern life. If you love flavorful food, wear perfume, use scented lotions or soaps, or drink herbal teas, herbs are as much a part of your life as they were for your ancestors.

Healer beware

The science of *phytotherapy* is the treatment of illnesses with plants or materials derived from plants. Herbalists have been doing this for centuries. But the knowledge needed to use herbs medicinally is complex. Consequently, it is not recommended that you make your own medicines from herbs. Any references to the historic use of a plant in this book should not be construed as medical advice. You can, however, use herbs in a variety of ways that are healthful and restorative. Always take care to test a new herb by using a small quantity, whether in food or applied to the skin. Understanding what herbs do, how they work, and how you react to them is the commonsense way to use them safely.

Native roots

Herbs offer a passport to the plants of the world. Discover where they hail from and how they immigrated to new lands—and new gardens.

Ancient herbalists experimented with the native plants of their regions. They learned about the talents (and possible dangers) of the plants that grew overhead and underfoot. Recipes and remedies were discovered and prescribed using locally available herbs and flowers.

The history of herbs as medicine
Everywhere in the world, herbs were an integral part of human life. Traditional cultures gathered and grew herbs because of their powerful restorative and medicinal uses.

We know that the history of herbs is intertwined with the history of humankind because herbal references are found in early texts from nearly all cultures.

For 6,000 years the traditional medicine of India, ayurveda, has employed herbs such as ginger, pepper, and mustard to help restore balance in the body. Since 2700 BC, traditional Chinese medicine has prescribed herbs such as angelica and ginseng. Traditional Western medicine has its roots in the herbal cures used by the Egyptians, Romans, and Greeks. The father of medicine, the Greek physician Hippocrates, wrote about using medicinal herbs. He said, "Healing is a matter of time, but it is sometimes also a matter of opportunity." Herbs offered that opportunity. In his texts he made reference to restorative and medical uses of rosemary, thyme, mint, fennel, and garlic.

Herbal homelands

Although most herbs today can be grown anywhere (and are!), herbs originally hailed from specific geographic regions. The availability of the native plants contributed to their cultural use. Herbs are indigenous by continent. For example, Europeans used medicinal herbs such as chamomile, licorice, comfrey, and feverfew because these herbs grew wild in the fields, meadows, and forests that surrounded their homes. North American herbal natives include burdock and echinacea. Medicinal herbs from Asia include ginseng and ginkgo. And ginger and garlic, Asian natives, also seasoned and flavored dishes there. South America gave the world cayenne, and Africa produced aloe vera.

The traveling herb trade

Spices and herbs became international citizens of the world thanks to the spice trade. As early as 2000 BC, trade in spices (and some herbs) was prevalent in the Middle East and Asia. In the Middle Ages, the import and export of exclusive spices such as saffron made fortunes. And with the discovery of the New World came the discovery of new spice/herb commodities. As people traveled, so did their herbs of choice. European culinary herbs such as dandelion and mint sailed with colonists to new lands. The Pilgrims brought herbs with them on the Mayflower.

Native to Africa, aloe vera is a popular garden and houseplant, and a common ingredient in healing lotions.

Unusual herb varieties can be bought as seedlings or seeds.

Search the catalogs of seed companies for specialty and regional varieties of herbs for your garden.

Growing a garden of cultures

Population shifts and the increase in world travel have enabled herb lovers today to enjoy a wider array of plants. Specialty herbs, once residents only in native lands, are available to anyone with a little garden space.

Specialty herb seeds are available from a variety of sources that include large seed companies (interested in cashing in on ethnic food trends) and small specialty companies that supply unusual varieties. Some of the rarest varieties can be obtained through seed-saver organizations. In addition, there are herb growers that supply garden centers with ready-to-plant seedlings of common and unusual herbs. There has never been a better time to be an herb gardener. With so many seed and plant choices, you can explore a world of herbs—all from your backyard garden or computer.

our
herbal past

Herb gardens were the grocery stores,
spice cabinets, and pharmacies of our ancestors.

Traditional herb gardens

TEST GARDEN TIP

Redefining weeds

There were no weeds in original herb gardens. All plants had value, even those that are now considered weeds. Some of the modern weeds that gardeners grapple with today, such as thistles, were welcome participants in herb gardens of the past. When planning and planting your herb garden, you might find yourself more liberal in plant selection, perhaps including ones you once considered weeds.

Today anyone with a spot of ground

or a container and bag of potting soil can have an herb garden. But herb gardens didn't use to be so egalitarian. In medieval times, traditional herb gardens were cultivated by the educated and the wealthy. The study of herbs and their powers became a science.

Cloister gardens

In medieval times, herb gardens were tended by monks and called cloister gardens. These gardens were an integral part of the monastery and served as a way to feed the brothers and provide a place of work, solitude, and prayer. Cloister gardens sometimes also provided an income for the monastery. Herbs played a role in making spirit-based drinks that were used as medicines and restoratives.

Benedictine monks in France created the liqueur Benedictine in 1510. This cognac-based drink, originally formulated to treat malaria, is made with fruit peels and more than 25 herbs that include angelica, coriander, fennel, hyssop, tansy, mint, and thyme. Chartreuse, another French herb-based liqueur, has been made by Carthusian monks since the 1740s. This light-green liqueur continues to be made using a secret recipe of more than 130 herbal extracts.

Physic gardens

Gardens cultivated for their healing and restorative powers were called physic gardens. They were, in practice, the first pharmacies. The Chelsea Physic Garden, the oldest surviving garden of its type, was founded in 1673 in London. First called the Apothecaries' Garden, it was a training ground and laboratory for medical apprentices.

Physic gardens weren't created to be pretty. Their aesthetics were driven by practicality and use. Beds were labeled by botanical classification and arranged by area of specialization. For instance, the Chelsea Physic Garden has a pharmaceutical garden that displays plants by specific cures. The oncology bed features numerous anticancer plants including Madagascar periwinkle (*Catharanthus roseus*), a plant that contains alkaloids used in anticancer drugs.

Potager gardens

Kitchen gardens or, as the French call them, *jardins potagers* or potager gardens, were an aesthetic way to raise vegetables, fruits, and flowers. Herbs had their own place in the potager. The Renaissance-era potager could be large or small. The design, as one might see on a large estate, could be elaborate, laid out in geometric patterns with shrubs, flowers, and trees amid the vegetables and herbs.

Above left: **Anise hyssop was used traditionally to relieve coughing. Native Americans used it as a breath freshener.**

Above right: **A potager garden often features walls that protect the garden from weather and grazing animals. The walls also create microclimates that allow more tender plants to grow.**

Opposite: **A knot garden can include herbs and flowers. Here agastache, tricolor sage, basil, and ornamental cabbage surround a bougainvillea standard (tree form).**

Classic herb garden designs

The pleasing symmetry of this knot garden comes from the patterned plantings of lavender, boxwood, germander, and red barberry.

Most herb gardens of the past followed a formal design.

Physic, cloister, potager, and knot gardens were designed for specific uses so the people harvesting the plants would not confuse them. The gardens could be viewed overall as a patterned, symmetrical whole, while individual beds contained herbs designated for specific purposes, such as foods, medicines, or dyes. Squares, rectangles, and circles were standard shapes within the formal garden's designs.

Paths were part of traditional herb garden design—for both utility and symmetry. Pathway materials included small pebbles or gravel, crushed shells, mulched plant material, or low-growing, treadable groundcovers, such as thyme.

Knot gardens

This formal garden concept was established in England during the reign of Queen Elizabeth I, coming into vogue at the time Shakespeare was penning plays. The framework of a knot garden is square or circular. It can be edged with boxwood, germander, lavender, santolina, or other shrubby herbs that are pruned into neat shapes, such as squared edges, pyramids, or rounded mounds. A knot garden may feature multiple beds or compartments within the outer framework.

A knot garden depends on the patterned combination of plants in repeated forms. Plants are set out to follow lines and fill in areas, giving the garden a sense of movement and continuity. The shapes intertwine, which is how the knot garden gets its name.

TEST GARDEN TIP

Edible edging

Use alpine strawberries, curly-leaf parsley, or fast-growing, shrubby 'Spicy Globe' basil for edible edging plants in a knot garden.

How to plant a knot garden

You can plant a knot garden in an afternoon. The plants used in a knot garden may include aromatic, culinary, and ornamental herbs, for example: germander, marjoram, winter savory, thyme, southernwood, purple basil, globe basil, rosemary, and santolina. Choose herbs that create color contrasts. Replace the annuals such as basil each year.

CREATE A SQUARE Measure and mark off the area for a square in a sunny area. Remove sod if present.

MARK A CIRCLE Within the square, mark a circle using a can of spray paint.

PLANT THE EDGES Using plants with contrasting colors, plant the circle first, then the edges of the square.

FILL IN THE GEOMETRIC SHAPED BEDS Plant the interior of the circle. Then plant the triangular bed shapes. Place a potted plant in the center as a focal point.

WATER WELL Water each plant deeply after planting. Spread a 2-inch layer of mulch among plants.

WATCH IT FILL IN Herbs such as lavender and sage grow quickly in hot weather. Trim plants regularly to keep them in shape as they grow.

America's herbal history

Modern herbs are steeped in ancient use.

Step into a health food store or the pharmacy section of your local grocery and you'll find more herbs than in the produce department. As the saying goes, "What's old is new again." It is also said that st. johnswort lifts your spirits, chamomile helps you sleep, and ginkgo improves your memory. Herbs, it seems, are a hot new health trend, even though many of today's remedies have been used for centuries.

Colonial herbal history

Modern herb use started centuries ago. America's herbal pioneers, like their ancient predecessors, gained plant-use knowledge from many sources. The herbs used in the colonial United States had roots in two cultures: settlers' own knowledge of herbs brought with them from England and native herbs introduced to them by Native Americans.

Native Americans shared indigenous herbs, such as sage, sassafras, and tobacco, with the colonists. In 1672, John Josselyn published *New England's Rarities Discovered*, a book that resulted from eight years of herbal research into Native Americans' use of plants. Throughout New England, housewives kept kitchen gardens that fed their families and produced herbs for seasonings, food processing, medicines, and household chores, such as cleaning and dying fibers. A kitchen garden was a way to be self-sufficient in a new land.

Bartram's Garden in Philadelphia is the oldest botanical garden in the United States. The living museum of plants includes a kitchen garden with medicinal and culinary herbs cultivated in the 18th century and growing there now.

America's oldest botanical garden

America's oldest living botanical garden, located in Philadelphia, was created by John Bartram in 1728. Bartram, a Quaker farmer, included varieties from old-world apothecary gardens as well as new plants that were native to North America. New-world herbs included bee balm (*Monarda didyma*), black snakeroot (*Cimicifuga racemosa*), and American ginseng (*Panax quinquefolius*). Today Bartram's Garden is a living museum and garden where you can follow the steps of his famous visitors, such as Thomas Jefferson and Benjamin Franklin. It features various theme gardens, including a kitchen garden with raised beds of herbs and vegetables. Like the kitchen gardens of its time, the herbs grown in Bartram's Garden have culinary, medicinal, and household uses.

The science of herbs

In the early 19th century, scientists became able to chemically analyze plants. Understanding herbs and extracting their properties led to the discovery of plants' active ingredients. Eventually scientists learned to modify plant ingredients, making their own version of plant compounds. Thus, modern drugs replaced herbal remedies—at least in the United States. According to the World Health Organization, 80 percent of the worldwide population still uses herbal medicines. The high cost of prescription drugs, coupled with a renewed interest in natural remedies, has increased medicinal herbal use in the United States.

TEST GARDEN TIP

Garden ideas

You do not have to be a garden or landscape designer to create a beautiful herb garden. Gather design ideas from books, magazines, garden tours, and historic herb gardens.

An especially fragrant English lavender hybrid is *Lavandula ×intermedia* 'Provence'.

What's in a name? Many herbs still bear common names that tell the story of their past use: lungwort was used to treat pulmonary infections; feverfew treated fevers or head ailments; and soapwort was used to clean household items.

The Latin name also reveals a plant's story: The botanical name of an herb consists of two parts: a genus and a species. This naming system was invented by Carl Linnaeus, a Swedish botanist and zoologist who is known as the father of modern taxonomy. The naming system is the same for all living things. For example, the genus and species for humans is *Homo sapiens*.

Here's how it works: The genus is a closely related group. The name always begins with a capital letter and is written in italics. The second part of a plant name, the species, is written after the genus and is also italicized. For example, *Lavandula* is the genus of lavender. *Lavandula* has dozens of species. *Lavandula angustifolia* is English lavender, *Lavandula stoechas* is Spanish lavender, *Lavandula dentata* is French lavender, and *Lavandula lanata* is woolly lavender. These species reflect similarities to the genus *Lavandula* but bear distinct differences—enough to make each an identifiably different plant.

A species can be further divided into varieties (also called cultivars or cultivated varieties). These are plants created through natural mutation, plant selection by breeders, or hybridization. Cultivars of lavender include 'Provence', 'Hidcote', and 'Silver Cross'.

For easy reading, plants are listed by their common name throughout most of this book. But in the encyclopedia, the full botanical name for each plant is also used, to help you find the same plant at the garden center.

our herbal present

Herbs are a versatile group of plants that can enhance nearly any part of a garden or yard with their diverse talents and charms.

p.22
HERBS IN CONTEMPORARY GARDENS
Learn how to choose the right plants for your herb garden, and get to know the ideal conditions for your favorite plants.

p.26
HERBS IN THE LANDSCAPE
Add herbs to your landscape plans and partake in an exciting new trend: edible landscaping. Mix herbs into flowerbeds and enjoy flavor and fragrance in every corner of your yard.

p.30
HERBS IN SURPRISING PLACES
Create herbal delights anywhere in your garden: in containers, in window boxes, between stepping-stones in pathways, and more.

Herbs in contemporary gardens

Modern herb gardening is all about you as a gardener

and a lover (and user) of herbs. Unlike herb gardeners of the past centuries, you can grow herbs as a supplement to a natural lifestyle and not depend on them for medicines and household products. Herbs can enhance your life rather than sustain it. Nothing says you have to plant every herb in this book. Instead, create an herb garden that reflects your lifestyle, your penchant for flowers, and your hobbies that include any of herbs' many facets, from preserving food to crafting.

Go formal or casual

An herb garden can be aesthetic, utilitarian, or both. You can follow a traditional herb garden plan that is highly organized, symmetrical, and even historical, including plants from a specific era or theme (such as a Shakespeare or Biblical herb garden). You can adopt a more utilitarian approach and plant a kitchen garden where herbs rub shoulders with vegetables and fruits. Herbs can easily be grown in containers—alone or in combination with other plants. By all means, add herbs to flower

Modern herb gardens can feature traditional elements such as topiary and organized raised beds.

gardens as planting partners with perennials and annuals. Tuck them into rock gardens or crevices in walls, or amid the paving stones or bricks in a pathway. Attract butterflies, bees, and hummingbirds to your yard with an herb garden made to sustain them. That's the beauty of modern herb gardening: There's no right or wrong way to do it. Whatever your goal—fresh herbs, dried herbs, herbs for cocktails or creative projects—you can plan and plant an herb garden that will fulfill your needs.

Your herb garden design

Think about size. Although herbs are a fairly easy-care group of plants, you should avoid committing yourself to a garden you can't maintain—one that is either too large or too complicated. Choose herbs that appeal to you based on their appearance and how you will use them. Fit planting, maintenance, and harvesting into your daily life.

Let your palate guide you

If you love Italian cuisine, pack your herb garden with the traditional herbs essential to the recipes: basil, oregano, rosemary, and fennel. If your family likes to spice it up with south-of-the-border dishes, plant hot peppers, cilantro, and Mexican oregano. If you want to raise fresh, organic herbs for teas, plant chamomile, bee balm, and mint. And if crafting is your hobby, plant herbs that you can use dried or fresh to make wreaths and sachets—lavender, artemisia, and roses.

TEST
GARDEN
TIP
Your nose knows too

Fragrance is a big draw for herb fanciers. Herbs that release their perfume with a simple touch include scented geraniums, mint, and rosemary. Even if you never harvest a leaf, flower, or stem, a scented herb garden can be a place of peace for you at the end of a long day. Just sitting amid the fragrances of an herb garden provides powerful relief from stress.

Left: **Add herbs to your garden for their textural and color appeal. Gray-leaved lavender, two-tone sage, and small-leaved thyme add three levels of texture as well as subtle color variations. Planting herbs in mass heightens the appeal.**

Below: **Lavender, rose, mint, and rosemary begin the list of fragrant plants most useful for homemade bath salts and other delightful concoctions.**

Growing your herb garden

Most herbs are so easy to grow

that they'll thrive without much attention. But they do have some preferences for light, water, and soil. Given adequate conditions, the plants will allow you to enjoy their charms with little tending.

The right light—sun!

Most herbs are sun lovers, requiring about six to eight hours of light a day. This allows them to grow vigorously and produce ample leaves, flowers, and seeds for harvest. There are some herbs, such as mint and sweet woodruff, that thrive in shady locations.

Well-draining soil

Site your herb beds in an area with well-draining soil. If the soil doesn't drain well, work in organic material such as compost, chopped leaves, and other natural amendments. Herbs that sit in soggy soil may succumb to root rot and fail to thrive. If your soil is too difficult to amend (such as heavy clay), build raised beds and add custom-blended soil (a mix of organic top soil and compost works well). Or plant your herbs in containers.

Annual herbs generally like richer soil with lots of moisture to help in leaf development. Leafy annuals such as basil and cilantro are perfect planting companions with vegetables, which are also annuals and need more moisture for fruit development. That's why you'll find basil and tomatoes planted together, or summer savory paired with green beans.

Pests aren't a worry

Keeping any plant healthy is one of the best ways to help protect it from pests and disease. Even so, most herbs aren't bugged by insects. This is because herbs have a natural immunity against insect infestations. The concentration of essential oils that makes the plants flavorful and fragrant also protects herbs from most insect attacks. Those same qualities are also why many herbal compounds are used as insect repellents.

Above: **New materials offer herb gardeners a variety of options. A raised bed, made with commerically available interlocking wall stone, makes for easy and long-lasting construction.**

Opposite, top: **Most herbs do best in well-drained soil. If your soil is too sandy, add organic matter. Clay soil is dense and drains slowly; amend it with coarse sand, perlite, and organic matter.**

The presence of herbs in the garden also helps repel insects that may be interested in other plants. This is why herbs make excellent companion plants for vegetable and flower gardens. Herbs can benefit the garden in several ways: they can deter bad insects, attract good insects, and enhance the flavors of the plants growing around them. For example, dill helps repel squash bugs while attracting important pollinating insects such as honeybees. Garlic, leeks, and onions stave off aphids from attaching themselves to surrounding plants.

Some apparent pests are, on closer examination, insects that you may want to welcome. For example, parsley, and fennel are host plants for the larvae of butterflies such as monarchs and swallowtails. If you want to encourage a healthy, wildlife-friendly garden, plant extras of these plants so you can allow these caterpillars to make themselves at home.

The easiest of the easy These herbs require little upkeep. Just plant them and wait for an abundance at harvest time.

ANNUALS

BASIL
Plants produce aromatic, flavorful leaves. Pinch back flowerheads to produce more leaves.

PARSLEY
Flat- or curly-leaf varieties are delicious used fresh or in cooking.

DILL
Thin, ferny leaves add fresh flavor to soups, salads, and fish.

CILANTRO
Harvest early and often before hot weather makes this annual bolt (develop seeds).

SCENTED GERANIUMS
Grown as annuals in cold climates, the aromatic plants suit Zone 8–11 gardens as perennials.

PERENNIALS

SAGE
The broad gray-green leaves of this drought-tolerant plant add to almost any garden.

THYME
The upright or creeping plants feature tiny, aromatic leaves and flowers.

CHIVES
Clip the young tender stems for use in cooking. The spring blooms are edible too.

MINT
Available in a wide range of flavors—spearmint, peppermint, apple mint—it's great for summer drinks.

FEVERFEW
Two-foot-tall plants offer finely cut foliage and daisylike flowers.

Herbs in the landscape

When it comes to herb gardening, think out of the bed. While it's tempting to put all your herbs together in one bed, they do nicely in other spots in the landscape. Herbs are versatile plants that can enhance a variety of landscape options.

Rock gardens

A rock garden is a handsome solution to several challenging landscape problems, such as eroding slopes, difficult-to-mow areas, and awkward grade changes. And since most herbs love hot, sunny locations and well-draining soil, they are good candidates for sunny-sited rock gardens. If you have a rocky slope in your yard, you can create a low-maintenance, natural-looking garden by adding herbs. (If you don't have a rocky area, you can create one by terracing with stone or making an outcropping of large and small rocks.) The nature of rock gardens—and the associated rocky and sandy soil that surround them—are exactly the venue in which herbs excel. Lean-soil lovers include marjoram, rosemary, and winter savory. Ground-hugging forms of herbs suit rock gardens. Try prostrate rosemary, or creeping varieties of thyme, oregano, and chamomile.

Adding herbs to a rock garden is easy. Using a narrow trowel, dig down into the crevices between the stones and, if there is enough soil, tuck in an herb. If no soil exists for a plant to get a roothold (even the scrappiest herbs need soil), add a couple trowelfuls of topsoil to create a planting pocket.

A stacked stone wall provides nooks and crannies for water to drain from the soil, as well as planting pockets for herbs, including thyme, lavender, and rue.

The stones in an herb garden can help spotlight a singular herb; a backdrop of rock helps define the plant's shape, leaf texture, or flower in the way a stage highlights a performer. Rock gardens can also accentuate and show off a plant's growth habit. For example, creeping rosemary looks more striking tumbling over stones than scrambling across flat ground. Rock gardens also provide a microclimate for plants, with stone heating the ground around plants as well as protecting them from weather extremes such as wind.

Plant vertical: walls

Herb gardens can go vertical when you add planting pockets to stone, brick, or concrete walls. Soften a retaining wall by inserting low-growing herbs into the wall, along the top (and cascading over), and as a frilly skirt at the base. In stone or paver walls, leave planting pockets for thyme, rosemary, catmint, or chamomile. When building a brick wall, leave unmortared gaps where you can tuck in small plants of marjoram, oregano, lavender, and thyme. Shrubby herbs that are native to the Mediterranean excel in wall pockets because they grow in loose, dry, stony conditions.

TEST GARDEN TIP

Walk this way

Pressure releases herbs' fragrance—which makes them ideal as underfoot plant selections. Thyme, chamomile, and Corsican mint can take a certain amount of foot traffic. Chamomile and woolly thyme tolerate slightly drier locations. Corsican mint thrives in damp, shady places.

How to plant a pathway Plant a fragrant path with creeping varieties of thyme, mint, pennyroyal, and chamomile.

1 START
Instead of allowing weeds or turfgrass to creep into the cracks of a stone pathway, plant herbs.

2 WEED
Dig weeds from the path. Amend the soil with compost or topsoil.

3 ADD
Remove plants from nursery pots and tuck the root balls into the planting areas. Add soil if needed.

4 ESTABLISH
Water newly planted herbs and keep the soil damp until they are well rooted. After that, water regularly when soil begins to dry to help plants become established.

5 PRUNE
Within a few months, the plants will fill in between the stepping-stones. Clip them into shape when necessary.

Edible landscaping

Adding herbs to your yard

lets you partake of a delicious trend: edible landscaping. Use herbs to replace turfgrass in lawn areas, and add them to flowerbeds. Herbs can add flavor and fragrance to every corner of your yard.

Go green with an herbal lawn

Low-maintenance herbs can fill in large open areas or hard-to-mow places, and even serve as a lawn replacement. Creeping herbs quickly create a carpet of green foliage that has the added benefit of seasonal blooms. Thyme is a favorite landscaping plant because it's hardy and treadable, and grows into a thick mat of foliage. Planted along pathways or between stepping-stones, thyme comes in various foliage and flower colors. Creeping mint offers a groundcover option that's both vigorous and

fragrant. Mint can even grow in partially shaded locations. This herb is so ambitious that it becomes invasive, so be careful to plant it in a contained area. Rosemary, especially a prostrate variety, is an excellent groundcover that bears blue flowers and gray-green foliage. Chamomile is a hardy perennial that excels in any location—from neutral to alkaline soil and full sun to part shade. It has pretty white, fragrant flowers that bloom from late spring until midsummer; the leaves of Roman chamomile are fragrant too. This low-growing herb is an excellent option for turf replacement. Both economical and eco-friendly, an established herbal lawn reduces the need for fertilizer, watering, and mowing.

Mix herbs with flowers

Herbs with colored or textured leaves make excellent companions in flower gardens.

Above: **Landscaping with herbs—even filling a front yard with the plants—proves possible when you mix a variety of creeping and shrubby herbs. Choose hardy perennials for low maintenance.**

Purple-leaved basil such as 'Red Rubin', variegated sage, and purple-flowering chives are as pretty as any ornamental annual or perennial. The colorful leaves of shiso (*Perilla*) can be used as an edible addition to pots or window boxes. Statuesque and ferny fennel, dill, and angelica add structure to a garden, rubbing shoulders with other tall perennials such as delphiniums, baptisia, and roses. Herbs can also be used as foils in a bed, helping highlight other plants. For example, tansy offers ferny dark green leaves that complement roses when growing near them.

Herbs and their interesting foliage can also be used in bouquets. Parsley, sage, and lemon balm offer beautiful foliage to enhance flowers in arrangements, and they have a long vase life too.

Choose colorful herbal blooms

One of the tenets of good garden design is using color effectively. Although many herbs are predominantly leafy and green, they also come in hues of green, gray, blue, and yellow. Grow herbs for their flowers too. For example, anise hyssop offers spires of pink, purple, or blue blooms that can be used in perennial gardens regardless of their herbal status. 'Golden Jubilee' offers lavender flowers and chartreuse foliage. Varieties of yarrow also feature colorful flower clusters.

Choose a color theme for your garden beds and select herbs that flower in those hues. Plant herbal blooms in cool hues: blue, purple, and green. These flowers create a calming effect and make a garden feel larger. Warm colors—red, orange, and yellow—are dramatic and exciting, and make the space feel smaller, more intimate. Repeat color themes throughout the garden to create a unified look. Aim for two or three colors; too many colors make the plantings feel busy.

Herb flowers
Herbs can play an important and colorful role in your landscape. Color your garden with bright-blooming perennial and annual herbs.

REDS/BLUES/PURPLES

BEE BALM
This prairie native has frilly flowers that bloom in jewel tones of red, pink, purple, and white. Zones 3–10

LAVENDER
Beautiful purple-toned blooms top foliage that exude fragrance on a sunny afternoon. Zones 5–10

BORAGE
Sparkling periwinkle blue blooms dance at the tip of borage's fuzzy stems and leaves. Annual

CHIVES
Chives grace the garden with bright green stems and pinkish-purple pompon blooms. Zones 3–10

CATMINT
Sky blue flowers and silvery foliage look great most of the season. Shear plants for repeat blooms. Zones 3–8

YELLOWS/ORANGES

CALENDULA
Cool-season blooms come in cream, yellow, apricot, or orange. Flowers are edible. Annual

TANSY
Bright yellow, buttonlike flowers appear throughout summer. Zones 3–9

CHAMOMILE
Dainty daisylike blooms with yellows centers and white petals make a fragrant groundcover. Zones 4–9

DILL
Producing yellow, airy umbels, dill's flowerheads beckon butterflies, bees, and other good bugs. Annual

MARIGOLD
Frilly, tightly packed flowers top sturdy plants with elegant dark green foliage. Annual

Herbs in surprising places

Create surprising herbal delights everywhere in your yard:
Creeping low, growing overhead, and everywhere in between, the exuberance of herbs is hard to contain.

Herbs underfoot
Herbs are superstars when used as groundcovers; left to their own devices they grow quickly and fill in open spaces. But many low-growing herbs can also be tapped for their landscape design talents. Inspired by chess- or checkerboards, a gridlike garden design uses commercially available paving stones mixed with herbs such as chamomile, thyme, or oregano. An herb checkerboard garden is ideal for a courtyard, entryway, or pathway. It can even be installed in a children's play area (you could adapt it to a hopscotch design), using some of the more treadable herbal options. To add color to the mix, use paving stones with alternating types of thyme, such as green- and gray-leaved varieties or thymes that bloom in different colors.

Herbs overhead
Within the category of climbing plants, hops are most notable. Some varieties are grown especially for their flowering cones. A golden vining form is especially ornamental.

Green roofs featuring gardens planted with herbs and other plants are an eco-friendly gardening concept being adopted worldwide. Green roofs absorb rainwater, prevent runoff, and control erosion. They also provide habitats for birds, butterflies, and bees, especially in urban areas. Many herbs are ideal for green roofs. Either sow herb seeds or plant small seedlings.

Herb-filled hanging baskets provide other ways to enjoy herbs in places where you'll use them the most: on patios and decks or near the kitchen. Many herbs, especially dwarf and creeping varieties, suit container culture. Plant hanging baskets with plants that meet a specific culinary use: a taste of lemon (planted with lemon thyme, lemon balm, and lemon basil), a salsa container (planted with a hot pepper, cilantro, and lime basil), or a pesto basket (planted with small varieties of basil, cilantro, and parsley—all of which make lovely pestos).

Herbs in containers
Whether you are short on space or just like to have herbs close at hand, containers allow you to grow any kind of herb regardless of your soil conditions or climate. Even if you lack a sunny spot in your yard, you most likely have a sunny spot on a porch or patio where sun-loving herbs can excel.

Tender and tropical plants, such as citrus and pineapple sage, can be grown in pots and taken indoors when the weather turns chilly. Any herb that you can grow in a garden can be grown in a pot. And for some herbs, such as mint, a container may be the best place to grow an invasive plant.

Grow herbs in any type of container—terracotta, concrete, plastic, wood, or iron, for instance. You can even use found objects, such as old teakettles, vintage tins, or wooden dresser drawers. Just make sure there is a drainage hole in the bottom of the container, because herbs don't like wet feet.

Above left: **Curly parsley is an ideal leafy and lush edger that can be clipped for salads and other recipes. Another compact, edible edger is 'Spicy Globe' basil.**

Above center: **Herbs in containers, set right into the landscape, allow you to grow tender perennials such as large rosemaries even when you live in colder climates. You can whisk the plants indoors before frost.**

Above right: **Although you might not think of herbs as candidates for baskets, hanging the plants overhead on porches and patios—near the kitchen and outdoor dining areas—makes delicious sense.**

Opposite: **A checkerboard of dense thyme plants interspersed with concrete stepping-stones makes an unexpected garden entrance.**

Unusual uses
for herbs

Herbs can be used in amazing and artistic ways.

Known for their culinary, aromatherapy, and medicinal uses, herbs also have an artful side.

Clad structures

Landscape designers and creative gardeners have long tapped the talents of herbs to add drama or whimsy to a landscape. For example, creeping herb varieties, such as thyme, mint, oregano, and marjoram, can be used to drape structures. Benches, chairs, and bed frames can be planted with a blanket of herbs to create the soft, tufted look of textural and luxurious fabrics. A bench clad with herbs is not a modern idea, however. Medieval paintings show plant-covered garden benches. And herbs such as thyme—because of the many varieties' low-growing, matting growth habits—make excellent upholstery for outdoor benches.

Topiary

Traditional topiary is the art of shaping plants to take on different forms. Famous topiaries include shrubs pruned into animal shapes or sculpted into undulating patterns. Some herbs, however, are quick-change artists that can magically transform from potted plants into formal sculptures or topiary ducks, chickens, and rabbits.

A popular topiary technique is to prune plants to resemble lollipops or miniature trees: a small round or square topknot of leaves on a thin trunk. The exposed stem grows a thick, woody layer with a barklike appearance. Topiaries of this type are best done with woody, shrubby herbs, such as lavender, rosemary, and santolina. But you can use your imagination and pruning skills to transform other leafy herbs, such as scented geranium or basil, into elegant formal topiaries.

Herbs may also be used to create intricate shapes that are grown through and around a wire frame. Herbs that are easy to train into forms include myrtle and germander. Animal topiaries look great in cottage gardens. Kids also love topiaries because of their fun shapes and hands-on qualities. Topiaries make decorative tabletop accessories in outdoor rooms or sunny indoor spaces.

Opposite: **Low-growing and blooming herbs are excellent choices for rock gardens, stone walls, or, in this case, a dramatic stairway. Blooming thyme is inviting, colorful, and fragrant.**

Artistic herbs Herbs are elevated to higher art when added to structures or containers, or clipped into exotic shapes.

HERBAL BENCH You can decorate a bench or old chair with herbs, creating a living cushion. For example, stacked stone forms the base for a bench and crevices filled with soil hold plantings of creeping herbs. Thyme and chamomile take root easily, covering the seat and spilling over the sides. Sitting on the bench releases the herbs' fragrances.

TABLETOP DECORATIVE HERBS A formal herb garden in miniature, swirling mini-labyrinth, or tiny checkerboard—all these tabletop marvels can be made using small herb plants. Start with a low bowl with adequate drainage. You can draw a design ahead of time, incorporating stones, creeping herbs, and focal points. The result: small gardens, tiny landscapes, and fragrant dioramas—a whole world within a bowl.

TERRIFIC TOPIARIES Some herbs can be clipped and sculpted into topiary forms. Rosemary, thyme, oregano, myrtle, and lavender can be pruned into geometric shapes (circles, squares, triangles) or animal forms (rabbits, dogs, chickens). These whimsically shaped plants take on another life in the garden and window boxes as growing sculptures.

design & grow an herb garden

Regardless of your yard and garden space, you can have an herb garden—from large formal plans to handy mini gardens in containers.

p.**36**
TRADITIONAL GARDEN PLANS
Circles, squares, and symmetry are the design hallmarks of historic and classic herb gardens.

p.**42**
CONTEMPORARY GARDEN PLANS
Raised beds and undulating borders make modern herb gardening beautiful, easy, and adaptable to any yard.

p.**48**
CONTAINER GARDEN PLANS
Patio herb gardens are easy to plant and a snap to maintain. Best of all, they provide easy access to fresh-cut herbs.

Celtic cross herb garden

Fragrant and culinary herbs, interplanted with flowers such as roses and cosmos, create a bountiful garden that's beautiful to behold from spring through autumn.

Inspired by the iconography of the Celts depicted in the stone walkway, this garden features easy-to-harvest beds with a mix of savory and scented herbs.

Ancient Celts populated what are now Great Britain and Ireland. Mysterious and magical, the Celts are associated with ancient romantic myths, brave and fierce warriors, cunning wizards, and a connection with otherworldly beings such as fairies.

Although ancient Celts may not have been dedicated herb gardeners, they used herbs for savory and medicinal purposes. Druids were skilled in the study of plants and employed herbs to make teas, salves, and tinctures, as well as potions and poisons. Herbs that were commonly used in Celtic times include some of the same herbs planted today: dill, juniper, lavender, mint, yarrow, valerian, and caraway.

A Celtic-style garden features a series of curved shapes and circles. A bird's-eye view of this garden shows a Celtic cross, an iconic shape that combines a cross with a ring. In the modern world, this symbol, used throughout the British Isles, denotes an association with all things Celtic; and it's a popular motif used in garden decor.

Traditional gardens are symmetrical and in many cases employ a central focal point. In this plan, a container planted with pineapple guava sits at the center of the garden. Although this garden is a picture of symmetry, the plantings do not mirror one another.

PLANT LIST

- **A.** **72 Alpine strawberries** (*Fragaria vesca*) Zones 4–9
- **B.** **16 Calendulas** (*Calendula officinalis*) Annual
- **C.** **2 Rosemaries** (*Rosmarinus officinalis*) Zones 7–10
- **D.** **10 Lavenders** (*Lavandula angustifolia*) Zones 5–10
- **E.** **1 French tarragon** (*Artemisia dracunculus*) Zones 5–9
- **F.** **3 Borages** (*Borago officinalis*) Annual
- **G.** **4 Italian basils** (*Ocimum basilicum* 'Genovese') Annual
- **H.** **5 Lemon basils** (*Ocimum ×citriodorum*) Annual
- **I.** **3 Sunflowers** (*Helianthus annuus*) Annual
- **J.** **19 Musk strawberries** (*Fragaria moschata*) Zones 6–9
- **K.** **1 Chives** (*Allium schoenoprasum*) Zones 3–10
- **L.** **1 Lovage** (*Levisticum officinale*) Zones 3–9
- **M.** **7 Dills** (*Anethum graveolens*) Annual
- **N.** **4 Sages** (*Salvia officinalis*) Zones 4–10
- **O.** **63 Tall cosmos** (*Cosmos bipinnatus*) Annual
- **P.** **3 Bay laurels** (*Laurus nobilis*) Zones 8–11
- **Q.** **12 Wooly thymes** (*Thymus pseudolanuginosus*) Zones 4–9

Each square = 1 foot

TEST GARDEN TIP

Herbs are a frugal choice

Regardless of how you get herbs—sown from seed, raised from cuttings, or purchased as prestarted plants— they generally are not very costly. Large herbs, some of which are sold in gallon containers, or those that are raised in a special way, such as topiary rosemary, may be pricier. Generally speaking, herbs are inexpensive plants. A seed pack costs a couple bucks. Seedlings may cost about the same per plant.

Knot garden

Weave a classic knot garden with low boxwood edging and then fill it with assorted herbs and flowers.

Since medieval times, knot gardens have been prized

in landscapes for their elegant lines and trim appearance. And in modern times they can be an oasis of order in the landscape.

Knot gardens can be quite elaborate, with low edges of different-color foliage creating an interwoven pattern. Or they can be simple, like the knot garden here. Its straightforward design makes it easier to achieve, lay out, and maintain.

Follow this pattern exactly or alter it to better fit your own yard and personal style. The planting plan includes excellent suggestions

for filling the shapes but you may substitute freely. Include more colorful annuals, herbs, or perennials to avoid replanting each year. Just be sure to use small plants that have a tidy growing habit to keep the neat, sharp appearance crucial to a well-tended knot garden.

Also select plants that contrast with the emerald green foliage of the boxwood hedges so the design stands out. Choose brightly colored flowers or plants with contrasting foliage in silvery grays, yellow-greens, or deep purples.

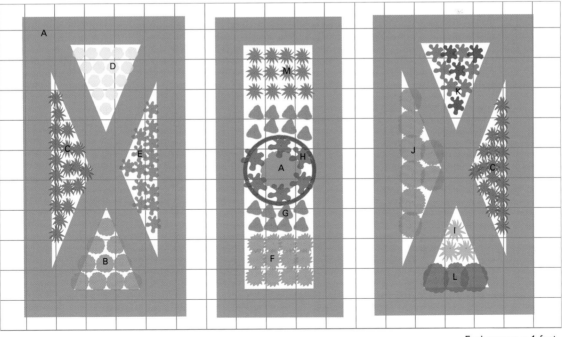

PLANT LIST

A. **136 Dwarf boxwoods** (*Buxus* 'Green Gem') Zones 4–9*

B. **10 Lantanas** (*Lantana*) Zones 9–11, annual elsewhere

C. **38 Zinnias** (*Zinnia*) Annual

D. **15 Vincas** (*Catharanthus roseus*) Zones 9–11, annual elsewhere

E. **14 Santolinas:** (*Santolina chamaecyparissus*) Zones 6–10

F. **12 Golden sages** (*Salvia officinalis* 'Icterina') Zones 5–11

G. **16 Common sages** (*Saliva officinalis*) Zones 4–10

H. **6 Petunias** (*Petunia ×hybrida*) Annual

I. **3 Chives** (*Allium schoenoprasum*) Zones 3–10

J. **8 Sorrels** (*Rumex acetosa*) Zones 3–8

K. **10 Mixed sweet and purple basils** (*Ocimum basilicum*) Annual

L. **3 Thymes** (*Thymus*) Zones 5–9

M. **12 Purple variegated sages** (*Salvia officinalis* 'Tricolor') Zones 6–9

* In Zones 4 and 5, wrap in burlap for winter protection.

TEST GARDEN TIP

A quick trim

Formal boxwood edging needs frequent shearing to stay its best. Trim it about four times a year in warm-winter climates; two or three times in colder climates.

Mark your cutting lines with string and stakes, and then use a power hedge trimmer (corded electric models are light and inexpensive) to make quick work of the task.

Each square = 1 foot

Wagon wheel herb garden

Whether you have a large planting space or a small one,

a circular bed is the ideal shape for an herb garden. This multisectioned bed offers enough space to grow ample amounts of your favorite herbs. Plus, a mix of annual and perennial flowers keeps the bed beautiful all summer long.

This raised bed can sit just steps away from your back door and supply you with herbs for spring, summer, and autumn meals. If you plant perennial herbs, such as thyme, oregano, and chives, you won't have to replant every spring—which makes this garden both economical and low maintenance.

Round herb beds are easy to make. Choose a site (make sure it receives at least six to eight hours of sun a day). Figure out approximately where the center of the bed will be, and pound a stake into the ground there, creating a pivot point. Measure a length of string a foot longer than half the size of the bed (for example, if you

want a 6-foot circle, measure off a 4-foot length of string). Tie one end of the string to the post. With a can of spray paint in hand, pull the string taut and walk around a circle at the end of it, painting a circle on the ground.

Each bed in this radial design uses the repetition of a few plant species, which helps to unify the beds. Repeating a dominant color, such as chartreuse, or a broader texture emphasizes the effect and makes the garden feel more cohesive. The rigid geometric shapes and construction of the bed provide a satisfying visual contrast for the loose, relaxed planting.

Adding a brick walkway gives permanent infrastructure to the bed so that it looks beautiful in all seasons. The triangular beds are accessible for planting from both the pathways and outer perimeter.

Opposite: **This easy-to-plant herb garden gets its great structure from a classic circle—with a round water feature as a focal point.**

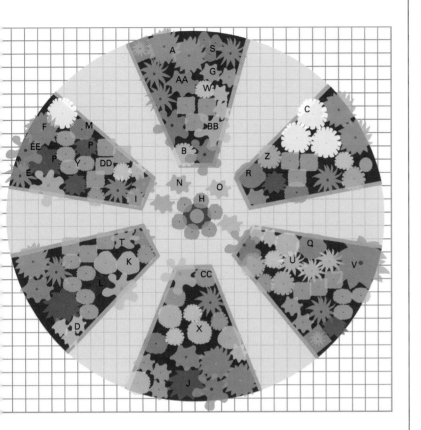

Tea garden

Kick back with a steaming cup of homegrown tea. Herb

tea is naturally decaffeinated and invigorating.

An undulating border packed with tea herbs is a beautiful landscape element as well as a great way to enjoy the restorative benefits of infused herbs. This border fits into a relatively small area and can be adapted to any sunny spot in your yard.

The scented geraniums are grown in lightweight pots, making it easy to move the tender perennials indoors over the winter. Lavender, bee balm, and a rose hip-producing rugosa rose (try 'Frau Dagmar Hartopp' with single-petal pink flowers) stand along the back of the border. Two-foot-tall, easy-care lemon balm makes a delicious and soothing pot of tea. The brewed leaves yield a lemony taste similar to that of lemon verbena. This hardy herb tolerates temperatures to -20°F. Lemon balm also withstands partial shade.

Low-growing alpine strawberries are grouped in front, where you can easily harvest the delicious fruit as well as the leaves, which you can infuse in hot water. Another tea favorite, Roman chamomile, bears flowers that taste and

smell like apples when infused. Chamomile is an age-old sedative and sleep enhancer.

Lavender's gray-green, sweet-smelling leaves make a flavorful and aromatic tea. Pick and dry lavender buds before the flowers open and add to hot water. You can also use these edible blooms in tea cakes and shortbread or as a fragrant addition to a brewed pot of tea.

PLANT LIST

A.	**2 Scented geraniums** (*Pelargonium*) Zones 8–11
B.	**1 Sunset hyssop** (*Agastache rupestris*) Zones 4–9
C.	**2 Lavenders** (*Lavandula angustifolia*) Zones 5–10
D.	**1 Bee balm** (*Monarda didyma*) Zones 3–10
E.	**1 Lemon balm** (*Melissa officinalis*) Zones 4–10
F.	**1 Rugosa rose** (*Rosa rugosa*) Zones 2–9
G.	**6 Roman chamomiles** (*Chamaemelum nobile*) Zones 4–8
H.	**3 Lemon thymes** (*Thymus ×citriodorus*) Zones 5–9
I.	**14 Alpine strawberries** (*Fragaria vesca*) Zones 4–9

The leaves of just-picked herbs such as chamomile and lemon balm may be used fresh to make tea.

SCENTED GERANIUM

SUNSET HYSSOP

LAVENDER

BEE BALM

LEMON BALM

RUGOSA ROSE

ROMAN CHAMOMILE

LEMON THYME

ALPINE STRAWBERRY

TEST GARDEN TIP

Refrigerator iced herb tea

Remember sun tea? Well, you can make herbal tea just as fast in the refrigerator. Clip your favorite herb leaves (or add herbal tea bags). Use about 4 bags for each quart of water. Place water and herbs in a pitcher or sealed jar (canning jars work well) and let them steep in the refrigerator overnight.

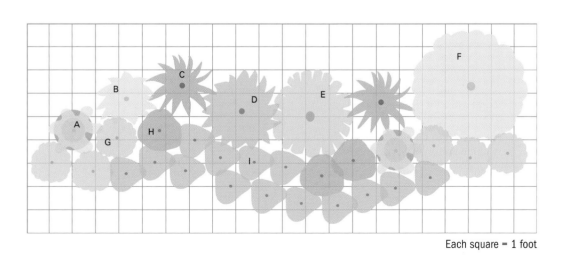

Each square = 1 foot

Raised bed garden

Growing herbs and vegetables together in the same bed is a modern spin on the dooryard herb garden of the past.

Colorful and easy-care, a raised bed garden allows

you to pack herbs and vegetables shoulder to shoulder to maximize space.

A raised bed is an herb gardener's dream space. You assemble a bed, then fill it ideally with amended soil. This soil in a raised bed warms earlier in the spring and drains faster in wet weather. A 4×4-foot square is an easy distance for people to reach the middle from all sides, making it simple to plant, weed, or harvest. Removing weeds is a snap because the soil remains soft and workable from year to year as long as you don't tromp on it.

Locate your herb-and-vegetable garden in a sunny location. Remove any turf, then rake and level the ground. Dress up a pressure-treated wood frame with a coat of exterior-type stain or primer and paint. (Here, a coat of teal stain gives the beds a bright, contemporary look.) Beds go together quickly with precut lumber (most lumber suppliers will cut to your specifications) and aluminum corner connectors.

Position the bed frame and drill in screws to attach the corner connectors. Use an angle square to make sure the sides line up at right angles. Measure diagonally in both directions across the planter bed to make sure the diagonals are of equal length and the frame is square. Eight easy connections later, you have a two-tier bed ready to be filled with soil.

Fill your raised bed with topsoil; the back tier is twice as deep as the front one. Add organic matter, such as compost, to improve the soil and help ensure the plants' success. Mulch to conserve soil moisture and minimize watering.

PLANT LIST

A. **2 Ginger mints** (*Mentha ×gracilis*) Zones 6–9

B. **1 Chives** (*Allium schoenopraesum*) Zones 3–9

C. **2 Stevias** (*Stevia rebaudiana*) Zones 8–11

D. **1 Thai basil** (*Ocimum basilicum* 'Siam Queen') Annual

E. **1 Cinnamon basil** (*Ocimum basilicum* 'Cinnamon') Annual

F. **1 Lemongrass** (*Cymbopogon citratus*) Zones 9–11

G. **1 Broccoli** (*Brassica oleracea*) Annual

H. **2 Hot peppers** (*Capsicum annuum*) Annual

I. **6 Purple basils** (*Ocimum basilicum*) Annual

J. **1 Pineapple sage** (*Salvia elegans*) Zones 8–11

K. **1 Summer squash** (*Cucurbita pepo*) Annual

L. **2 Tomatoes** (*Lycopersicon esculentum*) Annual

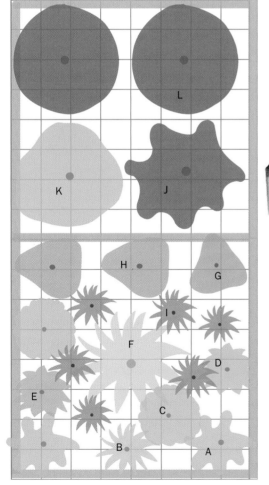

Each square = 6 inches

TEST GARDEN TIP

Rise above soil problems

If you have rocky or clay soil, or your herb bed is too close to a black walnut tree (the leaves and nuts of which cause toxicity in the soil), rise above the challenge with a raised bed. Fill the bed with a mixture of organic topsoil and compost, then plant with ease.

Welcome home garden

When you arrange a cluster of containers
filled with herbs, you get a double delight: You can step out your door to collect herbs while the eyecatching containers garner attention from the street level.

When you think curb appeal, herbs might not come to mind—in part because their charms are often enjoyed most up close. But there's a wide range of bold and colorful herbs that are nothing short of traffic-stopping—especially when planted in a cluster of colorful containers.

To create a grouped container garden resplendent with herb leaves and flowers, all you need is a group of containers tall and small that can be grouped together or strewn along the steps of a front entryway or backyard path. Choose a similar palette of pot colors, such as the Provence-inspired containers *above*, or mix it up with containers of different colors.

Amp up the color by planting showy flowering herbs such as calendula, nasturtium, and chives. Their edible flowers make ideal additions to salads and soups. Or they can be clipped for an impromptu bouquet.

Savory herbs such as thyme, oregano, basil, and rosemary are just a step away; clip container herbs often for recipes, garnishes, and herbal bouquets. Combine textural leaf combinations— such as curly- and flat-leaf parsley—to make visually interesting container plantings that look good even without flower power. Add smaller stature vegetables such as pepper, Swiss chard, and bush-variety summer squash for colorful edibles that look good with herbs.

With mixed plant combinations (or planted solo) herbs in containers make a welcoming— and appetizing—presentation.

Containers allow you to create a temporary garden wherever you live. At the end of the growing season, empty the pots and store them until they're needed again.

PLANT LIST

POT 1

A. **5 Lavenders** (*Lavandula angustifolia* 'Lady') Zones 5–10

POT 2

B. **1 Basil** (*Ocimum basilicum*) Annual

POT 3

C. **1 Calendula** (*Calendula officinalis*) Annual
D. **1 Nasturtium** (*Nasturtium* 'Buttercream') Annual
E. **1 Nasturtium** (*Nasturtium* 'Alaska') Annual

POT 4

F. **1 Flat-leaf parsley** (*Petroselinum neapolitanum*) Zones 5–9
G. **1 Curly leaf parsley** (*Petroselinum crispum*) Zones 5–9
H. **1 Pepper** (*Capsicum annuum* 'Gypsy') Annual

POT 5

I. **1 Meyer lemon** (*Citrus limon* 'Improved Meyer') Zones 9–11
J. **1 Silver thyme** (*Thymus vulgaris* 'Argenteus') Zones 5–9
K. **3 English thymes** (*Thymus vulgaris*) Zones 5–9

POT 6

L. **1 Daylily** (*Hemerocallis*) Zones 3–11
M. **1 Mint** (*Mentha*) Zones 3–10
N. **1 Summer squash** (*Cucurbita* 'Trombetta') Annual

POT 7

O. **1 Swiss chard** (*Beta vulgaris* 'Bright Lights') Annual
P. **1 Greek oregano** (*Origanum vulgare hirtum*) Zones 5–10

POT 8

Q. **4 Marigolds** (*Tagetes*) Annual
D. **1 Nasturtium** (*Nasturtium* 'Buttercream') Annual
R. **1 Sage** (*Salvia officinalis* 'Icterina') Zones 5–11

POT 9

S. **1 Rosemary** (*Rosmarinus officinalis*) Zones 7–10

POT 10

T. **1 Purple sage** (*Salvia officinalis* 'Purpurascens') Zones 5–9
U. **1 Lemon thyme** (*Thymus ×citriodorus*) Zones 5–9
V. **1 Purple basil** (*Ocimum basilicum* 'Purpurascens') Annual
W. **1 English lavender** (*Lavandula angustifolia*) Zones 5–10

POT 11

C. **1 Calendula** (*Calendula officinalis*) Annual
D. **1 Nasturtium** (*Nasturtium* 'Buttercream') Annual
E. **1 Nasturtium** (*Nasturtium* 'Alaska') Annual

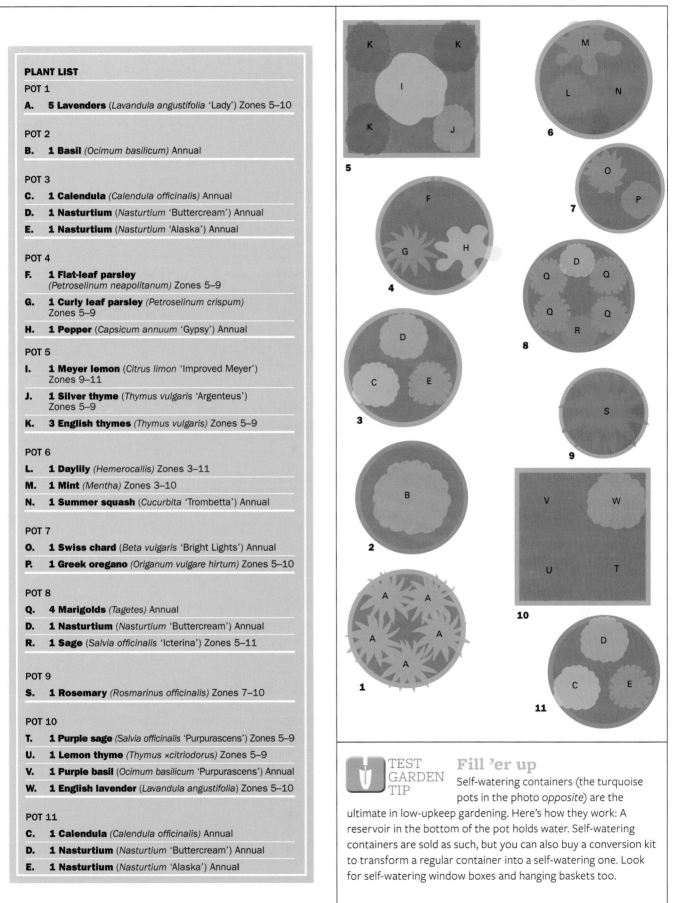

TEST
GARDEN
TIP

Fill 'er up

Self-watering containers (the turquoise pots in the photo *opposite*) are the ultimate in low-upkeep gardening. Here's how they work: A reservoir in the bottom of the pot holds water. Self-watering containers are sold as such, but you can also buy a conversion kit to transform a regular container into a self-watering one. Look for self-watering window boxes and hanging baskets too.

TEST
GARDEN
TIP

Container logic

Herbs benefit from quick-draining conditions, which these porous containers offer. Cast-stone, terra-cotta, and concrete pots are ideal containers for herbs. If you group unglazed pots so their sides are sheltered from the evaporating effects of the sun and wind, you'll be able to water less.

Set in stone

Large cast-stone or concrete planters offer a long-term home for perennial herbs. The thick walls of these heavy-duty containers insulate herb roots from temperature extremes. These hardy perennial herbs can remain in their pots for years in frost-free places.

Essentials

containers: 18×24- to 20×48-inch stone or stonelook pots

light: sun

water: when the soil feels dry

PLANT LIST

Pot 1

A. **1 Garlic chives** (*Allium tuberosum*) Zones 3–10

B. **1 Flat-leaf parsley** (*Petroselinum neopolitanum*) Zones 5–9

C. **1 Tricolor sage** (*Salvia officinalis* 'Tricolor') Zones 6–9

Pot 2

D. **1 Mint** (*Mentha*) such as peppermint Zones 3–8

Pot 3

E. **1 Lemon thyme** (*Thymus* ×*citriodorus*) Zones 5–9

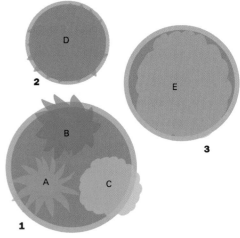

Try these herbs too

Other herbs that can grow with only a few hours of sunlight a day include perilla and any mint variety. Add a layer of mulch over the soil to help conserve moisture. To make containers nearly care free, install a container drip system with a timer.

Easy does it in the shade
Most herbs are sun lovers, but some tolerate shade. Pack these low-maintenance, unfussy herbs into a metal container that will shine on a partially shaded patio or terrace. Transplant perennial herbs into the garden by early fall.

Essentials

container: 18-inch galvanized pot

light: partial sun

water: when soil begins to feel dry

PLANT LIST

A.	**3 Foxgloves** (*Digitalis purpurea*) Zones 4–9
B.	**1 Lemon balm** (*Melissa officinalis*) Zones 4–10
C.	**1 Ginger mint** (*Mentha ×gracilis*) Zones 6–9
D.	**2 Sweet woodruffs** (*Galium odoratum*) Zones 4–9

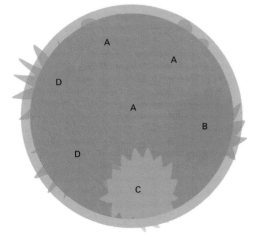

Grow better flavor

Go organic in your herbal window box garden, and you can snip and dine without worry. Herbs don't require fertilizer to grow well. And studies show that most herbs taste better when raised on the dry side. Avoid overwatering.

Tasteful window box

Enjoy the view out your window, then step outside and harvest snips of parsley, basil, and thyme. Tasty herbs make a lush green planter, and edible petals from violas and marigolds add dots and dashes of color. Position an herbal window box so it receives six to eight hours of sunlight a day.

Essentials

container: 48-inch window box

light: sun

water: when soil begins to feel dry

PLANT LIST

A. **4 Flat-leaf parsleys** (*Petroselinum neopolitanum*) Zones 5–9

B. **2 Basils** (*Ocimum basilicum*) Annual

C. **1 Marjoram** (*Origanum majorana*) Zones 8–10

D. **1 Lemon thyme** (*Thymus ×citriodorus*) Zones 5–9

E. **3 Spearmints** (*Mentha spicata*) Zones 4–10

F. **1 Cilantro** (*Coriandrum sativum*) Annual

G. **2 Violas** (*Viola tricolor*) Annual

H. **2 Marigolds** (*Tagetes*) Annual

I. **1 Thyme** (*Thymus*) Zones 4—9

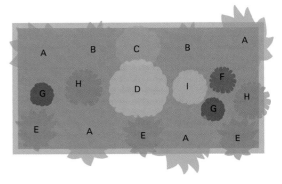

TEST
GARDEN
TIP

**Mint
smorgasbord**
Mix different types of
mint for a sweet culinary
garden: Try chocolate,
peppermint, spearmint,
and variegated types
to make a mint
smorgasbord for drinks
and desserts.

Contain your "excite-mint"
Keep a basket of mint
mixed with lemon balm near outdoor seating areas so you can snip garnishes
for drinks or desserts. Protect the basket by lining it with a sheet of landscape
fabric with added drainage holes.

Essentials
container: 17×11×9-inch
basket
materials: liner (sheet
plastic or moisture-
holding type)
light: part shade
water: keep soil moist

PLANT LIST

A.   **1 Peppermint** (*Mentha ×piperata*) Zones 3–8

B.   **1 Lemon balm** (*Melissa officinalis*) Zone 4–10

C.   **1 Spearmint** (*Mentha spicata*) Zones 4–10

D.   **1 Pineapple mint** (*Mentha suaveolens*
'Variegata') Zones 5–10

TEST GARDEN TIP

Sweeten the deal

Plant an all-sweet centerpiece with mint, chamomile, and sugary stevia for alfresco dessert parties. When the growth of these potted herbs slows, it's time to transplant them into the garden where they will have more room to reach their ultimate size.

Savory centerpiece

A snip-and-eat centerpiece keeps savory herbs, such as chives, rosemary, sage, and basil, where they will stimulate the taste buds as well as the conversation. An herb-packed bowl is as beautiful as it is delicious. Include a pair of scissors with each place setting so guests can snip and savor.

Essentials

container: 16-inch terra-cotta bowl

light: sun

water: when the soil feels dry

PLANT LIST

A.	**1 Chives** (*Allium schoenoprasum*) Zones 3–10
B.	**1 Rosemary** (*Rosmarinus officinalis*) Zones 7–10
C.	**1 Sage** (*Salvia officinalis*) Zones 4–10
D.	**1 Marjoram** (*Origanum majorana*) Zones 8–10
E.	**1 Thyme** (*Thymus vulgaris*) Zones 5–9
F.	**1 Basil** (*Ocimum* 'Spicy Globe') Annual

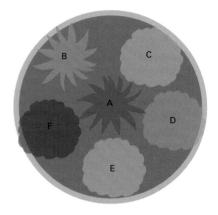

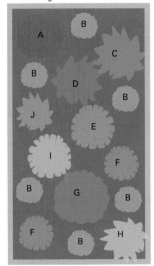

TEST
GARDEN
TIP

Natural pest control

Plants containing pyrethrum and citronella are natural insect repellents. They keep flying and crawling pests at bay. So it's no surprise that these same chemical components are found in the commercial pest repellents used today.

Don't get bugged herb garden
Some herbs have seemingly magical bug-repelling qualities. Standing on a patio or deck, this fragrant garden deters mosquitoes, moths, and ants. Solar lights add practicality.

Essentials
container: 39×16×32-inch
   self-watering planter
light: sun
water: when soil begins
   to feel dry

PLANT LIST

A. **1 Rue** (*Ruta graveolens*) Zones 4–9

B. **6 Marigolds** (*Tagetes*) Annual

C. **1 Southernwood** (*Artemisia abrotanum*)
   Zones 4–10

D. **1 Catnip** (*Nepeta cataria*) Zones 3–9

E. **1 Tansy** (*Tanacetum vulgare*) Zones 3–9

F. **2 Scented geraniums** (*Pelargonium*)
   Zones 9–11

G. **1 Variegated plectranthus** (*Plectranthus coleoides*) Annual

H. **1 Santolina** (*Santolina*) Zones 6–10

I. **1 Feverfew** (*Tanacetum parthenium*) Zones 4–9

J. **1 Variegated sage** (*Salvia* 'Tricolor') Zones 6–9

herbs in every season

Herb lovers can revel in a variety of herbal activities from spring through winter.

p.56
SPRING
Jumpstart the growing season by sowing herb seeds indoors, planning your herb garden, and planting transplants once the weather warms up.

p.70
SUMMER
Herbs love the sultry temperatures of summer that prompt warm-weather annual herbs to take off and produce in abundance.

p.92
FALL
Drying and preserving are autumn activities as the herb garden growing season draws to an end.

p.106
WINTER
Cold temperatures send tender herb indoors. Enjoy these herbs in the winter months as they lend flavor and fragrance to holiday gatherings.

SPRING:
Choosing herbs

Which herbs to select for your garden depends on the growing conditions.

Sunlight, climate (how cold your garden gets in the winter and how hot it gets in the summer), and soil play important roles in the success of the herbs you plant.

Seeing the light (and how to interpret it)
Most herbs are sun lovers, but there are a few herbs that can grow in shaded locations. The range from full sun to full shade is filled with varying degrees of light. Light requirements for plants are expressed in these terms:
Full sun. Herbs that require at least six to eight hours of sun per day.
Part sun. Herbs that need three to six hours of sun per day—preferably in the morning or evening.

Part shade. Herbs that thrive with three to six hours of sun per day, but that require shade during the afternoon, under a tree or near a building. **Full shade.** Herbs that require fewer than three hours of direct sunlight. This describes planting locations that receive filtered light or light shade created by trees or other structures.

Climate considerations

Each herb has the ability to withstand cold and hot temperatures. Temperature ranges are expressed by a hardiness zone. There are 11 zones from Canada to Mexico. Each zone is based on a 10-degree F difference. Once you know your hardiness zone (see the zone map on page 217 to find your zone), you can choose herbs that will thrive and flourish in your zone. The hardiness zone range for all perennial herbs appears on the plant tag (when you buy live plants in nurseries) or on the websites that sell herbs online. Temperature affects the growth and life cycle of herbs—something to consider when you plant. Some herbs, such as dill and cilantro, produce lovely edible leaves in cool weather, but once the weather turns hot, these annuals quickly develop seeds. Many perennial herbs, such as oregano and rosemary, really get growing when the summer weather sets in.

The right soil

For the most part, herbs are not picky when it comes to soil, except when it involves drainage. Most herbs prefer well-draining soil. If your soil is poor-draining or clay, amend it with organic matter (chopped leaves and compost). Test your soil's nutrient levels using directions from a county extension service or a nearby soil laboratory. If the soil pH factor is higher than 7.5, add sulfur; if lower than 6.5, add lime. Boost soil nutrients naturally with amendments. Find organic matter for your garden in a variety of places: Get composted manure from a dairy farm or horse stable. Compost made from collected leaves and grass clippings may be available from your municipal composting program. Purchase bagged products at your local garden center or from online or mail-order sources.

Opposite: **Most perennial and annual herbs do best in a sunny location. For herbs that prefer cooler, shadier spots, plant near a building for protection. Enjoy a long growing season by using cloches and cold frames to protect tender herbs in early spring and late fall.**

TEST GARDEN TIP
Cut back lavender

In the early spring, prune lavender, sage, and other woody herbs when you see new green growth. Prune back to new growth on short varieties; prune up to one-third of taller plants. This keeps plants nicely shaped and encourages new growth.

Frugal gardens: How to grow herbs from seed

Starting herb seeds indoors is easy. You need seed-starting supplies, a warm spot, and a good light source (a south-facing window or grow lights).

GATHER Get the supplies needed for starting herbs indoors, including premoistened soilless seed-starting mix, peat pots, and seeds.

FILL Add seed-starting mix to fill the peat pots or other multicell packs; then level the tops.

SOW Sprinkle several seeds per cell. Cover seeds with seed-starting mix following seed packet instructions.

WATER Gently sprinkle the plantings to avoid washing the seeds out of the mix. Set in a warm, sunny place.

Planting herbs

After you've determined what herbs grow best in your climate,

the next step is buying plants and seeds. Herbs are available from various sources these days: mail order, online, garden centers, grocery stores, farm stores, plant swaps, and herb society plant sales.

Buy healthy plants

There are several things to look for when buying herbs. Take a look at the leaves. Although most herbs aren't bugged by insects or disease, damaged leaves might indicate a problem. Also inspect the root system of the plant—roots that circle the bottom of a pot are a sign that the plant might be rootbound after living in the nursery pot too long. Before planting, gently loosen compressed roots.

Easy planting: Use potting mix

If you have less than optimal soil (remember, herbs like well-draining soil), use an all-purpose

Starting an herb garden from scratch is easy with young herbs. Buy your favorites and combine them in a bed or container. Look for healthy plants that show new growth.

potting mix, especially if you are planting in raised beds or containers. You can buy commercially prepared potting mix or make your own blend. Add together equal parts peat moss, topsoil, compost, perlite, and sand to create a soil mix that's light, retains moisture, and drains well. Since many herbs are indigenous to areas with coarse, sandy soil (think of the Mediterranean), some herbs benefit from having gravel and finely crushed limestone added to the planting hole to facilitate drainage.

Planting container-grown herbs

Herbs are sold in a variety of container sizes: 3- to 4-inch pots hold small plants; perennial herbs may come in larger quart- and gallon-size containers. Regardless of the size of the container or the plant (including your home-raised seedlings), plant herbs in the same way: Dig a hole. Remove the plant from the container by tilting it upside down (yanking the plant out of the pot by grabbing the foliage and pulling risks damaging the plant). Squeeze to loosen it, if necessary. Place the plant in the hole and backfill with soil, tamping gently to remove any air pockets. Water deeply.

Sowing herbs by seed

You can sow many herbs directly into garden soil in spring (or fall in warmer regions). Prepare the planting area by digging in compost and loosening the soil. Use a garden rake to smooth the area. Sow herb seeds according to their packet instructions. Cover seeds with a thin layer of soil, if required. Sprinkle the area with water daily until seeds sprout.

Planting depth

Most herb seedlings or plants do best when their crowns are planted at the same depth as they were in their nursery pots. Dig a hole, then set the herb in the hole. Adjust the planting depth to raise or lower the plant so the crown is even with the top of the hole.

Mulching herbs

Add a 2- to 4-inch layer of mulch (shredded bark, chopped leaves, cocoa shells) between plants to preserve soil moisture and deter weeds. Keep mulch about 2 to 4 inches away from plant stems to allow water and air to reach roots. Water after applying mulch—especially dry mulch. Watering will help hold it in place on windy days.

Planting tender perennial herbs

If you live in a region of the country where the temperatures dip below freezing, you can still grow tender perennial herbs—but you may need to plant them in a container if you want to keep them for next year. Tender perennial herbs such as rosemary and lemon verbena do well in containers in the summer and are easily transported indoors once warm weather is over.

TEST GARDEN TIP

Improve drainage

For plants that require lots of drainage, such as Mediterranean natives lavender and rosemary, toss handfuls of coarse gravel along with crushed limestone into planting holes to improve the soil's drainability.

Divide to make new plants

Many herbs benefit from a spring division. The mother plants are healthier, and you have plants to share.

1 DIG
Use a trowel or spade to dig up the plant. Make a trench around the plant on all sides. Dig under the roots to loosen the plant.

2 LIFT
Gently lift the plant from the ground, detaching the roots from below with the sharp end of the trowel.

3 DIVIDE
Pull apart the plant to make several smaller plants. Divide large plants with big root balls by cutting them with a spade or large knife.

Pairing herbs

Flowering herbs such as chives (still in bud in this photo) look right at home in a mixed flower and vegetable garden.

Herbs range in sizes—

from low-growing, creeping pennyroyal to magnificent 6-foot-tall angelica. So planting in your beds—both herbs and flowers—means you need to pay attention to all their attributes: size (height and width), leaves (size, texture, and color), and flowers (form and color).

Even at a distance, many herb gardens appear green and luscious. Herbs have been used for a plethora of purposes since antiquity, from medicines to seasonings and simply for their presence in a garden. Among all plants, herbs are considered beautiful in their own right. So be sure to consider the color and texture of herbs when planting your garden and include them with other plantings in spring.

Pretty planting partners

Depending on your herb garden design, certain herbs make ideal companions. Think about creating planting combinations so paired plants can show off each other's attributes. For example, dill and chervil pair nicely: one is spiky and the other feathery. Tansy and lovage make good partners; both are tall, and tansy's intricate dark green leaves and yellow flowers contrast nicely with lovage's flat green leaves. Contrast silver thyme and creeping thyme for color interest. Both are low-growing but have dramatically different leaf colors.

Spring herbs on the rise

In the herb garden, herbs come into their own each season. In early spring, shoots of chives rise from the ground like missiles. How pretty they are when paired with equally early species of tulips. Leafy, lacy fennel comes up around the same time violas are spreading their joy throughout the garden. And perennial herbs that don't die back in winter look stunning with early-rising bulbs: Woody-stemmed lavender greens up nicely near nodding narcissus, creeping thyme, and crocus; and sage and scilla look lovely together. Warm spring weather also brings forth a spate of self-seeders: Dill and cilantro germinate freely on their own and may have to be plucked from places you don't want them to grow.

TEST GARDEN TIP

Plant markers

One of the ways to add decorative interest to your gardens (as well as to keep track of what you plant) is with plant markers. This tradition goes back to the days when herbs were used as medicinals in physic gardens.

Herb pairings Herbs are known for their beneficial qualities such as repelling pests in the garden. Here are some tried-and-true pairings.

SAGE WITH BROCCOLI
Pair sage with broccoli, cabbage, and cauliflower to repel cabbage moths and black flea beetles.

HYSSOP WITH CABBAGE
Plant hyssop near cabbage and kale to deter cabbage moths.

MARIGOLD WITH TOMATO
Marigolds can help repel nematodes, aphids, whiteflies, and hawk moths (the parent of the tomato hornworm).

CHERVIL WITH RADISHES
Chervil planted near radishes and carrots improves the flavor of these root crops.

CHIVES WITH CARROTS
Plant chives near carrots and tomatoes to improve the flavor of the crops.

GARLIC WITH ROSE
Garlic deters the tiny bright green aphids that can infest roses.

Controlling invasive herbs

Some herbs are ruthless garden grabbers.

One season you have a well-behaved plant, and the next spring the same plant may have expanded in size or numbers and spread into other areas of the garden. Annual herbs can spread by self-sowing. Perennial herbs can self-seed or spread via above- and underground shoots. Self-propagation and spreading can be a good thing—until it goes too far.

Defining invasive species

Opportunistic plants that become weedy by growing where they shouldn't are called invasive species. The U. S. Department of Agriculture (USDA) defines invasive plant species as those that are "characteristically adaptable, aggressive, and have a high reproductive capacity." Some of the common herbs encountered in wild meadows and rural ditches today—mullein, st. johnswort, soapwort, elderberry, chicory, and others—are species the first Europeans brought with them. They have survived and spread across the country, but that does not make them invasive.

Imposing border control

Invasive plants outcompete others, cause problems in native habitats, and resist elimination. Aggressive herbs can be kept within bounds by planting them in containers or segregating them in areas of the garden where they can't spread and take over. Perennial herbs considered invasive include mints, pennyroyal, comfrey, and bee balm. Herbs that can reseed excessively include lemon balm, dill, garlic chives, and borage. If you have space in your garden and you like these plants, you may view their spreading habit as a good thing. It's up to you to decide whether a plant is a ruthless invader or a welcome colonizer.

But there are other reasons to put the brakes on invasive plants. They can spread into neighboring gardens. They can also adversely affect the use of the plants around them. For example, the unchecked intermingling of different types of mint results in the loss of the individual plants' scent and flavor: you can end up with chocolate mint that tastes very much like orange mint. Another reason to keep invasive species in check is to keep them from spreading to areas outside your garden, taking away resources from native plants.

How plants become invaders

Some annual herbs become invasive because they reseed themselves. Annual herbs do this by nature. In the case of all self-seeders, such as dill, garlic chives, catmint, and anise hyssop, you can simply cut off the seedheads as they form. Avoid allowing them to dry and produce viable seeds. If self-seeding occurs and you find a batch of seedlings growing around and beneath their parent plants, simply weed them out.

Some perennial herbs take over because they self-propagate by producing shoots that grow aboveground or rootstalks that creep belowground. These shoots are called rhizomes or underground runners. Members of the mint family produce this way. You can stop plants from spreading by runners by segregating them into their own planting pockets, creating deep edging around them so they can't spread, planting them in containers, or planting them in containers with the bottom cut out and sunk directly into the soil.

Opposite: **Aggressively growing mint is best sequestered in containers in the garden. Otherwise, this wandering herb may take over a garden bed.**

TEST GARDEN TIP
Is this a weed?

Sprouting herbs (especially those that may have self-seeded) are difficult to differentiate from weeds. Let plants grow a bit before yanking them, to identify friends from foes. Thin herbs to produce healthier plants. If the plants are weeds, pull them.

How to keep mint from spreading

Mint (and other members of the mint family) are notorious spreaders. You can solve the problem of invasions to other parts of your garden by corralling their roots. Here's how:

1 BURY
Cut the bottom out of a grower's pot and sink it into the garden.

2 PLANT
Set the mint plant into the grower's pot; only the roots will make contact with the soil. Runners will not form.

3 COVER
Add soil around the base of the plant and to cover the rim of the pot. Planted this way, the mint will be confined and not spread.

Planning a new herb bed

An herbs-only garden can be small but fully packed with plants. Although the footprint of this bed is tiny, it features nearly a dozen different varieties of plants.

Creating a new herb garden is just like creating any other type of garden. You decide on the style of herb garden you want—cottage, traditional, historical. Then determine its size. If you've never gardened before, it's a good idea to start small. A 4×4-foot herb garden is large enough to contain lots of different types of herbs, but small enough to care for easily.

Draw a plan

Use a piece of plain or graph paper to sketch a plan. You don't need to do it to scale; just make a rough drawing including overall shape and features, such as a path or fence. One way to design a garden is to borrow a classic geometric shape: square, circle, rectangle, or diamond.

Mark out your herb bed

An easy way to mark your bed is to use a can of spray paint. You can spray right on the ground to mark the area where you will dig.

Make a plant list

Determine which herbs you will grow and use. Make a list of the herbs you want to grow from seed, those you want to buy as established plants, and those you can get from friends' gardens. (Spring is the ideal time to divide plants, swap herb divisions with friends or neighbors, and attend plant swaps or sales.)

How many plants?

The plants and their space requirements will indicate how many you need. When you plant herbs, space them according to their mature size, leaving room for air circulation. If a plant grows 1 foot wide, place it at least 1 foot from the plant next to it. When you arrange young and small herbs in a bed, you'll see plenty of soil between plants. Overplanting or planting too tightly can increase problems with insects and diseases.

Prepare your soil

Till your soil and add appropriate amendments for your soil type. Digging in a layer of compost annually infuses the soil with organic material and nutrients, promoting healthy plants.

Water and mulch

After you plant your herbs, follow up with two more essential steps: watering and mulching. Water herbs to help them establish healthy root systems, even if they are low-maintenance and drought-tolerant varieties. Mulch helps maintain soil moisture and reduces weeding chores.

TEST GARDEN TIP
Mulching

Mulching herbs benefits them in many ways: It smothers weeds, helps maintain soil moisture, and unifies the look of an herb planting or flowerbed. Herb beds can be mulched with organic mulch such as finely shredded bark. Gravel mulch looks neat and clean when used in containers.

Herb garden decor **Many herb gardens have common decorative and utilitarian elements. Which ones to choose depends on style and need.**

BEE SKEP Traditionally used to house bees (the honey was extracted by crushing the skep at the end of the summer), these former bee abodes are purely ornamental.

BIRDBATH A birdbath provides water for drinking and bathing, helping to sustain birds in all seasons.

CLOCHE Glass bell-shape plant covers, cloches are used in the herb garden to protect tender plants.

PATHWAY Made from bricks, stones, pavers, or gravel, a walkway is essential for access to a large herb garden.

SUNDIAL A sundial is an ancient way to tell time. The classic ornament in herb gardens is often placed among thyme or lavender, which enhances the presentation.

SPRING:
Harvesting spring herbs

Clip herb leaves and flowers for use in recipes and bouquets.

Herb lovers have a special place in their hearts for spring herbs.

Among the season's first greens, aromatic and delectable herbs are as welcome as the season itself.

Pick small, pick often

Perennial spring herbs, such as sorrel and chives, are at their most tender and tasty in early spring. In cold climates they sprout before some of the spring-blooming bulbs break ground.

Sour savory sorrel

Young leaves of tart sorrel make excellent fresh additions to salads mixed with spring greens, such as arugula and leaf lettuce. You can also make a

hot or cold sorrel soup, called schav, from sorrel leaves, onion, lemon juice, and other ingredients.

Tender, strappy chives

Chive leaves are most tender in the early spring. Harvest and eat the shoots before the plants mature, producing buds and blooms. Snip the long, slender leaves, then dice and sprinkle into salads, soups, or sauces. Puree chive leaves with olive oil and almonds to create a chive pesto that adds flavor to bruschetta or pasta.

Spring herb harvesting tips

Harvest herbs early in the day, after the dew has evaporated from the leaves but before the sun bakes out the flavor and fragrance (essence). Herbs that are harvested early in the morning taste better because the plant's essential oil concentration is at its peak. Snip off the new growth of herb plants using scissors or pruners. Inspect the leaves before eating: They should be free from insect holes or leaf spots. Turn over the leaves and make sure there are no eggs or

larvae on the undersides. Wash herb leaves under cool running water to remove any soil. Shake off the water and pat dry with paper towels. Use herbs fresh, or bundle stems together and hang them in a cool, dry place to air-dry.

Fall planting for spring herbs

If you live in a warm climate, you can plant some herbs in fall and harvest them in spring. Parsley can be sown in autumn; this perennial prefers cooler weather. Cilantro also prefers the lower temperatures of autumn; it will germinate and grow, reseeding itself to come up in the spring. Combine spring-picked leaves of parsley and cilantro with garlic and olive oil to make chimichurri, an Argentinian sauce used as a marinade for meat.

Foraging in the wild

If you forage for wild-grown herbs, avoid harvesting leaves near roadsides where they could be affected by traffic emissions or roadside pesticides.

Transplant herbs grown from seed once they are large enough for garden life (they need at least two sets of leaves). Before you plant, help herbs become acclimated to outdoor conditions by setting them outside in a sheltered area. Water well.

Grow your own herb garden in a pot
Planting a snippable pot of spring herbs is easy. Using three containers, sow annual seeds of dill, cilantro, and chervil. The more you clip, the more the plants will grow.

1 SOW
In a container filled with potting mix, sow your favorite seeds. Keep the mix moist to prompt germination.

2 SPROUT
The seeds of chervil, dill, and cilantro sprout quickly in warm weather and bright sunlight.

3 CLIP
Harvest leaves as soon as they are big enough. Snip the plants regularly to keep them producing new leaves.

SPRING:
Herbal entertaining

Spring brings a flush of fresh herbs ready for picking.

Find perennial chives for soups and salads as well as sorrel for tarts and soups in the garden alongside spring daffodils. Mint and parsley leaves can be clipped as garnishes for sweet and savory dishes. Cilantro, self-seeded from last year's crop, can be picked just inches tall and tossed into salsa. Dill, with its ferny fronds, can be harvested as it develops—the newest leaves have a mild flavor. Plus, spring herbs offer materials for crafting, decor, and gift possibilities.

1. May basket

Celebrate the first day of May with an herbal May Day basket made with herb plants for the garden. Add fragrant herbs, such as lavender and thyme, and flowery violas too. Tradition would have you offer this gift anonymously, but you can add a card to make sure your recipient knows who was so thoughtful.

2. Herb butter or cheese

Almost any culinary herb makes a delicious herb butter. Some of the best options include herbs you can harvest in the spring: parsley, chives, dill, garlic chives, tarragon, and chervil. Mix ¼ cup butter with 2 teaspoons chopped fresh herbs. Let stand at room temperature for 30 minutes. Spread the butter on crackers or bread, corn on the cob, grilled or cooked vegetables, or pasta. You can also add herbs to soft cheese, such as ricotta, cream cheese, or chévre. Allow the cheese to soften by bringing it to room temperature. Add minced herbs and shredded hard cheese (such as cheddar or asiago) and shape the cheese into a ball, log, or rectangle. Chill before serving.

3. Mint juleps

Just in time for your Kentucky Derby party, harvest fresh mint leaves and serve mint juleps. Ingredients include crushed ice, 1 tablespoon mint simple syrup, 2 to 4 large sprigs of fresh mint, and 3 to 4 tablespoons bourbon. Fill a tall glass with crushed ice. Pour the mint simple syrup into a glass. (For a sweeter cocktail, add more syrup.) Slightly crush mint sprigs and add to the glass. Pour bourbon into the glass. Stir. Garnish with a mint sprig, if desired. Makes 1 serving. To make mint simple syrup: Pour ½ cup boiling water over ½ cup sugar in a small bowl; stir until the sugar dissolves. Stir in ¼ cup lightly packed fresh mint leaves. Cover and chill for at least 4 hours. Strain the mixture through a sieve. Discard the mint leaves. Store the syrup, covered, in the refrigerator for up to 2 weeks. Makes about ¾ cup.

4. Herb bouquet

Flowering herbs, such as chamomile and lavender, make a fragrant floral centerpiece for a spring party. Other perfumed herbs include scented geraniums, the leaves and flowers of which are long-lasting choices for bouquets. Choose aromatic and textured foliage from other herbs, such as artemisia, anise hyssop, and lemon balm.

TEST GARDEN TIP

Grow herbs organically

If you want to pick herbs from your garden and eat the leaves and flowers out of hand or sprinkle them into food, grow the plants organically. Avoid using chemical pesticides and herbicides on edible plants. Monitor pests and remove them by hand.

Edible spring herbal flowers
Clip, snip, and enjoy edible flowers from spring-blooming herbs. Always rinse herbs before serving.

CHIVES Crumble these peppery-tasting flowers into salads and soups. The purple blossoms of chives retain their color when dried.

GARLIC Garlic flower stalks are called garlic scapes. They offer a delicious oniony flavor.

ROSES Late-spring blooming rose petals can be shredded into salads to add color and flavor.

CALENDULA Sprinkle these orange and yellow petals directly into salads.

SUMMER:
Watering herbs

Water is essential to any plant's survival.

Many herbs are less thirsty than other plants. That's an advantage. Yet even though you will need to water young plants until they're established, you'll also need to provide established herbs with supplemental moisture (other than what Mother Nature provides).

How do you know when your herbs need water? You can look for the obvious sign of wilting leaves, but wilted, droopy plants may also indicate overwatering. It's important to feel the soil before watering. Poke a finger into the soil. If the first 1 or 2 inches (up to your first or second knuckle) feel dry, it's time to water.

A watering strategy: Group by needs

Some herbs, such as Mediterranean natives rosemary, lavender, and thyme, prefer dry soil. Other herbs, such as mint, prefer more moist soils. By grouping your dry-loving plants together—away from herbs that like wetter conditions—you can suit the plants' water needs more easily. In the process, you will make less work for yourself and keep your herbs happier too.

Low-maintenance watering options

There are a number of ways to water herbs—almost without lifting a finger.
Soaker hoses. These permeable hoses sweat moisture, allowing small beads of water to slowly seep into the ground. You can shallowly bury these hoses under mulch, making them discreet. Attach the hose to a timer and you can water the garden more efficiently and on a schedule.
Drip irrigation. This watering method uses in-ground hoses or PVC tubes to deliver water directly to a plant's roots. Instead of being permeable, drip irrigation hoses have attached emitters that drip water directly onto the ground.

Both soaker hoses and drip irrigation systems are efficient ways to water large herb gardens because moisture is delivered directly to the plants' roots without loss due to evaporation. This close-to-the-soil delivery method keeps herb foliage dry and helps prevent diseases that can develop and thrive in damp conditions.

Hand-watering options

If your garden is small or you want to water specific areas (such as herbs planted in containers, which require more frequent watering than herbs in the ground), you can use the following:
Watering can. This is an old-fashioned but still-effective way of delivering water to plants. Use a cans with a rosette for a fine spray (best for herb seedlings) or a thin stream (best for watering at the base of plants).
Hose and watering wand. A wand or stick waterer that is attached to a hose is an excellent way to water herbs in hard-to-reach places, such as window boxes or hanging baskets.

Opposite: **Herbs in containers need more moisture than herbs planted in the ground. Water at the base of plants to keep from wetting the leaves.**

TEST GARDEN TIP
Avoid excess water

Herbs are often drought resistant, and they can suffer from overwatering or too much rain. Also watch for signs of mildew or fungal disease, which can be caused by too much moisture. Water herbs early in the morning, allowing water on leaves to dry during the day.

Mulch options

Mulch helps conserve soil moisture so you don't need to water your herbs as often. Organic mulch breaks down, adding nutrients to soil and improving drainage. Here are some mulch options for your herb garden.

WOOD MULCH
Bark dust lasts up to two years and looks neat. Shredded bark looks better around the small leaves of herb plants than small pieces

COCOA HULLS These chocolate-scented pieces last for six months. This mulch is unsafe for use if you have a dog.

PINE STRAW
Regionally available and inexpensive, pine straw lasts for about one year. It is not good for windy locations.

CHOPPED LEAVES
Free in most places, leaves are best when used chopped and partially decomposed.

MUNICIPAL COMPOST
Available locally in some areas and often free for the taking, it lasts for a few months. Reapply seasonally or annually.

Fertilizing herbs

A tomato and basil veggie/herb combo in a container benefits from a dose of granulated organic fertilizer scratched into the soil's surface early in the season.

Here's the good news: Herbs need little fertilizer.

Like other plants, herbs make their own food, using light and water in photosynthesis. They also draw essential nutrients, including nitrogen, phosphorus, and potassium, from soil. If a soil test detects nutrients are lacking, you'll need to fertilize. Most fertilizers, whether synthetic or organic, contain these nutrients. The product package indicates the ratio of nutrients, such as 10-10-10, a balanced, all-purpose blend. Too much fertilizer can make herbs grow too fast, producing less flavorful, lush, leafy growth.

Liquid fertilizer blends

Water-soluble fertilizers can be applied to herb plantings using a watering can or sprayer. You can also use a foliar fertilizer, such as kelp, fish emulsion, or comfrey tea.

Granular fertilizer

There are fast- and slow-release granular fertilizers. Uncoated granular fertilizer releases nutrients quickly; the release is triggered by moisture. Even the moisture from your hands will start the release, so wear gloves if applying. Slow-release granular fertilizer is coated and releases nutrients at a slower, but constant, rate. To apply granular fertilizers, scatter the product over the soil's surface around plants. Scratch the fertilizer into the soil, covering the granules. Avoid letting the fertilizer remain on leaves or fall into the crown of the plant. If you add fertilizer to a mulched bed, pull the mulch away and apply the fertilizer, then reposition the mulch. Apply fertilizer to moist soil, or water after feeding. This enables plants to use the food, by taking it up through their roots.

Compost

Compost, a nutrient-rich mixture of well-rotted organic materials, is a great way to amend the soil in your herb garden. Use compost from commercial sources (available in bags at garden centers), or municipal sources (some towns and cities compost yard waste and give away compost for free), or make it in your yard or a composting unit indoors.

Timing and cautions

When do you need to fertilize? Before summer gets into full swing, when plants are putting on growth spurts, adding fertilizer improves growth. When using fertilizer, keep it away from water features and sweep up spills on hard surfaces such as sidewalks and driveways. Use fertilizer according to package directions. Overfertilizing can injure plants.

TEST GARDEN TIP

Stake tall herbs in spring

When you fertilize herbs it's also a good time to stake any tall plants, such as bronze fennel, to keep them growing upright. Use a grow-through type support that hides in the plant's foliage and keeps the plant from flopping over.

Comfrey tea liquid fertilizer Brew a strong herb tea for plants using comfrey leaves. This solution is rich in calcium, phosphorus, potassium, and other nutrients that will boost your plants' vitality and help your garden grow. Spray the fertilizer on plants' leaves or pour it onto soil.

1 PICK
Harvest comfrey leaves anytime during the growing season.

2 PACK
Fill a 5-gallon bucket with comfrey leaves. Pack tightly. Cover the leaves with water. Place a cover on the bucket.

3 STEEP
Let the leaves steep in the water for several days. The liquid will become quite smelly.

4 FERTILIZE
Strain the liquid and pour it into a garden sprayer. Use the spray at once. Do not store it.

SUMMER:
Grooming and deadheading

Pinching, pruning, and deadheading are actions that make herbs more productive.

Pinching back

When you pinch the top of an herb plant, it reacts by growing more at the bottom. Removing the growing tip stimulates the plant to produce hormones, causing the lower buds on the stems to sprout. This results in a bushier, fuller plant. You can pinch plants back in the spring, when they are putting out new growth, and throughout the summer to encourage lush, dense plants. Use clean, sharp pruners to snip woody or tough-stemmed herbs; pinch off soft stems or spent flowers between your thumb and forefinger. See the herb encyclopedia for advice about grooming specific herbs. Stop deadheading and pruning in late summer to allow perennial herbs time to prepare for winter.

Shearing back some herbs, such as garlic chives, after blooming revives the plant, neatens its appearance, and stops it from reseeding.

Shearing back spring bloomers

Many spring-blooming perennial herbs can be revived after they have flowered by cutting them by one-third. Herbs such as chives, viola, and comfrey appear spent and tired by summer. Prune the plants after they finish flowering to shape them and to produce new green growth. Other herbs that benefit from a revival pruning after they flower include catmint, catnip, sage, bee balm, and lavender.

Deadheading

Deadheading is the gardening term for removing faded flowers from plants. When an herb finishes blooming, some plants' flowers fade away on their own with little tending. Others linger, looking dead and brown and detracting from the plants' appearance. Clipping off spent flowers benefits plants in two ways: It neatens your garden and it stops seed formation. The second benefit is most important for herb plants that are voracious self-seeders.

And, with leafy edible herbs, removing the flower before it blooms (sort of pre-deadheading) is an important step in helping retain the most flavor. Literally nipping the plant in the bud halts the plant's seed production, which puts more energy (and flavor!) into the leaves. In fact, if you allow some herbs to flower, you'll notice the decrease in flavor in the harvested leaves. This is especially true for annuals such as basil, whose leaves are the main event of the plant.

When not to deadhead

You may not want to remove the head of faded flowers for many reasons. Some seedheads are beautiful, providing winter interest in your garden. For example, the waving heads of anise hyssop and the bright red hips of roses provide texture and color in the winter garden. Another reason to withhold the pruners is that if you deadhead, you cannot collect seeds at the end of the season. If you want to harvest seeds of coriander, dill, and fennel, you need to allow the flowerheads to fade and set seed.

TEST
GARDEN
TIP

Cutting tools

Keep your herb garden nipped, tucked, and flavorful by removing dead foliage and spent blossoms with the following:
Bypass hand pruners
Small scissors
Hedge or grass shears

Keep blades of cutting tools sharpened for the cleanest and healthiest cuts. Use lubricating oil when sharpening and cleaning cutting tools.

Create a rosemary standard
Standards, or tree-shape herb plants, are elegant ways to raise potted herbs. They're usually pricier too. You can breathe new life into a rangy, sparse rosemary by transforming it into a chic little standard. Then use your clippings in recipes. Here's how:

1 CHOOSE
Start with a sparsely growing plant that needs revitalizing or one that is newer and fuller from a local nursery or grocery store.

2 CLIP
Remove the side shoots by clipping them off with a hand pruner. Start at the bottom and work your way up.

3 SHAPE
Clip the branches close to the stem. Use the tip of the pruners to get in close. Snip and shape the top growth of the plant.

4 MAINTAIN
Keep your standard clipped into the desired shape, such as a globe or cone, by cutting off new growth every few weeks.

Ornamental and architectural herbs

Herbs are natural mixers in a landscape. In this entryway planting, potted rosemaries join a gardenia and a Japanese maple.

Herbs can play starring roles in landscape design.

Mixed with flowers, shrubs, and trees, many herbs offer textural, structural, fragrant, and edible options to home landscapes.

Landscaping with herbs

Perennial herbs can be used as long-term landscape participants. In warm, dry climates, rosemary flourishes as a drought-tolerant shrub. It can be shaped to fit any space while providing ample cuttings for recipes. Bay laurel and citrus trees provide structural assets to a landscape. Although these trees require warm climates, cold-weather gardeners can plant them in containers that can be brought indoors over the winter.

Tall perennial herbs, such as angelica and fennel, can be planted in mass for a lovely effect or used as background plantings in flower borders. A hedge of artemisia at the edge of a property provides ghostly gray foliage that can be enjoyed even after dark. Flowering perennial herbs, such as yarrow, chives, and tansy, can be tucked into herbaceous borders, where they hold their own amid other flowering perennials.

Walkway edgers

Create a welcoming walkway with low-growing herbs. Mounded clumps of parsley make a lavish, all-green border. This evergreen herb grows fast in sunny locations and maintains its good looks even after modest harvests. Shrubby, small-leaved basils such as 'Spicy Globe' or 'Boxwood' form tight, rounded mounds and look like topiaries. Add a colorful array of 'Tricolor' or 'Icterina' sage to highlight their gardening companions: They attract attention and provide a colorful, leafy foil. Their variegated foliage is as flashy as it is tasty.

Shady areas

Although most herbs prefer sun, a few excel in shade. Consider planting lady's mantle, sweet cicely, lemon balm, and mint in the dappled shade of a tree. Also, sweet woodruff, pennyroyal, and Roman chamomile are groundcovers that offer flowers and fragrance in partial shade.

TEST GARDEN TIP
Herbal bridal bouquets

Herbs make lovely additions to bridal bouquets, offering symbolic elements: Rosemary symbolizes love, lavender suggests deep devotion, sage means wisdom, and chamomile signifies patience.

Herbs by height
Plant herbs in your garden the same way you plant other annuals and perennials: Stagger the plants according to their heights so they all can be seen clearly.

LANDSCAPE HERBS: LOW TO MEDIUM (less than 3 feet tall)

LAVENDER

SANTOLINA

CATMINT

'TRICOLOR' SAGE

'SPICY GLOBE' BASIL

LANDSCAPE HERBS: TALL (3 feet and taller)

MULLEIN

FENNEL

TANSY

BORAGE

ANGELICA

Wildlife-attracting herbs

①  ②

③  ④

The leaves and flowers of many herbs attract winged wildlife to the garden.

Important garden pollinators, including hummingbirds, butterflies, and bees, find herbs both delicious and alluring. With declines in pollinator populations, it's especially important to offer a wide variety of nectar, pollen, and larvae food sources in your garden. A diverse herb collection does just that. In addition to diversity, pollinators also need chemical-free dining. If you want to attract and protect the health of pollinators, refrain from using pesticides in your garden.

1. Butterflies

Butterflies flitting about your garden is a treat. The fluttering creatures are colorful, ephemeral, and joyful. The insects with delicate crepe-paperlike wings are attracted to a variety of flowering annuals, perennials, shrubs, and trees—such as herbs. Butterflies are enticed to sip the nectar from herbs including mint, catmint, marjoram, chives, and thyme. As it happens, butterflies and herbs prefer the same kind of conditions: sunny spots in areas without a lot of wind.

2. Caterpillars

If you want to attract butterflies to your herb garden, you have to consider the whole life cycle of the butterfly. It starts out as a larva—a caterpillar. So to enjoy butterflies, you must also welcome their larvae. Before you destroy any caterpillars, first identify what they are. For example, the pesky tomato hornworm can defoliate a tomato plant quickly. This large larva of the hawkmoth can be controlled by picking it off the plant and dropping it into a cup of soapy water. However, the nearly equally large swallowtail or monarch larva should be left to munch leaves.

3. Bees

Bees busily buzzing from flower to flower are a sign of a healthy garden. Bees gather nectar (to make honey) and at the same time spread pollen. In honey from areas with lots of the same plants (such as lavender fields), you can actually taste the flavor of the flowers. The herbs bees love most include borage, chamomile, germander, hyssop, lavender, basil, lemon balm, bee balm, anise hyssop, hyssop, mints, sage, savory, rosemary, and thyme. Like butterflies, bees prefer flowers in sunny locations. They easily navigate single flowers; double-flower species are harder to sip from.

4. Hummingbirds

Hummingbirds dine on the nectar from many flowering herbs. The tiny birds' long beaks are best suited to tubular-shape flowers, such as those of pineapple sage, mint, hyssop, lavender, and bee balm. Hummingbirds also prefer the color red, so offer them red-blooming varieties of bee balm as well as pineapple sage. Other herbs that attract hummingbirds include anise hyssop, catnip, comfrey, and rosemary.

TEST GARDEN TIP

Create an anti-deer border

Some fragrant and flowering herbs can be used to deter deer in your garden. Plant rosemary, mint, bee balm, lavender, and yarrow *shown* near the edge of beds and borders to ward off deer.

Bee garden in a pot — Create a container that will delight the bees in your garden.

Gather. Choose nectar-rich, bee-attracting plants, such as hyssop, catmint, lavender, bee balm, thyme, borage, and salvia.

Pot. Use a spacious container or grouping, such as this tiered planter, to offer bees a diverse plant menu. Also include a saucer of fresh water.

Position. Set in a location away from entryways or dining areas; give your bees space to gather nectar and pollen away from people.

Herb harvests

Gather herbs in the early morning after the dew has dried to capture their peak flavor and fragrance.

Summer's heat brings on fast growth for the herbs that are hot-weather lovers,

such as basil, rosemary, and thyme. (Cool-weather spring herbs, such as cilantro, chervil, and dill are spurred to bolt—develop flowers and seeds, completing their life cycle—in hot weather.) Generous crops of summer herbs like basil will provide enough fresh clippings for cooking and enough to preserve for later use.

When to harvest

You can clip summer herbs anytime there is enough growth. Cut the stem ends of plants to prompt new growth. Cut herbs by midmorning, after the morning dew has dried from the leaves, but before the hottest part of the day cooks out their flavor. The peak flavor of most herbs develops right before they flower. Avoid snipping herbs during or after rainy weather unless you plan on using them right away. Generally you should cut no more than one-third of the stem's length. Exceptions to this rule include chives and lavender: When they bloom, you can harvest only the flowering stems at ground level.

Harvesting in hot weather

Perennial and annual herbs can be harvested all summer, but don't put added stress on plants by cutting them back too much during hot weather. Cut as many herbs as you want to use fresh. Allow them to stay on the plant until you want to use them. If you want to cut herbs for use within a day, cut the stems and place them in a small vase or glass of water to keep them fresh.

Prepping herbs for use

After you've clipped stems of edible herbs, rinse the foliage under cold water and pat dry with paper towels. Remove the leaves from tough or woody stems; set aside the stems and don't use them in cooking. Chop the leaves and tender stems with a knife or snip with scissors. Save the woody stems for later use, such as burning in the grill or fireplace to impart an herby aroma.

Experimenting with flavors

Try fresh and dried herbs in varying proportions to see how you like them best. Use herbs sparingly at first when adding them to recipes. Try them one at a time until you become familiar with the flavors. Mix and match herbs to your taste. Try some classic pairings, such as basil and oregano or dill and lemon. Then experiment and create pairings of your own.

TEST KITCHEN TIP

Savor the flavor

When you cut basil and other leafy herbs for use in the kitchen, treat them like a bouquet of fresh flowers: Harvest in the morning and place the cut stems in water. Refrigerate only if wrapped in plastic, otherwise the leaves will turn black. Parsley, dill, and basil are best used right away. Wrap any unused herbs in a moist paper towel and refrigerate.

What to do with fresh summer herbs Summer is prime time to pick, prune, and harvest.

DRY Bundle small-leaved long-stemmed herbs such as sage, tarragon, marjoram, and artemisia, and hang them indoors in a cool, dry, airy place.

GRIND AND FREEZE Wash and pat dry large-leaved herbs such as basil and parsley. Combine in a food processor with oil and grind into a paste. Spoon into ice cube trays to use later in soups, stews, and sauces.

ADD THEM TO THE TABLE Create small bundles of fresh herbs including colorful leaves and flowers, to grace individual place settings.

GATHER HERBAL BOUQUETS A textural mix of cut herbs in a simple vase looks as lovely as any cut flower arrangement.

MAKE INTO WREATHS Wire bundles of herb leaves and flowers to a wreath frame—a fresh herb wreath dries naturally and can be used in recipes all season. It's a flavorful gift from the garden.

SUMMER:
Culinary herbs

Rosemary, thyme, lavender—summer produces a bounty of herbal leaves and flowers to use fresh in recipes and bouquets.

Savor summer's herbs

Herbs come into their own during the hot months of summer. Here are some of the season's best, and tips on how to collect and use them.

LEAFY HERBS

BASIL
Large-leaved basil varieties produce ample leaves for pastas and pestos. Snip leaves as you need them. For larger quantities, harvest the entire stem.

THYME
Although savory, thyme is often used in sweets. To coat with sugar, wet leaves lightly with egg white and sprinkle sugar over top. Let dry two to three hours before using as garnish.

MINT
Use mint to make simple syrups for summer drinks. Or add leaves directly to iced tea, lemonade, or cocktails. Place leaves in each glass and bruise with a spoon to release their flavor.

PARSLEY
Cut up flat-leaf parsley to add to soups and stews. Add parsley to warm foods just before serving so it maintains its flavor and bright green color.

FLOWERING HERBS

HYSSOP
Use dried or fresh hyssop flowers to add a mintlike flavor to salads, stuffing, or vegetables.

BEE BALM
Pick the frilly flowers of bee balm while in full bloom and break apart for petals to sprinkle into salads and soups.

LAVENDER
Lavender flowers are used fresh or dried in in cooking as well as fragrant bath and body-care products.

CLARY SAGE
The small bracts of the flowers of clary sage can be used as a skin compress.

SEEDY HERBS

DILL
In late summer the yellow dill flowers develop brown seeds. Dill seed is used to flavor pickles, of course, and can be used in breads and biscuits.

CORIANDER
When cilantro plants have bolted, the flowers form seeds in midsummer. When the seeds (coriander) turn dry and brown, they can be used whole or crushed into powder.

FENNEL
Infuse a burst of licorice flavor by adding fennel seeds to sweet and savory dishes. To release the flavor, crush seeds in a mortar with a pestle before adding them to recipes.

CARAWAY
Caraway seeds can be used whole, such as sprinkled on breads and crackers, or ground and used in powder form.

TEST KITCHEN TIP

Clean cut

Snip herbs from the garden. Wash and cut tender stems and leaves such as basil into smaller pieces to use in recipes. Remove leaves from woody-stemmed herbs such as thyme.

Summer herb blends

Customize your own herb blends—using the herb combinations you like best—to dry or use fresh in soups, stocks, and stews.

Herb blends you grow and make yourself

allow you to create customized flavors for your food. There are several classic herb blends—herbes de Provence and bouquet garni—that are used in a variety of recipes. Here's how to make them yourself.

Herbes de Provence

Herbes de Provence is a blend of herbs that is used in the south of France, in Provence, as well as throughout the Mediterranean. The plants used offer strong flavors and resinous leaves, and can be added to foods that cook a long time. Typical herbes de Provence mixes include thyme, marjoram, savory, fennel, and basil. Both the leaves and flowers can be used. Dried lavender leaves and flowers are also often added, which give the blend a flowery taste.

Herbes de Provence is used to flavor grilled fish, meat, and poultry, and can be added to stews. This dried herb blend can also be added to oils and used as a marinade, or added to food during cooking. Here's how to make a classic recipe: In a small storage container combine 1 tablespoon each of dried marjoram, dried thyme, and dried savory. Add 1 teaspoon each of dried basil and dried rosemary. Then add ½ teaspoon each of dried sage and fennel seeds. Store in an airtight container up to one month. Crush before using. Makes ¼ cup (twelve 1-teaspoon servings).

Bouquet garni

This classic French herb bundle is bound together with string or added to a small sachet made with cheesecloth. It typically includes parsley, thyme, and bay leaf. It's tossed into soups, stocks, and stews to add rich aromatic and herbal flavors. The bundle is boiled with the other recipe ingredients and removed before serving. Bouquets garnis can include a variety of herbs, depending on the recipe. You can create bundles of basil, salad burnet, chervil, rosemary, savory, and tarragon. Vegetables can also be bound in bundles with herbs.

Fines herbes

An herb blend that also hails from the Mediterranean region, fines herbes is less pungent than bouquet garni. This mix is traditionally a combination of chopped parsley, tarragon, chives, and chervil. Marjoram and savory may also be added. Start with the same amounts of all herbs (for example, 1 tablespoon). Then experiment with the ratios to find the taste you like best. Use fines herbes fresh or make a mix of dried herbs.

Italian seasoning

Create a mix of fresh or dried herbs to season your favorite Italian foods. Chop equal amounts of basil, oregano, and thyme; then add 1 bay leaf. This blend can be used to flavor red pasta sauces or be tossed with olive oil and fresh garlic and served over pasta for a fast and flavorful summer meal.

TEST KITCHEN TIP
Bundle up

Tired of fishing herbs out of hot liquids? Bundling herbs in a piece of 100 percent cotton cheesecloth allows you to remove herbs from a cooked dish in one neat motion. A bouquet garni in cotton cheesecloth is especially handy for herbs such as bay leaves, which should always be removed before serving.

Variations on the theme: bouquet garni You can make your own version of this French classic using the herbs and vegetables that best suit your recipe.

ITALIAN Some Italian cooks tie their flavorings between two snuggly fitting pieces of celery, making removal from a hot dish simple and quick.

FRENCH A traditional French bouquet garni includes thyme, parsley, and bay leaf, but you can create one from just about any herbs, such as rosemary, tarragon, and lavender.

AMERICAN Casual American cooks often toss flavorings right into the pot, sticking cloves into an onion and poking a toothpick through the garlic, helping diners avoid unwelcome bites of seasoning.

Savory selections

Rosemary, garlic chives, thyme, and other herbs with stiff or woody stems make handy basting brushes for marinades. They also add flavor of their own.

Summer brings lots of outdoor entertaining possibilities:

grilling parties in the backyard, afternoon drinks on the patio, appetizers in the garden. Herbs lend fresh taste and leafy beauty to a variety of dishes—from drinks to appetizers to main meals. Here is an assortment of savory options.

Herbal meat brushes

Marinate meats with brushes made from herbs. Some of your favorite culinary herbs, such as rosemary and thyme, can be used to make flavorful brushes for dabbing marinade or sauce onto food as it cooks on the grill.

Grilled apricot appetizer

Grill lavender-infused apricots on lavender-stem skewers for a surprising (and easy!) appetizer. Remove and reserve half the buds from the lower portion of 6-inch woody lavender stems. Thread halved, pitted apricots onto the stems. In a saucepan combine ½ cup honey, ¼ cup butter, and ½ teaspoon lavender buds. Cook over medium-high heat until boiling. Reduce heat; cook, uncovered, for 10 minutes. Pour mixture through a sieve to remove lavender buds. Brush sieved mixture onto apricots. Grill on a greased grill rack directly over medium-hot coals for 1 minute on each side.

Cilantro pesto

Enjoy this bright green and flavorful pesto as an accompaniment with Thai or Mexican food. In a food processor bowl place 1 jalapeño pepper (halved and seeded), 2 cups cilantro leaves (stems removed), ½ cup loosely packed basil, ¼ cup loosely packed fresh mint leaves, and 2 large cloves garlic. Cover and process with several on-off turns until finely chopped. With processor running, gradually add ½ cup extra virgin olive oil and ¼ cup water. Stir in 1 to 2 tablespoons lime juice and ½ teaspoon sea salt. Makes 1 cup.

Lemongrass kabobs

Thread firm-fleshed fish cubes onto flavorful skewers to make a gorgeous, fast main dish. Strip the tough outer layers of 6 lemongrass stalks until they're pencil thin. In a bowl combine ½ cup coconut milk, 1 to 2 teaspoons green curry paste, and 1 tablespoon chopped lemongrass. Add 1 pound fish cut into 1½-inch cubes. Marinate for 30 minutes. Use a sharp knife to cut a point at one end of each lemongrass stalk. Skewer the cubes of fish onto stalks. Grill over medium heat for 2 to 3 minutes on each side or until fish flakes easily with a fork.

TEST KITCHEN TIP

Plant a cocktail garden

If you entertain a lot, plant an herb garden that provides you with all the makings for your favorite drinks: Mint for lemonade and mojitos, citrus for margaritas, lemon balm and lavender for garnishes, and marigolds and bee balm for edible flowers.

Herbal dressings, sauces, and marinades

Herbs can lend flavors in discrete ways—in dressings, sauces, and marinades. Here are some summer herb favorites and recipes you can use to enhance a variety of meals.

TARRAGON DRESSING
In a blender container combine ¼ cup mayonnaise, ¼ cup buttermilk or yogurt, 2 green onions, 2 tablespoons parsley, 1 teaspoon fresh tarragon, and 1 clove garlic. Cover and blend until smooth.

LEMON DILL SAUCE
In a small saucepan melt ¼ cup butter over medium heat. Stir in 1½ teaspoons cornstarch and ½ cup chicken broth, combined. Cook and stir until thickened and bubbly. Cook and stir for 2 minutes more. Stir in ½ teaspoon lemon zest, 2 tablespoons lemon juice, and 2 to 3 tablespoons snipped dill. Makes about ¾ cup sauce.

ROSEMARY MARINADE
Stir together 1 teaspoon finely shredded lemon peel, ⅓ cup lemon juice, ¼ cup olive oil, ¼ cup Worcestershire sauce, 1 tablespoon sugar, 1 tablespoon snipped fresh rosemary, ¼ teaspoon salt, and ⅛ teaspoon pepper in a small bowl. Pour over fish, chicken, or pork in a resealable plastic bag set in a bowl or shallow dish; close bag. Refrigerate 1 to 2 hours, turning bag occasionally. Makes 1 cup (enough for 2 pounds of fish or meat).

Sweet delights

Candied herb flowers and leaves, such as viola, rose, borage, lavender, and mint, can be used fresh or dried and stored for up to two weeks in an airtight container.

Sweeten summer days with fresh

herbs from the garden. Herbs add refreshing flavors to cool drinks and desserts.

Sugared herb flowers/leaves

Sprinkle sugar onto herb flowers and leaves to add to cupcakes, cakes, cookies, and other sweets. Rinse flowers or leaves gently. Let them air dry. Place an egg white in a cup. With a foodsafe brush, dab small amounts of egg white onto both sides of the petals and leaves. Sprinkle super fine sugar over both sides. Shake off excess sugar. Let dry for 1 hour before placing on sweets, such as cakes or cupcakes.

Verbena vanilla sugar

Infuse sugar granules with the citrusy flavor of lemon verbena and the mellow tones of vanilla. Use in teas, in baking, or sprinkled on your morning bowl of cereal. Harvest 1 branch (about 12 inches) of lemon verbena with leaves. Use a heavy-duty knife or sharp kitchen shears to cut the verbena stem in pieces about 3 inches long. Layer the verbena in the bottom of a glass container large enough to hold 4 cups sugar. Pour 2 cups sugar into the container. Stick 3 vanilla beans (split in half lengthwise) into the sugar at even intervals. Add 2 more cups sugar. Seal jar tightly and store at least one week before using. Once sugar is aromatic, remove verbena and vanilla. If sugar becomes hard or clumped, break pieces with a wooden spoon and sift before using. Makes 4 cups sugar.

Lavender whipped cream

Add a generous dollop of this herb-inspired whipped cream to a fruit crisp or pie. Or serve lavender whipped cream with scones for a summer afternoon tea party. In a small saucepan combine 1 cup whipping cream and 1 tablespoon crushed dried lavender. Bring to just a simmer. Remove from heat. Strain mixture and discard lavender. Cover and chill cream mixture at least 2 hours or until completely chilled. In a chilled metal mixing bowl beat whipping cream and 2 tablespoons superfine granulated sugar with an electric mixer on medium speed, beating just until soft peaks form. Use at once or cover and chill up to 2 hours. Makes 16 (2-tablespoon) servings.

Stevia extract

This leafy plant offers a natural alternative to sugar. Add 1 cup hot water to a heat-resistant jar. Drop in 1 cup freshly picked and lightly bruised stevia leaves. Cover tightly. Let the mixture steep for a day, then strain out the solids and discard. Use this sweetened extract in teas, coffees, and other recipes.

Stevia-sweetened mint syrup

Minty simple syrup is great to have on hand when whipping up summer drinks, such as mint juleps or mojitos. This recipe uses the sweetening charms of stevia instead of sugar. Add 1 cup hot water to a heat-resistant jar. Add ½ cup freshly picked mint leaves and ½ cup freshly picked stevia leaves. If desired, to thicken the liquid, add ¼ teaspoon unflavored gelatin to the hot liquid. Cover tightly. Let steep for a day at room temperature, then strain out the solids and discard. Store, covered, in the refrigerator up to 2 weeks. Makes 1 cup syrup.

TEST KITCHEN TIP
Fresh/dry herb ratios

When you substitute fresh herbs for dried, the general rule is to use three times as much. For example, 1 tablespoon (or 3 teaspoons) fresh tarragon equals 1 teaspoon dried tarragon.

Herbal substitutions
Although each herb has its own distinctive flavor, you can replace herbs in recipes with herbs with comparable flavors. Whether you're making an emergency substitution or experimenting with a new flavor, follow these suggestions for dry herb alternatives.

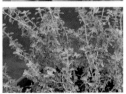

MINT = BASIL   **TARRAGON = CHERVIL**   **CILANTRO = PARSLEY**   **SAGE = SAVORY**   **OREGANO = THYME**

Herbal cooldowns

herbal spritz

1

2

3

4

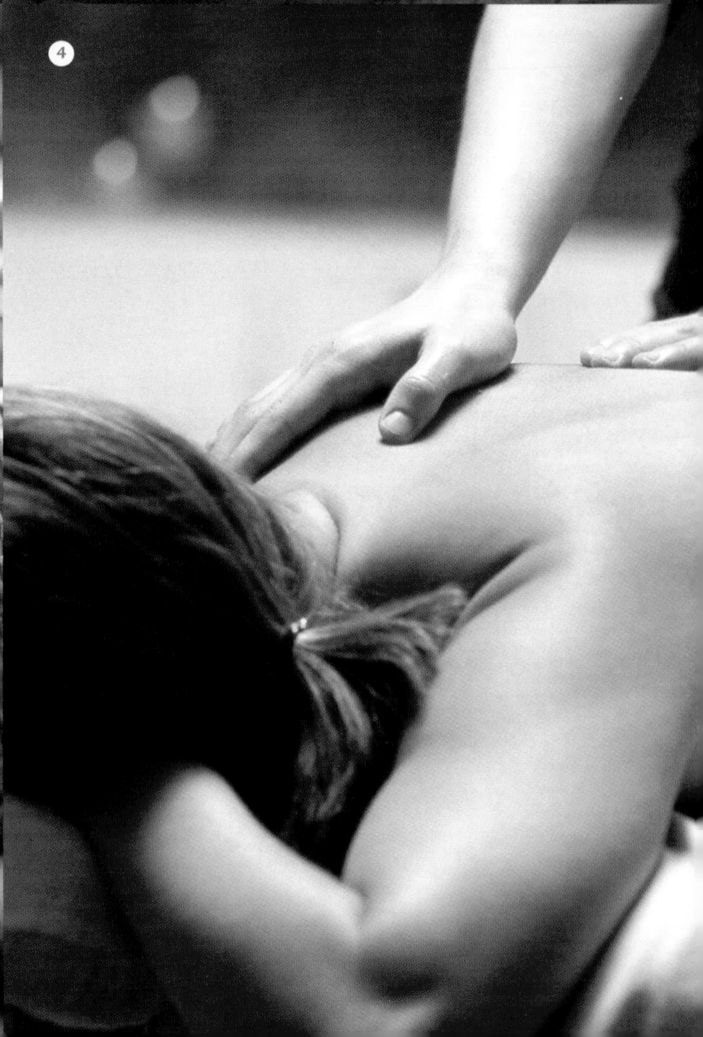

Cool down summer's heat with herbal possibilities—

there are so many scented ways to refresh and revive. Make these custom spa treatments at home and treat yourself to the charms of herbs for your skin, hair, and feet.

1. Herbal hair rinse

Benefit: Relieves a dry, itchy scalp.
Rosemary brings out the natural highlights in hair and it is also great for the scalp; it helps reduce dandruff. Place 1 large handful of fresh rosemary, sage, and/or chamomile in a 1-quart jar and pour 2 cups boiling water over the herbs. Cover loosely with lid or saucer and steep for 10 to 15 minutes. Allow the infusion to cool. Strain and discard herbs. To use, shampoo your hair, then pour the cooled infusion over rinsed hair. Do not rinse out.

2. Herbal spritz

Benefit: Quick cooldown after gardening.
Herbal refreshment is just a spray away when you make your own herb-infused cooling mist. Fill a quart jar with your favorite herbs, such as mint, lavender, rosemary, lemon balm, and rose petals. Cover with apple cider vinegar. Let steep for several days, strain out the solids, and pour the herb-infused vinegar into an atomizer or spray bottle. Keep the spritz in the refrigerator for an extra-cooling effect. Spray on your arms, legs, and face to enjoy a quick herbal refresher.

3. Peppermint foot soak

Benefit: Relieves dry, itchy feet.
Enjoy a foot soak every week of summer, thanks to the ease of this recipe and mint's assertive growth. Bring 8 cups (½ gallon) water to a boil in large pot; turn off the heat. Add 4 cups loosely packed fresh peppermint; cover with lid and steep 15 minutes. Transfer the infusion to a basin. Add enough warm or cool water to make a comfortable footbath. Sit in a shady area of your garden, soak your feet in the footbath for at least 10 minutes, and relax.

4. Soothing linament

Benefit: Moisturizes and soothes dry skin.
Create a calendula-infused oil for dry skin or massage. In an 8-ounce glass jar, combine 1 cup fresh calendula petals and 1 cup olive or almond oil. Allow the petals to steep in the oil for 1 week. Strain the oil, pressing the petals with the back of a spoon to extract as much of the oil as possible. Pour the oil back into the jar and discard the petals. Refrigerate the infused oil for up to 1 month.

TEST KITCHEN TIP

Flower ice cubes/ring

Edible herb-flower ice cubes make any drink look special. To make, fill ice cube trays half full with water and place an edible blossom or petal on the water in each cube. Freeze until firm, then top off the tray with water and freeze again. To make a flower-filled ice ring, fill ring mold half full with water and place edible blossoms or petals on water in ring. Freeze until firm, then fill the mold with water and freeze again.

Cool down summer's heat with herbal liquid and frosty treats

Herbs offer so many possibilities for unique and refreshing summer libations.

LEMON VERBENA TISANE
Place 12 sprigs fresh lemon verbena and 4 sprigs fresh mint in a warm teapot. Add 4 cups boiling water. Steep for 3 minutes; serve warm. To serve chilled, remove herbs and mint sprigs with a slotted spoon; refrigerate.

BASIL/CHAI PUNCH
Pour a 32-ounce container of chai tea concentrate (black tea) into a large pitcher. Stir in ½ cup sugar. Add 8-inch stick cinnamon, ¼ cup fresh, torn basil leaves, 1 medium sliced lime, and 1 medium sliced orange. Cover and chill for 4 hours. Strain mixture, discarding solids. Before serving, add 32 ounces of club soda to chai mixture. Serve over ice. Garnish with whole basil leaves. Makes 10 (6-ounce) servings.

GARDEN TEA PUNCH
Place 2 cups water, ⅔ cup sugar, 3 tablespoons snipped fresh mint, and 1 large stem of lavender or borage in a large stainless-steel pan. Bring to boiling; remove from heat and let steep for 20 minutes. Strain mixture, discarding solids. Add 1 cup orange juice, ½ cup lemon juice, and 2 cups strong brewed tea; chill. Before serving, add 32 ounces of chilled club soda. Garnish with a sprig of thyme. Makes about 3 quarts, 16 (6-ounce) servings.

BASIL MARTINI
Fill a cocktail shaker with ice, add a dash of vermouth, shake, and strain. Add 2 jiggers (3 ounces) basil-infused vodka. Shake vigorously; strain and pour mixture into a martini glass. Garnish with basil leaves. Makes 1 serving. To make basil-infused vodka, pour one 750 ml bottle vodka into a 2-quart container and add 1 cup lightly packed basil leaves. Allow to infuse for 24 hours. Strain vodka and discard basil leaves. Allow to age 1 week before using.

Propagating herbs

Fall is an ideal time to make cuttings from your still-lush, growing herb plants.

Cuttings are the most inexpensive way to multiply your plants. Plus they allow you to overwinter some of your favorite herbs—especially if you don't have room indoors to bring all your tender plants inside.

Start with healthy plants

Choose only the healthiest plants from which to take cuttings. Diseased, insect-infested, or stressed plants will not provide good cuttings. Select leafy, nonflowering stems for the best cuttings. Take cuttings in early morning because the plant usually has the most moisture at this time. Clip off stems and keep the cuttings cool and moist until you are ready to root them. Avoid leaving the cuttings in direct sun because they will dry out. You can root cuttings in two ways: in water or in soil.

Root in water

Rooting herbs in water may be the easiest method of propagation; it's a fun project for kids. But water rooting doesn't work well with all types of herbs.

The late summer and early fall garden is the culmination of the growing season—and it's the perfect time to make cuttings for next year's garden.

You can generally root soft-stemmed plants quickly (in less than a couple weeks)—think herbs such as mint, basil, and pineapple sage. Woodier-stemmed plants, such as lemon verbena and rosemary, will root in water, but they take much longer.

After clipping the stems of the plants you want to start, place the cuttings in a glass of water and set it in indirect sunlight. Change the water every day to keep bacteria from killing the roots. Once the stems have rooted, plant them in a small container in loose potting soil. When they have established a small rootball, you can plant them in the garden in spring.

Root in soilless mix

A lot of herbs can be started easily—and inexpensively—from stem cuttings. You can take cuttings throughout summer and into fall from plants grown in the ground or containers. Scented geraniums, oregano, lavender, and rosemary are best propagated through stem cuttings rooted in soilless, seed-starting mix. Other herbs, such as tarragon, catmint, feverfew, and hyssop, can be propagated using this method. The stems of woody herbs such as bay laurel should be scraped on all sides before rooting to facilitate growth. Most cuttings root fastest if they're kept in a warm, humid location. Misting the cuttings frequently helps them grow.

TEST GARDEN TIP
Compost for a greener world

Fall is the ideal time to start a compost bin. As summer-weary herbs require clipping and shaping, you can add their faded flowers and leaves to a compost bin. This recycles green refuse, turning it into nutritious compost over time. And it provides a free source of nutrients, which can be reapplied to the garden the following year.

How to make cuttings
Multiply your herbs by taking cuttings to make more plants. Within weeks, you'll have new plants to add to your garden or to share with friends and family.

1 CLIP
From summer into fall, cut 3- to 4-inch stems using a sharp pruner, a knife, or shears. Make the cut at an angle just below a node (where a leaf emerges from the stem). Pinch off the bottom leaves and any flowers or buds.

2 STICK
Dip cut ends in a rooting hormone powder to help them grow.

3 POKE
Use a pencil or chopstick to make a planting hole in a container of soilless, seed-starting mix (such as peat moss, perlite, and vermiculite) for the stem cutting.

4 PLANT
Stand cuttings 1 inch deep in the cells of seedling flats or in individual pots.

5 GROW
Cover the plantings with a sheet of plastic or a dome to help keep the soil moist; prop open the cover to let air circulate. Place the cuttings in bright light but out of direct sunlight. In four to six weeks, transplant into 6-inch pots or the garden as weather allows.

Saving seeds

Saving seeds from herb plants such as dill (*shown*), fennel, and caraway allows you to use the seeds in recipes as well as save some for planting next spring.

As you clean up the garden in fall,

gather seeds from your favorite herbs and save them for next year's garden. Some gardeners get great satisfaction from planting seeds they've collected in their gardens. Some want to propagate a sentimental favorite passed down through generations. Others aim to safeguard seeds' genetic diversity. In fact, seed saving was once the primary way to pass plants down from generation to generation.

Now with so many excellent sources to buy seeds, you may not feel compelled to save them. But if you are looking for a way to cut costs in gardening, this is one of the easiest. Plus, you can share seeds with friends and family.

The best plants for seed saving are old-fashioned varieties and open-pollinated plants. Seeds from these plants will grow into plants that look like their parents. However, seeds harvested from hybrids usually will not grow into plants identical to their parents.

Seeds follow flowers

Most seeds develop after the flowers have faded. Herb plants may produce seeds in pods (poppies), seedheads (dill and fennel), or fruits (rose hips). Herb seeds vary in appearance, size, and color.

Collecting seeds

No matter what the seeds look like, their size, or how they're held onto the plant, the key to successfully saving seeds is to wait until they have matured. You have a small window of opportunity here because you want to harvest seeds before they fall off the plant. The seeds of most flowering herbs can be harvested after they dry on the plant.

Storing seeds

Cool, dry, and dark are the keys to storing seeds. Place thoroughly dried seeds in small paper envelopes. Write the name of the plant, variety, and date stored on each envelope. Plan to use the seeds the next year. Place seed packets in an airtight jar. Store seeds away from light and heat to preserve their viability.

Seeds' shelf life

Many seeds remain viable for several years or more, although it's best to use seeds (whether collected or purchased) within a year of harvest for maximum germination.

TEST GARDEN TIP

Fall is the time to plant garlic

While you are busy harvesting herb leaves and seeds, it's planting time for garlic. Separate the cloves from the bulb at planting time (not before). Plant in the ground after your area's first killing frost (generally from late September to November). After you plant garlic, it will develop a root system in the soil, go dormant over winter, and send up leafy shoots in the spring.

How to save and store seeds

Harvesting herb seeds from your garden is easy—and a great way to jumpstart your spring garden.

1 SNIP
Harvest dried seedheads by clipping the stem at the base.

2 HANG
Place seedheads in a paper bag and tie it shut around the stems. The seeds will drop into the bag as they dry. Let seeds dry for several weeks. Remove the seeds from the bag.

3 PACKAGE
Place seeds in an envelope, jar, or handmade seed packet. Mark the date and type of seed. Store your dried seeds in a cool, dry place.

FALL:
Drying and storing herbs

Cutting, drying, and storing
herbs are delicious ways to reconnect with your garden. For centuries
herb gardeners have dried their herbal bounties, sewing them into sachets
and pillows, hanging them on walls, and storing them in jars for fall and
winter recipes. You can too.

Best cuts
The best time for harvesting herbs is in the morning after the dew has
evaporated from the leaves, but before the afternoon sun and heat sap the
plants' color and fragrance. For nonculinary use, select plants in full flower
and cut extras to allow for breakage. If you are cutting herbs to use in
cooking, do so before they flower. To preserve the health of the plant (if it
is a perennial), leave a few inches of the stem you cut so it can continue to
produce new growth.

There are several ways to dry herbs:

Air drying. This is the simplest method: You simply cut, bundle, and hang
herbs to dry. Gather three to six branches together and secure the stems
with a rubber band. The band will hold the stems even as they shrink

Bundles of clipped herbs
can be dried easily—
letting you sample the
flavors and fragrances of
your favorite herbs long
past the growing season.

TEST GARDEN TIP

Garden ristra

in drying. Hang the bundles upside down in a dry, dark place where air circulates (sunlight robs color, fragrance, and flavor). A well-ventilated attic or spare room works well. Your herbs will be fully dry and ready for storing within a few weeks.

Using desiccants. Moisture-absorbing substances can speed drying as well as preserve the colors and shapes of herb flowers for crafts. Traditional drying agents include sand, borax, and cornmeal. To dry flowers, place them in a container and cover them with clean, dry sand or a mixture of 1 part borax to 3 parts cornmeal. Leave the container open to allow for evaporation. The blooms should be dry in three to five days. Silica gel, available at crafts stores, has lighter granules that are less likely to damage leaves and petals. For most uses, pour about 1 inch of gel into a moisture-tight plastic, metal, or glass container; add your herbs; then cover them with more gel. Drying time will vary from about 2 to 10 days. Use a small paintbrush to remove crystals between the petals.

Microwave-oven drying. If you want to work with your herbs the day you harvest them, dry them in a microwave oven. Wash them and pat them dry. Lay them on a paper plate and microwave for intervals of about a minute each; allow standing time between cooking times.

Food-dehydrator drying. Cut, wash, and dry leaves. Then place them in a single layer on the tray of the food dehydrator. Dry herbs on the lowest setting possible; if your dehydrator doesn't have setting options, check often to avoid overdrying the herbs.

Pretty—and functional— a ristra is a traditional Southwestern way of drying and hanging chile peppers. You can supersize your ristra with other herbs, such as garlic cloves and stems of sage. Use the dried herbs in recipes or simply display them as a decorative accent in your kitchen.

How to store dried herbs Dried herbs can enliven meals throughout the winter.

1 ASSEMBLE
Assemble your materials: dried herb bundles, a tray to catch them in, and an airtight jar for each herb. Make sure the herbs are dry and brittle. Keep leaves whole. Crumble them only when using.

2 SIFT
Remove the leaves from the stems. Pick out the stems and any other chaff. Place the dried herbs in airtight jars or bags. Mark the herb type, the variety name (if you want to test the flavors of different varieties), and the date.

3 KEEP
Store dried herbs in a cool, dry place (not above the stove) to keep them at their peak of flavor. They will lose much of their flavor after a year—just in time to replenish them with herbs from next year's garden.

4 USE
When cooking, bring out the herbs you will need. Dried herbs are more potent than fresh herbs, so use less of them. If a recipe calls for 1 teaspoon fresh oregano, add $\frac{1}{3}$ teaspoon dried oregano (use one-third as much dried herb).

Freezing herbs

Freezing herbs is an easy and fast way to capture the fleeting flavors of the garden.

The best herbs for preserving are ones that have the most robust flavor, such as oregano, mint, tarragon, marjoram, sage, basil, thyme, and rosemary. For herbs that have a high water content in the leaves—such as basil, chives, and mint—freezing allows you to capture the flavor that doesn't come through as well when dried. The tradeoff is that these leaves don't retain their body; freezing makes them limp, albeit still tasty.

Some herbs keep their flavor better when frozen. For example, dill, basil, and sorrel retain their tart flavors better when frozen than dried. You can freeze herbs whole—in leaf form—or make them into an herbal paste with olive oil. You can freeze them in water. Or you can simply place them in freezer bags or containers whole—without even bothering to chop them—and use them later.

Freeze edible herb flowers and leaves into ice cubes to use them for parties and special meals. Viola, mint, and rose add their colors to these cubes.

Start fresh

Harvest the freshest, healthiest leaves. Rinse leaves and let them air-dry or gently pat dry with paper towels. Chop long, narrow herbs, such as chives and lemongrass, before you freeze them. These herbs are thin and will freeze within minutes.

Label and date

Push all the air out of freezer bags or boxes before sealing them. Add labels and the date the herbs were frozen, and place sealed containers in the freezer. In most cases, you can use these herbs without thawing.

Freeze for parties

Herbs can also be frozen to make decorative ice cubes for party drinks. Or freeze sprigs of mint and sweet woodruff into an ice ring or block. Boil the water first to make it clear. Once it has cooled, fill the bottom of the mold with the boiled water and freeze. Arrange the herbs you plan to freeze, then continue adding water until the mold is filled.

TEST
KITCHEN
TIP
Freeze a bouquet

You can prepare and freeze ready-to-use herb blends such as bouquet garni. Prepare sprigs of parsley, thyme, and a bay leaf. Wrap in cheesecloth and tie with kitchen twine. Place the bouquets in a freezer bag and use each as needed in sauces or soups.

Freezing herbs
Some herbs keep their fresh flavor when frozen—so you can taste summer long after it's gone. Here are some options.

FREEZE IN A PASTE To freeze herbs, chop them in a food processor, adding enough oil to form a paste or pesto, then freeze in ice cube trays. Once cubes are frozen, remove them from trays and place in a freezer bag; store in the freezer. Herbs that are good candidates for paste include basil, chervil, cilantro, dill, fennel, marjoram, mint, parsley, rosemary, sage, savory, and tarragon.

FREEZE WHOLE LEAVES Rinse the herbs and let them dry on paper towels. Spread the leaves in a single layer on a baking sheet without overlapping them. Freezing the leaves flat prevents them from sticking together. Set the baking sheet in the freezer. When the leaves are frozen solid, in an hour or two, place them in an airtight container and return them to the freezer.

FREEZE IN WATER Place several herb leaves (or a spoonful of chopped herbs) in ice cube trays. Fill the trays halfway with water. Place the half-filled trays in the freezer. Once the ice cubes are frozen, fill the rest of the trays with water. The leaves should be fully submerged. Place the trays back in the freezer to freeze solid. Once the ice cubes are frozen, remove from the trays and store in resealable plastic bags. As needed, toss ice cubes whole into your favorite stew or dish.

FREEZE IN PLASTIC BAGS/ CONTAINERS Simply rinse herbs, allow to dry, and place the leaves in resealable plastic bags or containers. Press all the air from the bags and seal them. Store in the freezer. To use, chop the leaves and add them to food.

Putting your herb garden to bed

In the autumn herb garden, growth slows,

seedpods thicken, and the time comes for preparing the garden for next year and completing the growing season. Here's what needs to be done.

Gather the last herbs before frost

Before a hard freeze or frost comes to your area, harvest the stems of the annual or perennial herbs you want to use, freeze, or dry.

Clean up beds

Begin fall cleanup by gathering fallen leaves to add them to your compost pile. After the first frost, your annual herbs—such as the lovely, leafy basils—will be reduced to a slimy black mess. Pull out frost-damaged plants and add them to the compost too. Avoid composting any leaves that show signs of disease. Empty out containers of annual herbs and compost the soil and foliage.

Compost and cut back

Give herbs an end-of-season nutrition boost by adding a thick layer of compost around the base of perennial herb plants. After frost, cut back leafy herbs such as catmint and bee balm. Leave herbs with seedheads intact for winter interest or to feed overwintering birds. For example, poppy, yarrow, and calendula seeds are sold in commercial birdseed mixes, so why not leave them in the garden for a natural snack?

Make design changes on paper

Take notes now about what you want to change in next year's garden. If some plants have become invasive, decide now how much you want to cut them back (or whether to remove them entirely). Now is also the time to mark perennial herbs to move in the spring; they're easier to locate now than when they are just coming up.

Water perennial herbs

Many perennials expand their root growth in the cooler temperatures of the fall, so watering throughout autumn is important to your herb plants' health. Strong root systems can help protect the plant through winter's freeze-thaw cycles, which can heave weaker perennials from the soil.

Continue planting

End-of-season sales can net some great deals on perennial herbs. And you can still plant these perennials in the warm days of autumn. If you haven't settled on a place for a specific herb, plant it anywhere; you can dig it up and reposition it in the spring.

Mulch

After the ground freezes, mulch newly planted perennials, as well as all perennials that are tender in your zone. Add chopped leaves or straw over the top of the plants. If you live in an area that has severe low temperatures, add up to 6 inches of mulch to your herb beds.

TEST GARDEN TIP

Comfrey compost

Cut back and compost comfrey leaves. This herb offers nitrogen and other nutrients that will help break down organic materials in your compost pile.

Opposite: **Use season-extending row covers to protect hardy herbs, such as parsley, from frosts. Cover on cold nights and you'll be able to use leafy herbs through fall and into winter.**

Make end-of-season herb bundles With cold weather and the holidays in mind, harvest the last of the season's herbs to bundle as gifts.

FRAGRANT BURNING BUNDLES Save the dried stems of fragrant herbs, after stripping off the leaves for cooking or crafting. Gather the stems of lavender, mint, rosemary, juniper, and others and use them as kindling in the fireplace. Add a bay leaf to a bundle of twigs; wrap with colorful thread.

WINE BOTTLE BUNDLES Snip stems from your favorite herbs to make tie-on bundles for wine bottles. Forgo gift bags, and make a greener choice by adding bundles of fresh herbs to dress up gift bottles of wine.

Bringing herbs indoors

Many herbs that excel outdoors can make the transition to houseplants. Although the "climate" indoors is dramatically different from the outdoors, with a little help some herbs can grow indoors.

What herbs to bring indoors

Some herbs will do better than others inside your house. Depending on the amount of space you have—and the amount of south-facing light—you may need to pick and choose which herbs get the invitation indoors.

Leave annuals outdoors

If you want to bring herbs indoors to use in recipes, it might make better sense to dry or freeze herbs for this purpose. The payoff for raising basil indoors will not be that great; make pesto with what's left of the plant instead. The same goes for other annuals; they've lived for a season and are nearly at the end of their natural lifespan.

To enjoy a few herbs indoors over the winter, move plants long before cold weather sets in. A chore of hoisting a heavy container into a quick and easy task for two.

Bring in selected perennials

Tender perennials—especially pricey ones such as topiaries—are definitely worth taking indoors. So are plants you can take cuttings from, such as scented geraniums. Perennial herbs that you love to cook with should also make the cut: rosemary, oregano, thyme, and marjoram—you decide.

Check for insects

Before you bring your plant indoors, thoroughly inspect the tops and the undersides to make sure you aren't bringing any hitchhiking pests indoors. Insects such as aphids could infect your other indoor plants. Spray all plants with a forceful blast of water to chase away any pests.

Acclimate your herbs

Outdoor plants need to adjust to indoor air and light levels. After you pot up the herbs to bring indoors, set them out of direct sunlight outdoors for a few days to help them acclimate to the lower light levels they will experience indoors. Bring them indoors for a few days; then set them back outdoors for a few days. Finally, bring them in to stay.

Find the best light

Most herbs prefer full sun. Indoors, herbs need at least six hours of sunlight a day. A south- or west-facing window can provide that. If you need to add supplemental light, place herbs under grow lights.

TEST KITCHEN TIP

Terra-cotta is tops

Because most herbs hate wet soil, unglazed terra-cotta containers are best for potting up plants to bring indoors. Terra-cotta allows moisture to seep out not only through the drainage hole but also through the permeable sides. Most herbs prefer soil on the dry side.

Transplanting herbs from the garden for indoors
Many perennial herbs can transition from outdoors to indoors with the right treatment. Herbs that do best being transplanted to an indoor location include chives, garlic chives, lavender, rosemary, thyme, and mint.

1 PICK
Choose the healthiest herb plants to bring indoors. Dig up herbs before the first frost. Dig up the entire root ball. Divide larger plants (if you prefer), and replant the divisions, keeping one division to take indoors.

2 PLACE
Plant the herb in a container that is slightly larger than the root ball. The container should have a hole in the bottom to facilitate drainage. Fill in spaces with potting soil.

3 SET
Water well. Add extra soil around the root mass and tamp down to eliminate air pockets around the roots. Take your newly potted plant indoors and set it in a sunny, south- or west-facing window.

FALL: Herbal entertaining

1

2

3

4

Enrich autumn gatherings with herbs from the garden

Gather the last of the season's bounty in fragrant armloads of foliage and flowers.

1. Herb-baked olives

Serve as a rustic appetizer with any meal.
In a 15×10×1-inch baking pan combine 1½ cups mixed imported Greek and/or Italian olives, ½ cup dry white wine, 1 tablespoon olive oil, and two 4-inch sprigs fresh rosemary. Bake in a 375°F oven for 45 to 60 minutes or until most of the liquid is absorbed, stirring occasionally. Meanwhile, for dressing, in a small bowl combine 3 tablespoons olive oil, 1 tablespoon finely shredded orange zest, 2 tablespoons orange juice, 1 tablespoon snipped fresh rosemary, 1 tablespoon snipped fresh parsley, 3 cloves garlic, minced, and ⅛ teaspoon ground black pepper. Pour dressing over olive mixture; toss gently to coat. Transfer olive mixture to a serving bowl. Cover and chill for at least 2 hours. Makes 6 servings.

2. Thyme wreath

Clip end-of-the-season thyme and fashion it into a fresh and savory wreath.
Harvest thyme by cutting at the base of plants so the branches are as long as possible and about the same length. Use a wire wreath base and add bunches of fresh thyme to it, attaching them with fine-gauge wire. Wrap the wire tightly around the cut ends of a bunch, securing it to the base.

Keep adding bundles until you have completed the wreath. The wreath can be hung fresh and allowed to dry. Use the leaves in cooking, if you like.

3. Herb bowl centerpiece

Enjoy autumnal meals with fresh snips from a leafy centerpiece.
Plant small herb plants into a decorative bowl and serve with dinners as the freshest way to add seasonings—just clip fresh herbs directly into food. You can also make a cut-herb bowl by harvesting small bundles of fresh herbs and standing them in water. Use a flower-arranging frog to hold them in a bowl.

4. Sage stuffing

Fresh sage makes this classic poultry stuffing even better. Preheat oven to 325°F. In a large skillet cook 1½ cups chopped celery and 1 cup chopped onion in ½ cup hot butter over medium heat until tender but not brown. Remove from heat. Stir in 1 tablespoon snipped fresh sage and ¼ teaspoon black pepper. Place 12 cups bread cubes in a large bowl; add onion mixture. Drizzle with enough chicken broth to moisten (1 to 1¼ cups); toss lightly to combine. Place stuffing in a 2-quart casserole. Bake, covered, for 30 to 45 minutes or until heated through. Top with fresh sage. Makes 12 to 14 servings.

TEST KITCHEN TIP
Autumn grilling

Instead of composting the woody stems of rosemary, use them to infuse flavor in grilled meat. Soak twigs in water for 10 minutes, then lay them directly on hot charcoal or the ceramic briquettes of a gas grill. The herb will flavor chicken, fish, or pork.

How to make herbal tea
Infuse herbs in steaming hot water to make tea—healthful, soothing, and satisfying. Use mint, chamomile, rose hips, licorice root, or ginger.

1 PLACE TEA IN A POT
Sprinkle 2 teaspoons of dried herb leaves (or use a tea bag) for each cup of water. A teapot adds to the ritual.

2 BOIL WATER
Bring water to a boil, then cool a few minutes; pour water over dried herbs, cover, and let the herbs steep for 5 minutes.

3 SERVE TEA
Pour or release the prepared tea into a teacup.

4 SIP AND ENJOY
Allow your tea to cool a bit. Sip and relax!

The right light

Whether indoors or out, herbs have a few essential needs:

soil, water, nutrients—and sun. When you bring herbs indoors, you need to provide them with enough light to thrive.

Herbs have special needs when growing indoors. And not all herbs can grow indoors (short-lived annuals such as cilantro and dill are poor candidates). Most herbs need at least six hours of sunlight a day, and the short, often-cloudy days of winter make for less-than-ideal growing conditions. But herbs can tough it out indoors with your help. The right light and a few other indoor climate considerations will help your herbs survive the winter indoors.

Winter growth expectations

Unless your indoor location has plenty of light, most indoor herbs will slow or even stop growing during the winter. They won't sprout many new leaves or flower as they do outdoors. When their growth slows, you should reduce leaf harvests.

Potted herbs do best indoors when placed in the bright light of a south- or west-facing window.

Best natural light

Herbs grow best in south- or west-facing windows where the direct light is the strongest. These sun-loving plants can't thrive in north-facing windows or any indoor location that receives less than four hours of direct light a day.

When herbs don't receive enough sunlight, they will try to grow toward a light source. This is why plants that are grown indoors grow elongated stems; they are actually reaching toward the light and becoming leggy. Plants that don't get adequate light produce thinner, more delicate leaves.

Supplemental lighting

Even if you can grow your herbs in brightly lit southern windows, they may still need more light. Weak winter light can be supplemented with grow lights. Indoor lighting used to grow plants is different from regular lightbulbs.

Grow lights offer the full-spectrum light that plants need to grow. You can purchase stacked shelflike units with long lights on several levels; these are ideal for starting seeds. Or you can rig your setup using fluorescent shop lights. Use one warm lightbulb and one cool lightbulb to mimic full-spectrum light. Suspend the lights about 4 inches above the plants. Set the fixture to turn on and off with a timer.

Climate control

Most herbs should be kept away from windows and doors where cold drafts and blasts from the outdoors can damage them. Herbs can thrive in consistent indoor temperatures as low as 60 to 65°F. And, of course, they like it warmer.

Some herbs, such as French tarragon and chives, benefit from a short period of cold temperatures; they can be placed in cool locations, such as your garage or basement, as long as the temperatures stay above freezing. These herbs can stay in a cool area for a month or two, then be reintroduced into warmer, brighter locations for the rest of winter. The cool hiatus may stimulate new growth.

Minimizing leaf drop

Plants drop leaves when they are introduced to lower light levels. It's a self-preservation reaction: When plants can't produce enough food due to lower light levels, they let leaves go. To minimize leaf drop before you bring plants indoors, help adapt the plants to lower levels by moving them to a shaded location outdoors first.

TEST GARDEN TIP

Brighten up with grow lights

Use grow lights to start seedlings or to grow herbs indoors during winter. You can get kits with fluorescent bulbs or brighter high-intensity lights, also called high-intensity discharge (HID) lights. Check with commercial lighting sources for the best option for your indoor herb-growing situation.

Growing an herb garden on a windowsill Create a snippable indoor herb garden in a sunny spot in your home.

1 ASSEMBLE
Bring together all the supplies for your indoor windowsill garden: plants, such as basil, oregano, thyme, and flat-leaf parsley; lightweight potting mix; terra-cotta pots and saucers.

2 TRANSPLANT
Start with young plants for best results. Give them new homes in terra-cotta pots. Dress up the pots using acrylic paint.

3 WATER
After you transplant each of your new herb plants, water it well to help it adjust to its new pot.

4 GIVE LIGHT
Place plants in a sunny window; south- or west-facing is the best and brightest light.

Watering and humidifying

Amp up the humidity for your herb plants by setting them on a water-filled tray of stones or gravel. Keep the tray filled with water to the top of the stones. Set herb containers on the stones so plants can benefit from the humidity.

Most herbs prefer well-draining soil and hate soggy

roots when outdoors, and this doesn't change for indoor plants.

Indoor versus outdoor conditions

Indoor plants have fewer drying elements to contend with than outdoor plants: There is less sun (and consequently less growth) and less wind. In lieu of that, indoor plants have to contend with dry air from forced-air furnaces or fireplaces. Overall, indoor herbs need less water than when they are living outdoors.

Water when the soil is dry

To determine when your herbs need water, test the dryness of the soil in the container. If it feels dry to the touch, the plant needs water. The touch test is more accurate than watering on a schedule.

How to water

Use a watering can to water herbs. Direct the flow of water directly at the soil. Pour the water at the base of the plant rather than wetting the leaves. Keep watering the plant until the water runs out of the bottom of the container. If no water comes out, the pot's drainage hole may

be blocked; check and unplug it so the soil can drain properly. You may need to repot the plant.

Misting

To raise the humidity level around your plants in a home with dry forced-air heat, use a mist sprayer. If your herbs develop any fungal diseases, such as powdery mildew, stop misting.

Use mulch in containers

Outdoors, mulch helps keep the soil damp in beds and pots. Indoors, it serves the same purpose, conserving soil moisture. Apply a layer of chopped bark, clean gravel, or other material to cover the surface of the soil in the container. Make the layer 1 to 2 inches deep. You can use decorative materials for mulch that will enhance the look of your containers.

Err on the side of dry

Overwatering your herb plants is the most common way to kill them. Too much water creates soggy soil, which can cause roots to rot. Allow the soil in the container to dry out completely between watering.

TEST GARDEN TIP

Cut and savor

Grow a kitchen garden container with a mix of herbs so you can snip the plants and use the leaves in cooking throughout the winter.

Pests and diseases
Although insect pests and diseases don't bug herbs much outdoors, they can pose a problem indoors.

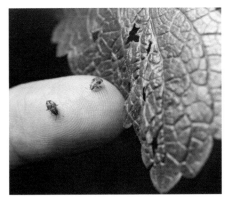

SYMPTOM: Curled leaves; tiny insects

PEST: Aphids are small insects that suck the life out of plants along the stems and leaves. Fill a spray bottle with water, add a few drops of liquid soap (not detergent), and spritz the top and undersides of the leaves. Rinse herb leaves before using them in recipes.

SYMPTOM: Holes in leaves

PEST: Leaf holes are usually caused by insects, not disease. A number of insects may be the culprit. Check the undersides of leaves for pests. Use a spray of water, soapy water, or insecticidal soap to treat. Start with the least-toxic solution.

SYMPTOM: White powdery foliage

DISEASE: Powdery mildew is a fungus that needs humidity and a dry sruface to thrive. Good air circulation and growing disease-resistant plant varieties help prevent it.

Planning next year's garden

Winter is an ideal time to page through your collection of herb and gardening books for planting inspiration. Your local library will also have a selection of books to help you plan the herb garden of your dreams.

Plan your next year's herb garden while the snow flies.

Gorgeous summer herb gardens start with herbal dreams during the cold months.

Order seeds early

After the first of the new year, seed catalogs begin to arrive in the mailbox. To get a jump on the planting season, order herb seeds in the winter. This is especially important if you are planting hard-to-find or rare varieties; seed supplies often sell out fast.

Grow a healthy lifestyle

Rethink your eating habits and incorporate more herbs into your diet. Herbs offer fresh flavors without fat or calories. Plan your next garden to include the herbs you like best as well as some herbs that are especially known for their healthful characteristics, such as chamomile to help you sleep, and oregano and sage, which offer antioxidants.

Plant the way you cook and eat

Before you plan your herb garden for next spring, pull your cookbooks off the shelf and review the herbs you most often use to flavor your favorite recipes. Your standard recipes will taste fresher with herbs that you grow yourself (and can harvest anytime you need them). Then pull the world atlas off the shelf and think about which ethnic foods you like best. Create seed lists with herbs that are indigenous to those geographic regions. Do you like Thai food? Add lemongrass and cilantro. Want to try your hand at rolling your own Japanese sushi rolls? Add shiso (perilla) to your list. Herbs add ethnic flavor to recipes—you can actually taste the place through the use of seasonings.

Plan theme gardens

Let your family's food favorites be your planting guide. If pizza is a big hit at your home, plant an herb garden with those flavors in mind: savory oregano, leafy basil, spiky rosemary, and pungent garlic. If tacos are a staple, plant a garden with cilantro, peppers, tomatoes, and onions to grow your own backyard salsa.

TEST GARDEN TIP

Plan ahead

Open your calendar and mark the dates to start seeds. Generally, you can start herb seeds six to eight weeks before the last frost date in your area.

Engage the kids
Herbs that are tasty and fragrant are the perfect plants for young cooks. Here are some herbs that appeal to all the senses:

Taste: basil Use freshly harvested and rinsed whole basil leaves to top homemade pizzas. A favorite: Margherita pizza with red sauce, leafy basil, and mozzarella cheese.

Touch: scented geraniums Rub the leaves of scented geranium varieties to unleash the scents of nearly everything: apples, chocolate, mint, roses, and spices.

Smell: lemon-scented herbs It's amazing how plants can mimic other scents. Plant an all-lemon garden in a bed, container, or window box that includes these citrus poseurs: lemongrass, lemon balm, lemon verbena, and lemon thyme.

Taste: mint Planted in pots, mint offers kids delicious leaves for harvest from spring through fall. Make minty simple syrup (with mint leaves, sugar, and water) to drizzle into drinks, over ice cream, or onto a stack of chocolate chip pancakes.

Smell: catnip Kids with cats can make small aromatic bags of catnip for the family feline. Buy or make small cloth bags and fill with dried catnip leaves. Seal the bag tightly before giving it to Fluffy.

WINTER:
Herbal decor

Trimmed herb topiaries add their charms to any home. Keep them in a sunny window and pinch the branch tips often to promote lush growth.

Decorating with herbs is

easy because they have so many pleasing qualities: They are aromatic, colorful, and textural. And best of all, they infuse a bit of the summer garden into your home in the midst of winter.

Herb topiaries

Shapely herb topiaries are an elegant way to enjoy herbs all winter. The best herbs for topiaries are rosemary, bay laurel, lavender, scented geraniums, and lemon verbena. Topiaries of various sizes and shapes can be grouped for maximum effect. The thought of topiary brings up images of traditional English manor houses or French country estates.

Rosemary centerpieces

Rosemary is a popular choice as a winter gift plant, in part because when the fragrant herb is sheared into a cone shape, it mimics the classic shape of a holiday tree in miniature. Set a mini holiday rosemary tree in a colorful container, and it becomes an instant centerpiece with an added value—foliage can be clipped directly at the table and added to soups, salads, and stews.

Indoor kitchen garden

Plants brighten a room, herbs enhance a dish—so indoor herbs in the kitchen pack a double bonus. Place culinary herbs in a bright, south- or west-facing kitchen window. Clip foliage to shape plants. You can harvest leaves and stems for recipes all winter, but don't remove more than one-third of the plant at a time if you want to keep it alive until next spring. Meting out your herbs to last all winter isn't such a problem because kitchen herbs are now readily available in grocery stores in the winter months. If you want to make more aggressive harvests (like using the whole plant), feel free; you can replace the plant once you've used up the herbs.

Herb garlands

For holiday celebrations and special winter dinners, cut fragrant sprigs of rosemary, lavender, thyme, and sage and bind them together into bundles with green florist wire. String the bundles together to make an herb garland to drape along a stair railing or fireplace mantel.

Herbal incense

Toss dried herb stems into the fireplace just before guests arrive to add a spicy, herbal scent to the house—both indoors and out.

TEST GARDEN TIP
Winter warmup

Brew a sweet, lemony herbal tisane by combining two flavorful herbs: lemon verbena and stevia. For the lemon flavor, harvest several lemon verbena leaves and crush them in a teacup. Add a leaf or two of crushed stevia to add sweetness. Pour boiling water into the cup and steep for about five minutes.

Deck a rosemary topiary with lavender A cone-shape rosemary becomes a fragrant holiday centerpiece when dressed up with flowering lavender sprigs and twinkle lights.

1 FIND
Start with a large, unadorned cone-shape rosemary plant from the grocery store or nursery.

2 INSERT
Add dried or fresh flowers and sprigs of lavender. Insert the stems into the dense foliage of the rosemary.

3 ENCIRCLE
Twine a strand of twinkle lights around the rosemary tree. Use a battery operated light string when displaying the tree as a centerpiece to eliminate contending with a cord.

4 ENJOY
A lavender-studded rosemary topiary makes a holiday decoration that lasts beyond the holidays. The warmth of the twinkle lights releases the herbs' fragrances in a subtle way.

Herbal entertaining

Bring potted rosemary plants indoors in late summer and they'll prosper throughout the winter when placed in a cool room and watered often enough to keep the soil damp. Tuck baubles at the base of the plants for an instantly festive touch.

Winter meals can be brightened

with the pungent tastes of the garden. Fresh or dried herbs infuse flavor and fragrance into meals that recall the warmer and sunnier days of summer.

Orange-fennel marinade

Flavors of sage and fennel seeds blend to make a marinade for meat or fish.

In a small bowl stir together ⅔ cup orange juice, ⅔ cup water, 2 tablespoons thinly sliced green onion, 1 tablespoon snipped fresh sage (or ½ teaspoon ground sage), 1 tablespoon Dijon-style mustard, and 1 teaspoon fennel seeds, crushed. Pour over meat or fish and turn to coat. Marinate in the refrigerator at least 30 minutes or up to 4 hours. Drain the meat or fish, discarding the marinade. Grill. Makes enough for ¾ pound of meat.

Lemon-mint water

Serve this refreshing drink to counterbalance a heavy desert.

Place slices of 4 lemons in a large pitcher. Gently squeeze 1½ cups of mint leaves to slightly bruise them. Add the mint to the pitcher with lemon. Pour in water. Cover and chill for 1 to 8 hours. Strain the lemon-water mixture. Discard the herbs. Divide additional lemon slices and fresh mint (or basil sprigs) equally among 6 to 8 tall glasses or pint canning jars. For each serving, add 1 cup of ice cubes; fill with the lemon water. Makes 6 to 8 servings.

Five-spice powder

A Chinese spice and herb blend that features five flavors: sweet, sour, bitter, pungent, and salty.

Combinations vary, but this fragrant blend usually includes cinnamon, anise seeds or star anise, fennel seeds, black or Szechwan pepper, and cloves. In a blender combine 3 tablespoons ground cinnamon, 6 star anise or 2 teaspoons anise seeds, 1½ teaspoons fennel seeds, 1½ teaspoons whole Szechwan peppers or whole black peppercorns, and ¾ teaspoon ground cloves. Cover and blend until powdery. Store in a covered container. Makes about ⅓ cup.

Jamaican jerk seasoning

Add a Caribbean twist to winter meat dishes.

Combine in a bowl: ¼ cup sugar, 2 tablespoons dried thyme, 2 tablespoons ground allspice, 1 tablespoon ground black pepper, 1½ teaspoons salt, 1½ teaspoons cayenne pepper, 1½ teaspoons ground nutmeg, ¾ teaspoon ground cloves. Rub over meat before grilling. Makes about ⅔ cup, or enough for 3 pounds of poultry, pork, seafood, or vegetables.

TEST GARDEN TIP

Green up holiday tabletops

Herbs go with every tabletop decor—from minimalist meals to totally blinged-out occasions. Even parsley appears snazzy when cut and placed in a cut crystal saltshaker vase. Snip fresh herb tips and place in tiny vases as part of each place setting, rather than going with a large central table centerpiece. A bit of green brings a lot of life to the table.

Herbal flavor ranges

Herbs are generally categorized as strong or mild. Most foodies agree that using one strong-flavor herb per dish keeps herbs from overpowering a recipe. Mild-flavor herbs can be used with a free hand.

ROSEMARY

SAGE

WINTER SAVORY

PARSLEY

DILL

CHERVIL

STRONG HERBS These herbs are more resinous than mild herbs, and their flavors tend to dominate a dish. Generally, use just one of these herbs per dish.

MILD HERBS These herbs add subtle undertones of flavor to a dish. Use fresh or dried and add to a dish just before serving. You can use multiple mild herbs in the same preparation.

WINTER:
Herbal gifts

1

2

3

4

basil

Give the gift of scent and flavor

with herbal-inspired gifts you can grow and make.

1. Good taste basket

Dress up small herb plants to make an herbal gift basket. Give each pot a colorful paper wrapper, then insert four different herbs into a compartmentalized basket. Go with a culinary theme: French herbs, Italian herbs, tea herbs, or sweet herbs. For the gift marker, insert a fork (handle first) into the soil of one of the pots. Thread a gift tag hand-printed on a slip of paper between the tines. If you like, include an envelope with a few of your favorite herbal recipes hand-copied onto recipe cards.

2. Exfoliating scrub

Customize your own skin scrubs using herbs from your garden combined with supplies from your pantry. To make a soothing exfoliating scrub, use coarse kosher salt or sea salt. Combine with a natural oil, such as jojoba, grapeseed oil, olive oil, or sweet almond oil. Drop in the oil from a couple punctured vitamin E capsules. Add a handful of dried powdered rosemary and lavender. Add 10 drops of your favorite essential oil (rose, lavender, lemon verbena) and mix well. The salt scrub will have a grainy consistency. Spoon it into decorative jars or tins. Tie on a sprig of rosemary with a length of cotton twine.

3. Mini greenhouse

For a frugal and tasty gift, grow herb seedlings in repurposed milkshake cups. Cost: the price of a packet of herb seeds. Fill cups with potting soil and sow three to five basil seeds in each. Cover lightly with soil and add water. Set under grow lights or in a south-facing window. After the seedlings sprout, pinch them back to make bushier plants. Wrap the base of the cup with yarn, twine, or ribbon. Add a matching gift tag and top the cup with its greenhouse dome.

4. Herb-infused bath oils

Fragrant and skin-soothing oils are easy to make. First sterilize and let dry any small, pretty bottles you have on hand. Drop into each bottle a few fresh or dried stems of lavender or rosemary. In a measuring cup with a spout mix together the oils. For a soothing bath oil, mix 16 ounces almond oil with 24 drops lavender essential oil and 8 drops rose essential oil. For a stimulating bath oil, blend 16 ounces soy or olive oil with 24 drops rosemary essential oil and 8 drops juniper essential oil. For each mixture, break open 8 capsules of vitamin E and stir the contents into the oil mixture. Using a funnel, pour the oil mixture into the bottle and cork it. Seal the cork with paraffin. Tie dried flowers to the neck of the bottle with raffia or ribbon.

TEST GARDEN TIP

Make your own simmering potpourri

Scent your house with an herbal mix you can simmer on the stove. Mix together ¼ cup each dried bay leaves, cedar tips, sage leaves, rosemary leaves, lavender leaves, marjoram blossoms, juniper berries, cinnamon sticks (broken into pieces), and dried orange peel. Use in a potpourri burner (1 tablespoon at a time) or simmer in a pan of water on the stove (¼ cup potpourri in 2 cups water, set on lowest heat). Makes about 2 cups.

How to make lavender sachets

With cut and dried lavender bundles, you can make your own lavender sachets that will scent your clothing and keep away insect pests.

1 THRESH
Remove the lavender flowers from the stems by rubbing the stems together over a tray. The flowers will drop off the stems.

2 SIFT
Place the lavender blossoms in a bowl and remove any stems or chaff.

3 FILL
Using a small scoop, place lavender buds into a small bag with a pull string. Use cloth or fine mesh bags (which allow you to see the lavender flowers).

4 GIVE
Box several of your creations and give them all as a gift. Or use individual bags as stocking stuffers.

herbal
lifestyles

Herbs are inspiring on so many levels.
Meet nine chefs, crafters, and gardeners who
express their creativity in herbal ways.

CULINARY:
The taste of Ireland

Chef and teacher
Catherine Fulvio harvests
chives and dill for her
menus and classes.

The Irish Sea lends a salty tang to the air of County Wicklow, Ireland.

Except, that is, among the green meadows and forested hills a few miles inland near Ballyknocken House and Cookery School. Here, along Lucky Brook Lane, the aromas are tormentingly lush and mouthwatering. They waft from the windows of the renovated milking parlor where innkeeper and head chef Catherine Fulvio gathers her classes around four stoves.

Weekends often provide exotic fragrances as Catherine and her guest chefs help students master barbecue, pizza, Mexican, and Asian dishes. On Monday, though, the kitchen perfume is as comfortably familiar as the breeze riffling through the tawny leaves of the inn's 200-year-old copper beech. That's the day Catherine introduces international guests to the tastes of Ireland, and reconnects native Irish with the country-style traditional fare of what once was an island of farmers.

Local foods comprise traditional Irish dishes

Plump ovals of soda bread bake in ovens while pots of stew bubble on the hobs, or burners, next to pans of simmering whiskey and butter sauces. Catherine and her students craft meals from renowned County Wicklow lamb; trout from the Avonmore River; vegetables, butter, milk, and cheese from local farms and creameries; and fruits and herbs from Ballyknocken's own gardens. The inn also serves traditional meals, often with sophisticated twists, to its guests after they spend the day exploring the walking trails, historic sites, and flowerbeds of the county known as the Garden of Ireland.

Catherine combines Ireland's bounty with the mastery of a classically trained chef who also is fond of the flavors and traditions of Irish country cooking. "We can count back six or seven generations of farmers," she says of her family.

Although the inn and cookery school keep Catherine running, she finds time to tend Ballyknocken's Victorian-style herb garden. "The herb garden is my baby," she says. Catherine grows chives, mint for lamb sauces, fennel, and bay. Catherine's thyme and sage often find their way into the inn's soda breads, which are the centerpiece of Irish country food. Her favorite herb, lemon verbena, adds an intense, lemony flavor to desserts.

The front yard entryway to Ballyknocken House and Cookery School features edible landscaping.

Fresh Mint, Onion, and Apple Chutney

Serve this relish with lamb dishes. It is best fresh, but you can make it up to one day ahead. Start to Finish: 20 minutes

Ingredients
3 cups lightly packed fresh mint leaves
2 medium cooking apples, peeled, cored, and cut up
1 medium onion, cut up
3 tablespoons sugar
½ teaspoon salt

In a food processor combine mint, apples, onion, sugar, and salt. Cover and pulse with on-off turns until mixture is finely chopped. Season to taste with additional salt and/or sugar if necessary. Makes 3 cups.

Herbal edibles

Raised beds are the best way to grow herbs, which thrive in soils that drain quickly.

Daring, dynamic, and sensual, the gardens at Tangled Garden in Nova Scotia

provide herbal inspiration to Beverly McClare, one of Canada's premier herbal chefs. Located in Grand Pré in the scenic Annapolis Valley, Tangled Garden has become a destination for herbal enthusiasts and for foodies who seek the fresh and quirky.

Designwise, Beverly has gone far beyond the prim four-square Colonial plots in which herbs were initially grown. Her garden is a delicious blend of flowers, herbs, and fruit trees. She masses plantings for clouds of subtle color. Although "tangled" may conjure images of a jungle, the garden is actually sweet and welcoming, with picket fences and pergolas.

Raised beds overflow with herbs

Tangled Garden is planted on heavy clay, so the soil needs amendments. Beverly opted to grow her garden in raised beds. The boxes she built shimmer with green, gold, and silver herbs. When those herbs are at their peak, she plucks fresh herbs daily from late spring through early winter. With them she creates alluring pairings for the products she creates: jams, jellies, vinegars, and liqueurs.

Beverly McClare's business is a licensed distillery, and she makes and sells herbal liqueurs onsite. Basil, orange mint, and lavender are just some of the herbs that flavor her custom-made liqueurs. Lemon Gemelo is flavored with lemon balm; Cafe Diablo features anise; and sweet basil plays a starring role in her Dazzling Damson Plum Liqueur.

She combines herbs and fruits to create signature flavors in her recipes: anise hyssop with cherry, sage with apples, rosemary with quince, and angelica with peach. Lavender, thyme, and fennel are other additions. Her fruit and herb jellies are produced the old-fashioned way—in a kitchen onsite, cooked in big pots, just as Grandma used to do. She makes delectable jellies in small batches, six jars at a time.

Beverly McClare harvests herbs early in the morning and then whisks them to the kitchen.

Lemon Thyme Ice Cream

Prep: 30 minutes **Chill:** overnight **Freeze:** according to manufacturer's directions; 4 hours

Ingredients

1½ cups whipping cream
1½ cups milk
⅔ cup sugar
3 egg yolks
1 teaspoon vanilla

1 cup coarsely chopped lemon thyme or thyme
4 teaspoons finely shredded lemon peel
3 tablespoons Tangled Garden Lemon Gemelo Liqueur or limoncello liqueur

In a medium saucepan stir together cream, milk, and sugar. Heat over medium heat until sugar is dissolved and mixture is just starting to simmer. Do not allow to boil. Whisk the egg yolks lightly in a small bowl; gradually whisk in about 1 cup of the milk mixture. Pour the egg yolk mixture back into the saucepan. Cook, stirring constantly, over medium heat for 6 to 8 minutes or until mixture thickens and coats the back of a metal spoon. Remove from heat and stir in vanilla. Immediately place saucepan in a large bowl of ice water and stir mixture for 2 minutes to cool slightly. Stir in lemon thyme and lemon peel. Transfer to a storage container; cover and chill overnight. Strain the custard mixture through a fine-mesh sieve; discard solids. Stir liqueur into strained custard. Freeze in a 2-quart ice cream freezer according to manufacturer's directions. Transfer to an airtight storage container and freeze for 4 hours before serving. Makes about 3 cups ice cream (six ½-cup servings).

Naturally flavorful

A love of plants became a business model for Jim and Theresa Mieseler

of Shady Acres Herb Farm in Chaska, Minnesota. In 1977 the couple started a Minnesota wildflowers business. The next year they added herbs to the gardens and their for-sale list. When they started their business with just one plant shelter, some herb plants were hard to find. They've remedied that problem over the years by collecting new varieties as well as creating some of their own. *Rosmarinus officinalis* 'Shady Acres' is a rosemary hybridized by Theresa in 1999. Since then, Theresa has been awarded the Helen de Conway Medal for Excellence in Horticulture from the Herb Society of America.

Organic gardening protects wildlife

Shady Acres is located southwest of Minneapolis amid hills of rich and rolling farmland. The herbs at the farm are grown organically—the Mieselers use neither insecticides nor fungicides to raise healthy herbs. Instead they employ the natural predatory skills of beneficial insects to control harmful ones. To keep fungal diseases at bay, they space their herbs so good air circulation keeps plants healthy. In the event of a pest outbreak, they use insecticidal soap. It's important that their herbs are free from chemicals so they are safe to eat and provide healthly nectar resources for butterflies, hummingbirds, and other visitors to their gardens.

From aloe to watercress, the herbs at Shady Acres Herb Farm are fresh and organic. The Mieselers grow and sell about 150 varieties of herbs (as well as 200 varieties of fruits and vegetables). They sell onsite as well as participating in the Minneapolis Farmers Market. In addition to selling herb plants, they make a variety of herb-inspired foods, such as salsa, pickles, and sauerkraut. The peak of summer finds them canning tomatoes and drying herbs. Come fall, they turn their efforts to making herbed vinegars and pesto.

Opposite: **More than 150 herb varieties are sold at Shady Acres Herb Farm, including bronze fennel, sage, and Thai basil (shown growing with redbor kale).**

Above: **Jim and Theresa Mieseler have been growing herbs for more than 30 years.**

Making herbal vinegar For personal use or for gift-giving, herbal vinegars make beautiful additions to anyone's pantry and kitchen.

1 GATHER
Assemble the ingredients: fresh herbs (tarragon, thyme, mint, rosemary, basil, bay), garlic, dried hot pepper, and apple cider vinegar.

2 WASH
After you've washed the herbs and sterilized the bottle, insert the garlic clove, pepper, and any other nonleafy herbal addition.

3 COMBINE
Collect the herbs into a bundle and insert into the bottle.

4 PUSH
Use a toothpick or kabob skewer to push the herbs into the bottom of the bottle.

5 FILL
Top off the bottle with apple cider vinegar. Cover the bottle with a tight-fitting, nonmetallic lid. Let stand in a cool, dark place for one week. Strain the vinegar, removing the herbs.

In love with lavender

Lynda Dowling's passion for lavender began in 1986 when an elderly lady gave her a massive old 'Munstead' lavender from her garden. Lynda made 500 cuttings from the big plant, rooted them, then planted them in rows. "It was my first lavender block, and I was hooked," she said.

She and her husband, Michael, propagate lavender cuttings as a business now. Their Happy Valley Lavender & Herb Farm is located in Victoria on Vancouver Island, British Columbia. They grow lavender in long neat rows on an acre of their farmland, where they also run a nursery and sell lavender, and herb and veggie plants, as well as their dried lavender, teas, cooking blends, soaps, and seasonal lavender cosmetics.

Happy Valley Lavender & Herb Farm is a family business run by Lynda Dowling and her husband, Michael.

From essential oils to soothing products

The Romans used lavender to scent their baths; its name is derived from the Latin *lavare*, which means to wash, and refers to its ancient use in soaps and bath products. Like the Romans, Lynda uses the essential oils from her harvested flowers to make soaps, spritzes, lip balms, and hand salves, which she sells at the farm and online. "In aromatherapy, lavender oil is used to soothe, balance, and relax," says Lynda, who also makes lavender wands, cookies, brownies, and iced tea from her crop.

Lavender is a family affair. Lynda and her family sell lavender by the pound to chefs, crafters, and dried-flower arrangers, and plants to people who want to grow their own beautiful, fragrant lavender. The fields are mostly English lavender (*Lavandula angustifolia*). In the nursery they offer more than 30 varieties of lavender from French bold lavandin hybrids to Spanish (*L. stoechas*) with their "butterfly" tops to the latest woolly (*L. lanata*) crosses with velvety grey foliage and elegant dark blooms. Lavandins are especially popular with commercial growers in the Provence region of France because of their abundant essential oil.

Although lavender tolerates poor soil, Lynda always amends her planting blocks. "I like my lavender full and glorious," she says. "Our land has fir tree fringes and therefore the soil is on the acid side. So we add dolomite lime to sweeten the soil before we plant lavender. Also before planting we put in old manure and compost made of leaves, weeds, lawn clippings, food scraps, and old peat-based potting soil from the nursery. We rototill the soil and grow buckwheat on it as a summer cover crop. We want our lavenders to thrive, not just survive!"

At their Happy Valley Lavender & Herb Farm, lavender flowers are harvested during the third week of July. In summer, the farm evokes the lavender-smothered hill of Provence.

Freshly picked and bundled lavender will be hung up to air-dry, preserving it for crafts projects.

Lavender wands
Bring the sweet scent of lavender indoors with these wands. Both English lavender and lavandin make richly fragrant, long-lasting wands for perfuming a closet—or an entire room.

1 GATHER
Pick 15 to 20 long-stemmed sprigs of fresh flowering lavender. Also assemble scissors, strong thread, and ribbon.

2 BUNCH
Collect the lavender sprigs into a bunch and tie with the thread just under the flowerheads. Working in one direction, bend back each stem to enclose the flowers.

3 TIE
After all the stems are bent back, tie thread around the bundle, just past the flowers. Cover the thread with a decorative ribbon. Place the wands with stored clothes and linens to add a fresh lavender scent.

Living the herbal life

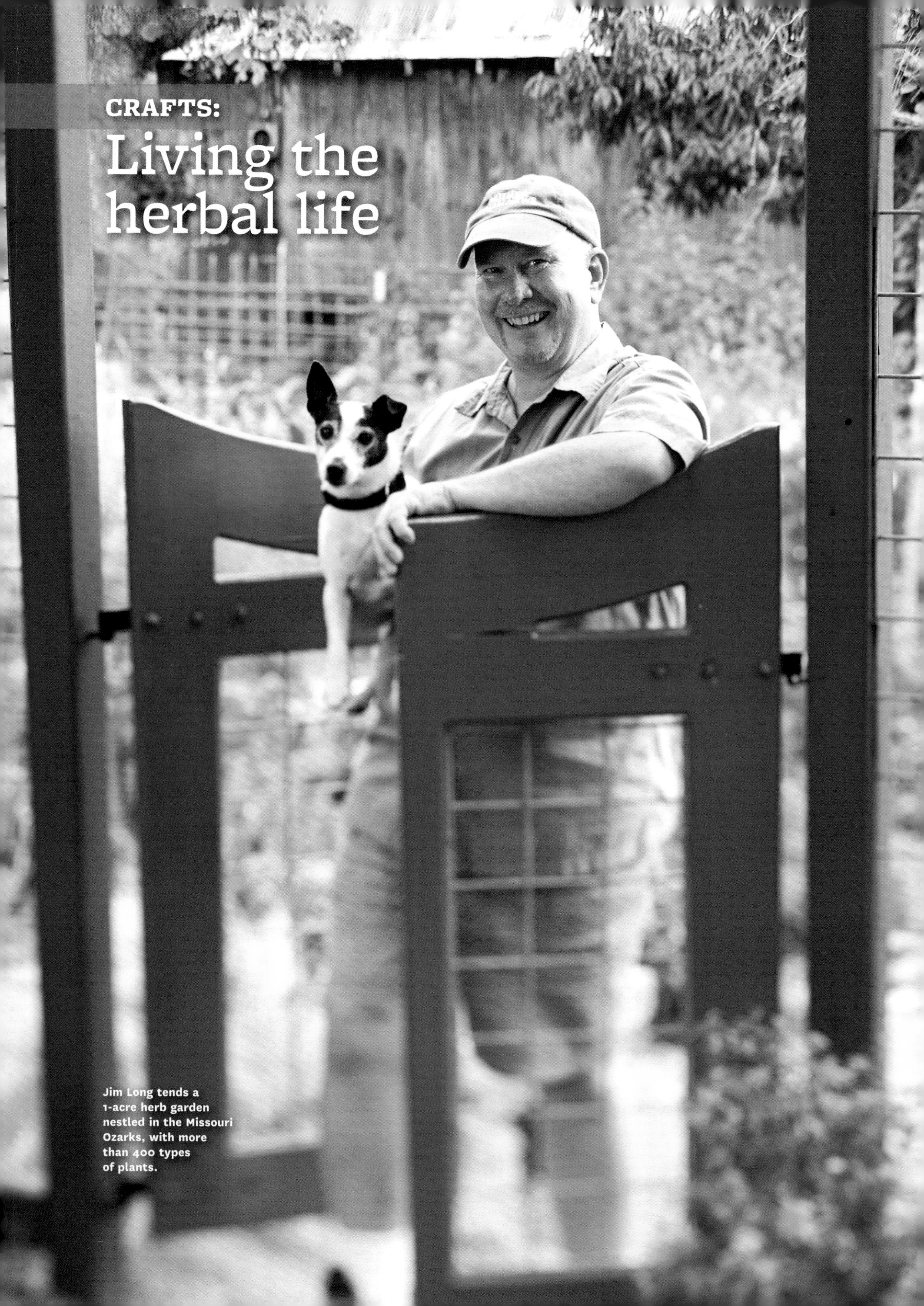

Jim Long tends a
1-acre herb garden
nestled in the Missouri
Ozarks, with more
than 400 types
of plants.

Nestled in the southern Missouri woods,

Jim Long and his partner Joshua Young are surrounded by herbs—it's their business and their passion. Long Creek Herb Farm, through their website and catalog, sells an extensive line of products ranging from Jim's books about using herbs and creating herbal projects to bulk herbs, seasonings, and herb-stuffed dream pillows.

The 1-acre garden is surrounded by the farm's 27 acres. The informal beds are filled with more than 400 plant species, both medicinal and culinary including many rare Asian herbs and vegetables. Unusual plants, such as the Bhut jalokia ghost pepper, rated as the world's hottest seasoning pepper, and the Udorn dancing tea plant (*Codariocalyx motorius*), with its odd habit of "dancing" when exposed to music or song, find space alongside more traditional herbs in the farm's raised beds. Also grown is mugwort, which is used to fill dream pillows and aromatic sachets made popular during the 18th century and still popular today. The blend of mugwort and other fragrant herbs are thought to inspire tranquil, dream-filled nights.

Edible and indigenous herbs

Culinary herbs feature lemongrass, which Jim uses on fish, and angelica, which he uses in desserts. Bronze fennel is a favorite. "It's a shame more people don't grow this plant," says Jim. "It's a tough perennial with tasty seeds, and their ornamental feathery leaves are sublime stuffed in trout. It grows easily in any soil, and a bonus is the black swallowtail butterflies it attracts."

Jim is interested in herbs that are indigenous to his part of the Ozarks, so sweet goldenrod and st. johnswort are grown in beds. Goldenrod is the locals' anise-scented substitute for tarragon, says Jim. "Ozarkers used st. johnswort to keep witches away."

Jim's books offer information for budding herbalists who want to learn how to grow and use herbs, make bentwood trellises, dream pillows, herbal cosmetics, flavorful sorbets and herbal crafts.

Indigenous plants from the Ozark region inhabit the beds and borders at Long Creek Herb Farm.

Pot-size bentwood trellis
Jim recycles saplings and prunings into attractive bentwood trellises. Here are steps for making a small, container-size trellis.

1 BEND
Choose pliable wood such as willow, honeysuckle, or grapevine. For bent pieces, use right after cutting, while the wood is still flexible.

2 TACK
For straight pieces, you can use dry wood. Cut off side branches so you have long, straight pieces. Hammer small nails to attach and secure the crosspieces.

3 CLIP
Snip off the ends of the crosspieces with a pair of pruners.

4 ADD
Make more bent pieces to add to the design. You can make the trellis as simple or elaborate as you want.

5 INSERT
Place the trellis in a container. It makes a great climbing structure for small herbs and also serves as an ornament for nonclimbers.

Flower and herb pairings

Pamela's trademark raised planters are lushly packed with flowers and herbs.

Pamela Crawford is a successful author and gardening expert

who has pioneered new garden design in a relatively small space: containers. She is known for her lavishly large and overpacked containers that feature dramatic layers of flowers and foliage. Her specialty: huge, extravagantly spilling containers—at least 14 inches in diameter but some as large as 27 inches across the top—that are set on posts so they look like flowery orbs floating in the air.

But is there a place for herbs in giant flower-packed pots? Pamela thinks so. In her book *Easy Container Combos: Herbs & Flowers* she features containers filled with herbs and flower pairings, making plants usually planted in separate beds seem like old friends.

Cutting-edge, colorful containers

Through her container designs, Pamela has moved herbs out of staid beds and into wildly colorful containers. Recognizing that many herbs are just as beautiful as flowers, she uses fragrant, textural, and edible herbs throughout her large containers. There's a side benefit in using such large pots—they don't dry out as fast as smaller pots.

Good-quality potting mix, a soilless combination of peat moss, perlite, and vermiculite—rather than potting soil, which is heavier—is essential to success. "New potting mixes are one of the greatest things that has ever happened to container gardening," Pamela says. "All you have to do is dump them into the pot, and they are almost the perfectly draining medium."

Pamela slips lots of herbs into her containers: lavender, sage, basil, rosemary, oregano, and thyme. Rosemary is her favorite, followed by basil. Both are easy to grow, fragrant, and delicious.

Above: **A surprising choice for a window box, tall rangy dill plants crown a flower-packed view.**

How to plant an herb-and-flower container

Combining herbs with flowers is easy. Pamela shows how to make a bold container garden that's edible too. This planting scheme includes 'Tiger Eye' black-eyed susan, bright globe amaranth, 'Dragon Wing' begonia, variegated oregano, and rosemary in a 19-inch blue-glazed pot.

1 ASSEMBLE
Start with a colorful container with a drainage hole. Fill with a good-quality potting mix. Assemble a mix of small to tall plants in a specific color palette.

2 PLANT
Remove the plants from their pots and insert them into the container at the same depth they were growing in their pots.

3 ARRANGE
Pack the taller annuals at the back or middle of the planter, depending on how it will be viewed. Snuggle plants together for the most instantaneous impact.

4 INSERT
Add lower-growing herbs such as rosemary and thyme to the front of the container. This allows for easy clipping access.

5 ENJOY
Created in just minutes, this colorful and flavorful container gets its good looks from flowers, herbs, and a well-packed planting style.

Body and Soul

Michelle King, owner of Martha's Herbary, sells raw materials to make natural herbal-inspired cleaning products too. "We use a lot of lavender oil for making home cleaners," she says.

"Herbs are so beneficial—both inside and out," says Michelle King, owner of Martha's Herbary in Pomfret, Connecticut. Michelle has been owner of the herb shop since 2009. She worked with shop founder Martha Paul; Michelle carries on the shop and garden's mission, which is to promote and provide organic herbs in various forms and uses.

Making your own herbal spa, cosmetic, bathing, and home cleaning products is easy, says Michelle. Using organically grown plants, flowers, leaves, roots, and stems, she offers classes that teach budding herbalists how to use restorative lavender, soothing calendula, invigorating mint, and other natural ingredients to make bath salts, herbal waters, and sugar scrubs.

Restorative recipes include an easy and soothing herbal bath—simply place fresh or dried herbs in a small cloth bag or washcloth to hang under the faucet to scent and condition the water. Or blend a few drops of essential oil (Michelle's favorite is lavender) with a carrier oil such as sweet almond or avocado. Use the oil in bath water or directly on your skin during dry winter months. "Lavender essential oil is so versatile," she says. "It's antifungal, antibacterial, and you can put it directly on your skin to soothe the itch of a bug bite."

Michelle also offers classes in making body scrubs. Lavender and vanilla—two of Michelle's favorite scents—create a fragrant sugar scrub. She combines white sugar, vanilla bean scrapings, and lavender essential oil mixed with a carrier oil (such as grapeseed or almond oil). "This makes a great sugar scrub for your hands," she says. "The lavender relaxes you." The same mix, substituting peppermint oil for the lavender, makes an invigorating foot scrub. "The peppermint wakes up your feet," she says.

Other herbal pick-me-ups include flower water. "Take your favorite herb, pour hot water over it and steep it like tea, then strain it. Cool it and bottle it," she says. "I use it in bathwater. I add it to witch hazel for a summer facial spritz. I also make linen sprays using distilled water."

Martha's Herbary features a ½-acre garden that includes 13 raised beds, a traditional English-style garden, and a sunken garden with medicinal herbs.

Herbal cosmetics
Make delightful concoctions for personal use with various ingredients including herbs from your garden and simple items you can find in your pantry:

CLEANSING GRAINS AND BATH SALTS Add dried rose petals and lavender flowers and leaves to coarse salt.

CHAMOMILE TEA BAGS Add chamomile flowers to a teabag or cloth mesh bag and soak it in cool water. Place the bag on closed eyes or daub it on your face for refreshment.

HERB VINEGAR ASTRINGENT Add calendula, spearmint, peppermint, and other herbs to vinegar for an excellent astringent.

herb encyclopedia

Herbs have many alluring talents in the garden, kitchen, and bath. Snip their leaves and flowers to use their flavors and fragrances.

WHERE TO PLANT

Choose the best planting spot for annual and perennial herbs to ensure the most bountiful and flavorful harvests. Check out planting tips for each herb on the pages that follow.

HARVEST TIPS

Learn the ideal harvest time and method for each herb. Picked at their peak, herbs season recipes, make healthful teas, and offer fragrant leaves and flowers for aromatherapy.

USE GUIDELINES

Find out the popular uses of herbs from all over the world—fresh, dried, and in classic recipes. Discover the best varieties of herbs to suit your specific needs.

Aloe Vera (*Aloe vera*)

Talk about easy care. Aloe vera has simple needs: Sunshine and a little water make it very happy. In return, the plants provide you with handsome, spiky foliage that contains a gel-like sap used to soothe burns and moisturize skin.

YOU SHOULD KNOW
Aloe vera is a versatile plant that grows just as well in a container indoors on a sunny windowsill as it does outdoors.

Aloe vera is a perennial tropical plant native to hot, dry regions of Africa. It has been used in traditional medicine around the world, and can be traced to early Egypt (nearly 6,000 years ago), where an image that resembles an aloe vera plant is depicted on stone carvings. Carl Linnaeus identified and named aloe vera in 1753 as *Aloe perfoliata* var. *vera*. It is referred to as the plant of immortality and the first-aid plant because of its healing properties.

Best site
Full sun is ideal. This plant does best in arid climates. Throughout much of the country, aloe vera is grown in containers that can be moved indoors when frost threatens. In frost-free regions it can be grown outdoors.

Planting
Aloe vera can be grown from seed, but it's faster and easier to buy young plants at your local garden center or greenhouse. Pot them in a soil mix designed for succulents. As plants mature, they develop offsets that can be divided and potted individually.

Growing
Set aloe vera in a location that receives at least six hours of sun a day. Because this is a succulent plant, the leaves have a high water content so it's important not to expose it to freezing temperatures. Water when the soil feels dry to the touch. Indoors during the winter, keep plants in bright light; water less often. In the spring, give your plants a diluted solution of liquid houseplant fertilizer. Zones 9–11.

Harvest
Leaves can be broken off and used at any time.

Uses
Healing touch Aloe vera gel can be applied as a soothing balm for cuts or second-degree burns and is thought to have antioxidant and anti-inflammatory properties. It is found in many skin products, including lotions, sunblocks, and salves. Aloe vera gel is not to be confused with aloe juice and should not be taken internally.

Landscape design Aloe vera makes a dramatic edging plant for garden beds.

Succulent bowl Combined with other succulents, such as jade plant, panda plant, and echeveria, aloe vera is an excellent addition to succulent containers.

Angelica
(*Angelica archangelica*)

Angelica is a tall, hardy biennial. It has dramatic stalks that can be candied and used on cakes or cookies. It also is used to flavor liqueurs such as Chartreuse. It bears ball-shape pale green to cream flowers with a pleasant fragrance.

In ancient times angelica was an herb of protection from witchcraft and illness, including the plague. Angelica is associated with protector angels—specifically Michael the Archangel—from which the herb gets the species name *archangelica*.

Best site
Plant angelica in full sun in a location where it has plenty of room. It can take dappled shade. This easy-care herb grows 4 to 6 feet tall. Place it at the back of the border.

Planting
Angelica can be grown from seeds, root divisions, or transplants purchased at your local garden center or nursery. The first year, the plants produce lots of beautiful frilly green foliage. The second year, angelica shoots up flower stalks and then produces seeds.

Growing
This herb does best in a rich, organic soil that remains slightly moist. In poor soil, add rotted manure or compost to the bed at planting time. Angelica is somewhat drought tolerant. Plants may self-sow, but as a precaution, plant new angelica each year. Mulch the soil around the plants to prevent weed competition and to maintain consistent soil moisture. Zones 5–9.

Harvest
Use all parts of the plants: seeds, stems, and roots. Pick leaves and stems in the plant's second year—early in the season, when they are tender. Gather seeds in autumn, then dig the roots.

Uses
In garden beds This big, bold bloomer offers flowers and foliage as a tall, back-of-the-border accent in perennial gardens.

Tea Angelica root can be dried and used for tea.

Candied treats The celery-flavor stems can be candied. The stems may be eaten raw.

YOU SHOULD KNOW Bees love angelica, so if you want to increase the pollinators in your garden, include this plant.

①

varieties:

① **PURPLE ANGELICA** (*Archangelica gigas*) Plants have pretty reddish-purple stems and flowers.

Anise Hyssop
(*Agastache foeniculum*)

This 2- to 5-foot-tall plant produces upright columns of fuzzy, purplish-blue blooms in late summer. The scent of anise hyssop is a marriage of licorice (anise and licorice are synonymous) and mint (because this plant is also a member of the mint family).

YOU SHOULD KNOW
Anise hyssop self-seeds with abandon. If you don't want this lovely herb to spread (and to avoid having to hand-weed seedlings every spring), deadhead the flowers as soon as they fade.

Anise hyssop was used extensively by Native Americans, who called on it to relieve depression. It was also used in medicine bundles.

Best site
Plant in full sun in moist to well-drained soil. Anise hyssop can also grow in light shade. To improve the fertility of the planting area, add 2 inches of compost to the soil.

Planting
Plants spread 1 to 3 feet wide, so space them accordingly. Plant transplants or seedlings (if you have a friend who has this plant, self-sown seedlings should be readily available).

Growing
Start anise hyssop from seeds about eight weeks before your last frost date. You can also sow seeds directly in the garden. If buying seedlings, wait until the threat of frost has passed before planting. For established plants, divide large clumps in spring. Zones 4–10.

Harvest
Gather leaves from established plants any time of the season. Start from the base of the plant and harvest leaves in the morning. The plants combine beautifully with silver-leaved herbs such as artemisia and sage. Anise hyssop attracts bees and provides them with generous forage. To dry leaves to use as seasoning later or for tea, cut whole stems, make into bundles, and hang upside down to dry. Remove dried leaves and store. Cut fresh flowers when they are about three-fourths open. Use the flowers in bouquets.

Uses
Deer-resistant gardens These plants don't taste good to deer, so they are ideal for gardens in deer-heavy areas.

Pollinator attractant Loved by hummingbirds, butterflies, and bees, anise hyssop is a must-have plant for gardeners who want to attract and feed winged wildlife.

Scent blends The leaves and flowers make pleasant additions to fragrant potpourris and sachets.

varieties:

❶ **'BLUE FORTUNE'** (*Agastache foeniculum*) grows 3 feet tall and blooms July through September. Zones 4–9.

❷ **'GOLDEN JUBILEE'** (*A. foeniculum*) produces chartreuse foliage and lavender-purple flower spikes. It grows 2 to 3 feet tall in Zones 4–10.
KOREAN HYSSOP (*A. rugosa*), This agastache grows 4 feet tall and has a sharper scent and flavor than anise hyssop. Zones 5–9.

Artemisia
(Artemisia)

Artemisias are prized for their beautiful silvery foliage that complements other perennials and herbs in the border. The different members of the family go by various common names, such as wormwood, prairie sage, and sagebrush.

Artemisia was a folk remedy used to treat digestive system disturbances. Chinese herbalists used artemisia to treat fevers in ancient times.

Best site
Plant in full sun and well-drained soil. Artemisias thrive in hot, dry conditions. All species can grow quite large and make poor candidates for containers.

Planting
Start artemisia from nursery-grown plants, spacing them at least 2 to 3 feet apart. Many species will self-sow, providing you with artemisia seedlings for friends and family. Taller species may topple in high winds and may require staking.

Growing
Artemisias are drought tolerant. They thrive in sandy soil with only an occasional watering to keep them looking good. Hold off on fertilizer. These plants prefer soil low in nutrients.

Harvest
Artemisia foliage can be clipped at any time. You may also cut the plants back severely if they start to flop over their neighbors in the border.

Uses
Insect repellent This pungent herb can be used to deter insects in closets or dresser drawers.

Flower foil Artemisia provides an elegant backdrop for flowers such as dahlias and roses.

Nature gardens Artemisia is the host plant for several species of butterfly larvae. Plants are so vigorous that caterpillar leaf damage is typically not noticeable.

Everlastings The frosty gray foliage dries well and provides an ideal addition to wreaths, swags, and other decorative arrangements. Cut 4-inch stems, gather them into bundles, and attach the sprays to a base for an elegant wreath.

YOU SHOULD KNOW
Trim the new growth of artemisias by a few inches to shape them and prevent them from flopping over later in the summer. Cut plants to 6 inches in fall.

varieties:

1. **WHITE SAGE** (*Artemisia ludoviciana*), the variety used to make Owyhee oil, is a fruity-smelling artemisia with a hint of peach. Zones 4–9.
2. **'SILVER KING'** (*A. ludoviciana*) grows 4 feet tall, creating a tower of silver foliage for back-of-the-border locations. It spreads easily. Zones 4–9.
3. **'POWIS CASTLE'** grows 3 feet tall with feathery, finely serrated silver leaves. Zones 4–9.

Basil (*Ocimum*)

If summer had a flavor, it would taste like basil. An ideal companion to tomatoes, basil offers spicy flavors when used fresh or cooked in sauces. This popular annual herb is easy to grow and comes in many varieties: sweet big-leaved selections, lemon-flavor, purple-hued, and compact dwarf types. The flavors range from citrus to spicy, with a touch of anise.

Basil has a rich history. It is a sacred herb in India and Thailand; in Italy it is a traditional symbol of love and romance. As a medicinal it has been used to relieve sore throats, headaches, and nausea. There are more than 150 varieties of basil.

Best site

Plant basil in full sun. Although it grows best in moist soil, it will tolerate drought conditions for short periods as long as it has an established root system, which develops about six weeks after planting. Basil grows well in garden beds, whether in a traditional kitchen garden or mixed with perennials and annuals in a flower garden. It also grows well in containers. Use a well-drained potting mix and plant in a container that holds at least 5 gallons of soil.

Planting

Start from seeds or transplants. Basil is a tender herb. Plant only after the threat of frost has passed. It grows slowly in cool weather, but once the weather warms, basil flourishes. Sow seeds indoors in early spring and transplant into the garden after the danger of frost is over. Thin seedlings to 1 to 3 feet apart. Seedlings are a great way to grow different basil varieties.

Growing

Cover plants with cloches, cold frames, or protective cloth in cool regions or anytime frost is predicted. To encourage bushy growth, cut or pinch off flowers as they form. Basil does not need extra fertilizer; in fact, excessive nutrients result in poor flavor. Average garden soil provides all the necessary nutrients. Keep the soil around plants consistently moist and free of weeds. To help satisfy moisture needs and stifle weeds, spread a 2-inch-thick layer of mulch around plants when they are about 6 inches tall.

Harvest

Begin harvesting basil as soon as the plant has at least four sets of leaves. For the most intense flavor, harvest leaves just as the flower buds begin to form. Pinch out the topmost set of leaves and any flowers as needed for use in the kitchen. After harvesting, store unwashed basil in plastic bags in the refrigerator for a day or two. Basil cuttings won't last long; the foliage begins to turn black after a few days. You can also stand cut stems in a glass of water and keep them handy on your countertop. Preserve fresh leaves by pulverizing them in a food processor with olive oil, then placing the paste in an airtight bag or other container and storing it in the freezer for up to a year. Basil can be dried, but dried basil is neither as flavorful nor as colorful as basil preserved with oil.

Uses

Tea Steep 2 teaspoons dried or fresh leaves in 1 cup boiling water. Strain out the leaves and sweeten the tea with honey or sugar.

Chiffonade Large-leaved basils are ideal for cutting into thin strips and sprinkling on dishes. This preparation technique is called chiffonade: Stack large basil leaves, roll them tightly, then cut across the roll using a sharp knife. Use the ribbons of flavorful basil to top soups, sauces, and salads.

Edible flowers The spicy sprays of basil flowers can be used to spark salads and soups.

Breath freshener Chew a basil plant stem to freshen your breath.

A few full-size basil plants provide plenty of leaves to make several batches of pesto, a paste made of basil, garlic, nuts, and oil. Use pesto on pasta, pizza, and bread; freeze small amounts in freezer bags to enjoy in the winter. Large-leaved basils such as 'Genovese' make excellent pestos.

varieties:

❶ 'GENOVESE' grows 2 to 3 feet tall and 2 feet wide. The large, fragrant leaves can be harvested all summer. This tall, productive basil grows at least 2 feet tall.

❷ 'PESTO PERPETUO' has variegated foliage (cream-edged pale green leaves) and forms a columnar plant that reaches 3 feet tall. It seldom blooms. Use it in pots or the landscape.

❸ 'MRS. BURNS' LEMON' is a tall and narrow basil that's a green-leaved version of 'Pesto Perpetuo'. It grows 18 inches tall. It has a delightful lemony fragrance and flavor.

❹ 'SWEET THAI' has a pronounced spicy, anise flavor and pretty reddish purple stems on 12- to 18-inch-tall plants.

❺ 'RED RUBIN' looks as gorgeous in flower borders as it does in bouquets. This purple-leaved beauty grows 2 feet tall and 14 inches wide.

❻ 'SPICY GLOBE' is one of the best basil varieties for use in small spaces, reaching only 6 to 10 inches tall. It has a spicy flavor, tiny leaves, and a compact form.

❼ 'CINNAMON' has tasty, cinnamon-flavored leaves. Plants grow 18 inches tall.

Bay Laurel
(*Laurus nobilis*)

A mainstay in every chef's arsenal, bay is a warm-climate tree that's easily grown in containers in northern gardens. Where it is hardy outdoors, bay can grow to 30 feet tall, but in a container it typically tops out at 3 to 5 feet.

YOU SHOULD KNOW Bay is a slow-growing plant, so buy the largest plant you can find. The bigger the plant, the more leaves you can harvest.

The leaves of bay laurel have a heralded and symbolic past. In ancient Greece laurel wreaths indicated high status, and in Rome laurel was a symbol of victory and accomplishment.

Best site
Bay needs a sunny spot that receives at least six hours of direct sunlight a day. Start with a young plant from a local nursery or greenhouse, or start cuttings taken from branch tips.

Planting
Plant bay in a good-quality potting soil that drains well. Water whenever the soil's surface feels dry to the touch; bay prefers to be on the dry side and will suffer in wet soil.

Growing
Bay is a slow-growing plant that benefits from a dose of liquid houseplant fertilizer in the spring. In late spring or early summer, move the plant outdoors where it will benefit by spending the season in a sunny spot. New leaf growth can be targeted by aphids. If you notice the tiny green insects on the plant, blast them off with a jet of water from the garden hose. Bay cannot tolerate temperatures below 25°F and must be moved indoors to protect it from cold weather. Once indoors, keep the plant in bright light, away from cold drafts. Indoors, if a bay tree becomes infested with scale, spray the plant with insecticidal soap. Zones 9–11.

Harvest
Leaves can be harvested at any time, but you can snip off extra leaves in the late spring as the plant puts out new growth. Bay leaves can be dried and used for up to three months after harvest. Their flavor dissipates quickly.

Uses

Soup and stew seasoning Use fresh or dried bay leaves to season food. Bay is an ideal seasoning for poultry and fish dishes. Add the whole leaves to soups and stews, and be sure to remove them before serving to eliminate a choking hazard.

Topiary Bay can be clipped into shapes, most commonly the classic ball topping a bare trunk.

Wreaths The stiff almond-shape leaves of bay make it ideal for wreath making.

Bayberry
(*Myrica pensylvanica*)

A North American native, bayberry forms a beautiful semi-evergreen shrub that can grow up to 8 feet tall. An adaptable coastal shrub, bayberry is most prized for its grayish-white berries that have a waxy covering.

The Choctaw tribe used the bark of bayberry for a variety of medicinal uses, including fever reduction. In the Colonial era, bayberry was favored for its waxy berries, which were used for candle making. Bayberry candles are fragrant when burned and offer a bright light. Bayberry is also called candleberry and tallowbush.

Best site
Bayberry will grow in full sun or partial shade. It prefers coastal areas, where it thrives in poor, sandy soils. The roots of bayberry have nitrogen-fixing bacteria on their surface that allows the shrub to grow in extremely poor soil. Bayberry tolerates salt spray, making it a good choice for landscapes along the east coast.

Planting
Buy bayberry plants at your local nursery or garden center. Because these plants can grow 8 feet tall and wide, be sure to give each plant enough space to stretch out. Plants are either male or female; to ensure berry production, always plant at least two to three shrubs in the same landscape.

Growing
Once planted, bayberry requires little care. The plants bloom in the early spring, developing small white or green flowers that eventually form prized grayish-white, waxy berries. The berries are about $1/8$ inch in diameter and are popular

with a wide range of songbirds. Pruning is rarely necessary, but the plants can be shaped at any time. Zones 3–6.

Harvest
The berries appear on the plants in late fall and, if left alone, they will remain on the plant throughout the winter. To harvest the berries, simply pluck them from the branch.

Uses
Essential oils Bayberry leaves can be used to produce a delightfully fragrant essential oil.

Candle making Harvest the berries, cover them with water, and boil. The waxy coating from the berries will harden on the surface of the water as it cools. Skim the wax and use it to make candles. Four pounds of berries yields a pound of wax.

 **YOU SHOULD KNOW**
If you live in an eastern coastal area, bayberry makes an excellent landscape plant. You need to plant several shrubs to ensure the best berry production.

Bee Balm
(*Monarda didyma*)

Bee balm, also known as bergamot, attracts pollinators such as butterflies, hummingbirds, and bees in droves. For that reason alone, it's good to have this plant in your garden. Herb fans enjoy this plant for its flowers because they are edible. The aromatic, citrusy-minty leaves are a plus.

YOU SHOULD KNOW Bee balm or bergamot is not the source for the essential oil known as bergamot. That citrusy essence is derived from a fruit (*Citrus bergamia*) that provides the distinctive flavor in Earl Grey tea.

Also called Oswego tea, the leaves of bee balm were used by the Oswego tribe of New York. Native Americans discovered medicinal uses of bee balm and shared them with the settlers in America. They used the plant for poultices to cure skin infections and tea that promoted dental health. It's no surprise that bee balm has been found to contain antiseptic qualities.

Best site
Although bee balm prefers full sun, it tolerates some shade. Plants grown in partial shade, however, produce fewer flowers. Bee balm can grow in a wide variety of soil conditions, although it does best in moist, well-drained soil. In dry soils plants do not grow as vigorously. This plant does not do well in climates where winters are warm and humid.

varieties:

1 **MONARDA DIDYMA** has a citrus aroma. Plants grow 2 to 3 feet tall in Zones 3–9.
2 **'CAMBRIDGE SCARLET'** has leafy clumps of 3-foot-tall stems clothed with aromatic oval leaves. The terminal whorls of bright red two-lipped flowers are surrounded by brownish-red bracts. Zones 3–9.

Planting
Bee balm is slow to start from seed, so buy established plants. Transplants will generally bloom the first year. Plants vary in size by variety but are generally 3 feet tall and wide. Allow room between plants to avoid fungal diseases.

Growing
This perennial is loved by flower gardeners because it blooms all summer, producing shaggy blooms, from lavender, pink, white, red, or magenta. Plant bee balm in perennial borders where it can spread out. Prune plants almost to the ground in fall. Powdery mildew and rust can affect plants, but most bee balms are resistant to most wilts and viruses. Slugs can be a pest early in the season. Zones 3–10.

Harvest
Both the leaves and flowers are edible. To dry leaves and flowers, cut stems, bundle them in small groups, and hang upside down in a cool, dry location. Or dry stems, leaves, and flowers on a screen.

Uses
Sage substitute Use dried bee balm leaves as a citrusy substitute for sage in seasonings for poultry and pork. It makes a tasty dry rub.

Potpourri Because of its minty and citrusy scents, bee balm leaves and flowers are ideal for sachets and potpourris.

Edible flowers Remove the flower petals from the fringy bee balm heads and scatter them into salads or use to garnish dips.

Pollinator attractant Bees love bee balm—hence the name.

Betony
(*Stachys officinalis*)

Commonly called wood betony or bishop's wort, betony is a close relative of the common perennial lamb's-ears. This sturdy herb has nectar-rich flowers that attract bees and butterflies to the garden in late summer.

YOU SHOULD KNOW
Early herbalists claimed betony could cure a variety of ailments and often called this versatile plant self-heal or heal-all.

For centuries betony was credited as a cure-all for many ailments and was used as a talisman against evil spirits. In Europe it was frequently planted in physic gardens and churchyards. Ancient healers prescribed betony for nearly everything from curing coughs to deworming. Today it is grown mostly to draw pollinators to the garden.

Best site
Betony prefers a sunny spot, but it will grow in partial shade. The drought-tolerant plant prefers soil enriched with organic material such as compost. Although drought-tolerant, it does best when watered on a regular basis.

Planting
Start betony from seeds, cuttings, or divisions. Because it's not a particularly common plant, you may have some difficulty finding seeds locally, but there are seed sources available online. Once started, betony requires little care. Sow seeds ½ inch deep.

Growing
As plants sprout, cultivate frequently to eliminate weed competition. Betony thrives in moist conditions. Mulch between young plants to help conserve soil moisture. It takes two years for betony to mature and flower. The plant's attractive flowers are a deep reddish-purple and lure bees and other pollinators. Mature plants grow to about 2 feet tall. Zones 4–8.

Harvest
Cut stems just as the flowers are beginning to open. Pluck the leaves and dry them on a rack or screen in a well-ventilated, dark location. Store the dried leaves in an airtight container.

Uses
Tea Use the whole dried leaves to make tea. Use 2 teaspoons of leaves for every cup of boiling water. Allow the tea to steep, covered, then remove the leaves. Betony tea is reputed to cure headaches, sore throats, and nervousness.

Cut flowers Harvest flowers as they are just opening for herbal bouquets.

Attract pollinators The sweet nectar of betony flowers attracts bees and butterflies.

Perennial garden The purple blooms of this plant make stunning additions to perennial gardens alongside yellow flowers such as yarrow and daylily.

varieties:

1. **'ROSEA'** (*Stachys officinalis*) provides a summerlong display of spires of small pink flowers above compact, healthy clumped foliage. Zones 5–8.
2. **'SUPERBA'** (*S. macrantha*), also called big betony, grows 24 inches tall and is topped with lovely pink flowers. Zones 4–8.

Borage (*Borago officinalis*)

Borage has an outstanding presence in a garden, growing 1 to 3 feet tall and 2 feet wide. The plant appears as natural in an herb garden as it is mingling with perennials. The plant has notably fuzzy stems and leaves. Gardeners especially appreciate this herb for its edible periwinkle blue blooms—and so do bees!

YOU SHOULD KNOW
Borage has a reputation as a self-seeding plant. To prevent the herb from becoming too gregarious, weed out early-spring seedlings.

Borage was thought to instill courage in ancient times. A native of the Mediterranean region, this distinctive herb was used as a remedy for sore throats and skin disorders. You can buy borage seed oil pills, which have shown anti-inflammatory effects. Borage is also called starflower for its bright blue blooms, and its leaves and flowers are edible.

Best site
Plant borage in a sunny spot in well-drained soil. Borage will, however, do well in poorer soils if fertilized with compost.

Planting
Start seeds indoors a month or so before the last frost in cold climates. Transplant seedlings or purchased plants into the garden once the threat of frost has passed and the soil is warm.

Growing
Although borage is classified as an herb, flower gardeners use it in mixed perennial borders. It is also a popular addition to vegetable gardens because of its ability to attract pollinating insects. Borage is considered a good companion plant for tomatoes, strawberries, and squash. Allow enough space for this rangy plant to spread out to 2 feet. Borage continues to bloom throughout the summer. This herb is an annual but it readily self-sows to come back each year.

Harvest
Harvest borage flowers when they are fully open. Harvest new leaf growth; the leaves are fuzzy, but blanching them makes them more palatable.

Uses

Edible flowers The flowers are a bright blue (and sometimes pink or white). Harvest the flowers to dress up salads, summer drinks, or desserts. Pluck flowers moments before serving time, remove the prickly back, and rinse flowers before serving. Sprinkle these bright edibles into fresh greens. Because vinegar discolors flowers, add borage flowers to salads just before serving. If not using the blooms right away, store them in a glass or plastic container in the refrigerator.

Desert garnishes Borage flowers can be candied in sugar and used to decorate cakes or cupcakes.

Ice cube adornments Freeze borage flowers with water in ice cube trays to add to summer drinks.

Leaves Borage leaves can be used in recipes such as rustic raviolis, soups, or fritters.

Salads Harvest young leaves of borage plants for salads. The flowers and the leaves have a cucumber flavor.

Herbal bouquets Borage leaves and flowers make beautiful additions to herbal bouquets to give as gifts or use as a centerpiece.

Calamint
(Calamintha nepeta)

Calamint looks as much at home in the perennial border as it does in the herb garden. This compact plant develops small leaves that have a refreshing, minty fragrance. Calamint is dotted with masses of tiny white flowers that attract butterflies.

Calamint, because of its minty aroma, was often historically used in the kitchen and as an herbal remedy for stomach problems. It's also called lesser calamint.

Best site
Calamint grows well in any sunny location with well-drained soil. It tolerates heat and drought and because it only grows 18 inches tall, it makes an excellent edging plant along walkways and paths. In the extreme southern part of its range, plant calamint where it's protected from the hot afternoon sun.

Planting
This herb can be grown from seeds that germinate easily. Start four to six weeks before last frost date in spring. For faster results, buy started transplants at your local garden center or from a mail-order garden catalog. Space plants about 15 inches apart.

Growing
Once established, calamint requires almost no maintenance. It develops pretty, light-green leaves that resemble oregano. In late summer the plant produces waves of tiny white or lavender flowers until frost. Although calamint is resistant to dry spells, mulch between plants to maintain soil moisture. This healthy plant has few problems with pests or disease. Typically, calamint is a short-lived perennial and may not return after four or five years. Otherwise, the plant may self-sow and reappear in your garden. Zones 4–9.

Harvest
Use leaves as needed from spring to fall to make teas or to flavor soups and stews. Harvest whole stems. Leaves can be used fresh or dried.

Uses
Deer garden As a member of the mint family, this herb is uninteresting to deer.

Pollinator attractant The tiny flowers attract butterflies and bees.

Oregano substitute This herb is sometimes used in Italian cuisine as an oregano substitute. In Tuscany, it is used to flavor mushroom and meat dishes.

YOU SHOULD KNOW You can't beat calamint for its minty foliage and beautiful late-summer flowers. It's also a snap to grow in any sunny spot.

Calendula
(*Calendula officinalis*)

Beautiful and edible, calendula flowers will brighten your spring garden. The cool-season annual is easy to grow. You can harvest the bright petals and use them to add color and zip to soups and salads. These bright beauties also make long-lasting cut flowers.

YOU SHOULD KNOW
Calendula is versatile. It looks great in herb gardens, in mixed flowerbeds, and even in containers planted with salad crops, such as Swiss chard or lettuce.

A native of southern Europe, calendula was named by the ancient Romans for its nonstop blooming habit. It was used by ancient Egyptians as an herb of rejuvenation. In Europe, calendula flowers were used to color cheese.

Best site
Calendula requires a sunny spot in the garden that receives at least six to eight hours of direct sunshine a day. The plants prefer well-draining soil enriched with organic material.

Planting
Calendula grows easily from seed, whether started indoors or planted directly in the garden. Or start with transplants from a local nursery or garden center. Space plants 6 to 8 inches apart. They will grow up to 3 feet, depending on variety. Calendula also grows beautifully in containers. It goes by the common name pot marigold.

varieties:

1 **'CANDYMAN ORANGE'** develops showy double orange flowers on compact 1-foot-tall plants.

2 **'DAISY MIX'** has single flowers in a variety of colors that include yellow, apricot, and orange on 1-foot-tall plants.

Growing
The key to success with calendula is to remember it prefers cool weather, so plant early in the spring or fall. Heat is calendula's biggest enemy. When the temperature soars, calendula will die back. In the southernmost parts of the country, you can grow calendula for winter color. To keep your plants blooming, remove flowers as they fade. However, at the end of the season, let a few flowers mature and form seeds. Your calendula may sow itself for next season's display.

Harvest
The petals of calendula can be harvested at any time, but it's best to pick them as soon as the flowers open. The petals of young blooms will be more tender than those of older flowers. You can dry the petals on screens for use later.

Uses
Saffron substitute For rice dishes such as paella, use calendula flowers to take the place of the more expensive saffron.

Skin oils Infuse flowers in olive or jojoba oil to make skin treatments for bee stings, bug bites, and rashes.

Edible flowers The cream, orange, apricot or yellow flower petals of calendula add vibrant color to a salad.

Caraway (*Carum carvi*)

Caraway has been cultivated for centuries. This versatile plant—a member of the carrot family—produces tasty edible seeds. The leaves and parsniplike roots are also edible. As a biennial, the plant blooms in its second year.

YOU SHOULD KNOW
Caraway is a biennial, meaning you'll have to wait until its second year in the garden for the plant to produce flowers and seeds.

In ancient times, caraway was favored as a remedy for digestive tract disturbances. The seeds were used in various other medicines. It is still known for its antiflatulence qualities. Today, caraway seeds bring their distinctive flavor to rye and other breads. All parts of the plant are edible.

Best site
Caraway prefers a sunny location and rich, well-drained soil. Because the plant develops a large taproot, loose soil is best. Although the plant tolerates drought, the soil should not be allowed to dry out completely.

Planting
Grow caraway from seeds sown directly in a garden bed. Sow seeds about ½ inch deep. The seeds may be slow to germinate. When seedlings have developed several sets of leaves, thin them to about 8 inches apart. Gently pull out or snip off the extra plants.

Growing
Cultivate around caraway plants every few weeks to eliminate weeds. Once the plants are several inches tall, spread mulch between them to help keep weeds at bay. Weed prevention is essential while the plants are young. Water the plants thoroughly during dry spells. Caraway has few insect pests, but some foliage diseases may affect your crop. To avoid this, keep the foliage as dry as possible by hand-watering with a hose early in the day or using drip irrigation. Zones 5–8.

Harvest
Gather seeds before they fall. Cut the stalks as soon as the seeds begin to ripen and turn brown. Then bundle the stems and hang them upside down in a dry, airy place over a large tray until the seeds are completely dry. Hold the dried seedheads inside a large paper bag and shake them to release the seeds. Store the seeds in an airtight container and use them within one year.

Uses
Salads Harvest the young leaves for use in salads or as a seasoning for soups and stews.

Root dishes The roots can be boiled in the same manner as parsnips or carrots.

Seasoning for baking The seeds are a flavorful ingredient in breads, cakes, cookies, soups, sauces, and vegetable dishes.

Catmint
(*Nepeta* ×*faassenii*)

Catmint is a tough perennial herb that excels in hot, dry weather. Plants feature mounding sprays of silvery-green foliage with a flush of blue flowers. Although the name suggests cats are attracted by this herb, they aren't as tantalized by it as they are by catnip.

YOU SHOULD KNOW Catmint is easy to divide. After the flowers fade in late summer, dig up large plants, separate them into smaller plants, and replant them with room to grow.

Catmint was used historically for brewing tea that was enjoyed as a relaxing hot beverage as well as a medicinal drink to relieve fever. An ancient attribute is that catmint gives strength to timid people.

Best site
For best results, choose a sunny location with average, well-draining soil. Catmint is a drought-tolerant plant and can grow in partially shaded locations, although it will not bloom as well.

Planting
Sow catmint seeds indoors or directly in the ground. Mature plants self-seed. Transplant these seedlings elsewhere in your garden. Space plants according to the variety's mature size. Most varieties range from 6 to 36 inches tall and from 2 to 4 feet wide.

Growing
Catmint is easy to grow. The tall types may need gentle staking, but otherwise it is a easy-care plant. Deadhead or cut back hard after first flush of bloom to encourage more flowers. Zones 5–9.

Harvest
To dry leaves, cut the stems and bundle them; hang the bunch to dry in a cool, airy location. After the stems are crisp-dry, strip off the whole leaves and store them in an airtight container.

Uses
Tea Catmint makes an interesting tea with a mild minty-spicy flavor.

Rock gardens Catmint is a long-blooming option for rock gardens.

Lavender substitute In cold climates, include the blue-purple bloomer in the perennial garden as a good alternative to more tender lavender.

Garden edger Catmint is a pretty edging plant. It spills over pathways and blooms nearly all summer long.

varieties:

1. **'SIX HILLS GIANT'** is one of the tallest growing catmints. It reaches up to 3 feet tall. Zones 5–9.
2. JAPANESE CATMINT (*Nepeta subsessilis*) reaches 30 inches tall and develops bluish flowers. Zones 5–9.

Catnip
(*Nepeta cataria*)

A member of the mint family, catnip is the recreational drug of choice for cats. The fragrance of fresh or dried leaves attracts some cats. You may find your cat rolling around near your plant in ecstasy. The leaves are used as filler for cat toys. Catnip is also a proven mosquito repellent.

Best site
Give catnip a sunny location and evenly moist, well-draining soil.

Planting
Start from seed about eight weeks before the last frost in your area. Or plant transplants directly into the garden after frost.

Growing
Plant this aromatic perennial in flowerbeds or near vegetables to deter flea beetles and aphids. Zones 3–9.

Harvest
Snip fresh leaves all summer. To dry, cut stems in early morning and hang bundles upside down in a dry, airy, shaded place. Strip the dried leaves from the stems and store in a glass jar.

Celery
(*Apium graveolens dulce*)

Growing celery in your garden allows you to try smaller, more tender, and milder-flavor celery than you get at the grocery. This crunchy, low-calorie vegetable offers its fresh flavor for soups, stuffings, and stews. Celery seeds are used widely in French and Indian cuisine.

Best site
Plant celery in full sun or partial shade. Mulch the soil to help keep it evenly moist.

Planting
Celery takes 80 to 120 days to mature. Start seeds indoors 10 to 12 weeks before your usual spring planting time. Transplant seedlings when the soil has warmed.

Growing
Space plants at least 6 to 8 inches apart. If you plant in rows, leave 2 to 3 feet between the rows.

Harvest
When the stalks reach about 10 inches tall, cut them at the base of the plant using a sharp knife. Allow the plant to flower and set seeds, then harvest them before they dry and scatter.

YOU SHOULD KNOW Used as a mosquito repellent, catnip has been found to be 10 times more effective than DEET, the chemical found in many commercial insect repellents.

YOU SHOULD KNOW Blanching gives celery stalks a milder flavor. To blanch stalks, place a light-blocking structure, such as a terra-cotta drainage tile or a PVC pipe, over most of a plant. Remove the cover and harvest two to three weeks later.

varieties:

① **CUTTING CELERY** (*Apium graveolens*) grows well in containers. It produces flavorful leaves for vegetable salads. The greens also add flavor to homemade tomato juice.

Chamomile
(Chamaemelum nobile, Matricaria recutita)

Two plants called chamomile are easily confused. Both have similar white-and-yellow daisylike flowers that bloom from late spring into summer. and have an applelike scent. The plants has subtle-but-notable differences.

YOU SHOULD KNOW Roman chamomile offers a fast-spreading, aromatic groundcover for moist climates. As an alternative to a lawn or pathway, it can be mowed and smells delicious when cut or walked upon.

Chamomile was considered one of the nine sacred herbs by the Anglo-Saxons. It was strewn on floors to improve the ambience (and odor) during gatherings. Chamomile comes from the Greek *chamaimelon*, meaning ground apple—a reference to the plant's fragrance.

Best site
Plant chamomile in full sun or partial shade and well-drained soil.

Planting
Sow seeds indoors four to six weeks before the last frost date. You can also sow seeds directly in the ground. If you garden in a warm climate, you can sow seeds in the fall. Plant chamomile seedlings 12 inches apart. If you use chamomile as a groundcover, set the plants 6 inches apart.

varieties:

❶ ROMAN CHAMOMILE (*Chamaemelum nobile*) is a perennial herb that grows from 6 to 12 inches tall. Some gardeners use it as a lawn alternative. It has a stronger flavor than German chamomile. Zones 4–8.

❷ GERMAN CHAMOMILE (*Matricaria recutita*) is a more common plant, an annual that reaches 2 feet tall. The flowers are apple scented, but the foliage has no fragrance.

Growing
In spring, sow seeds directly in the garden where they will germinate readily. Set out transplants, if you prefer. For best results, keep the soil evenly moist. Cold climates are hard on Roman chamomile. Cover plants with 4 to 6 inches of mulch after the ground freezes to protect them from the damage of freeze-thaw cycles. German chamomile may reseed itself and come back year after year.

Harvest
In spring and summer, gather flowers and leaves to use them fresh or dried. To dry the harvest, gather stems into a bunch, secure with a rubber band, and hang upside down in a dry, airy place. Or spread the plant material on a rack or screen. Store dried flowers and foliage in an airtight jar.

Uses
Groundcover The foliage is deep green, finely cut and matlike, making Roman chamomile an ideal groundcover.

Tea Brew a relaxing tea using 2 teaspoons of chamomile flowers and 1 cup of freshly boiled water; cover and steep 5 minutes. Women who are pregnant or lactating shouldn't use chamomile. People allergic to ragweed may react to chamomile. Handle it carefully and use sparingly.

Chervil
(*Cerefolium crispum*)

This cool-season annual has fine-texture, fernlike leaves and grows from 12 to 18 inches tall. Chervil has a mild flavor and appearance similar to parsley. Used to flavor eggs, soups, sauces, vinegars, and butters, this herb is essential in French cooking.

This native of eastern Europe has long been associated with new life, which is why chervil soup may be served as part of a traditional Easter feast. It is also reputed to cure hiccups.

Best site
Grow chervil in a partially sunny location. Plant it in well-drained soil. Chervil prefers moist soil and shaded roots.

Planting
This annual grows easily from seed. Scatter seeds in beds or containers several times throughout the growing season for an ongoing harvest. Sow seeds where you want them to grow because the plants do not transplant well. The seeds need light to germinate. Leave them uncovered after sowing and keep the soil well watered until the seeds germinate.

Growing
In the garden, let a few flower stalks set seeds and self-sow for a continuing crop of chervil. If aphids become a problem, remedy it with a strong spray of water from the garden hose.

Harvest
Snip tender young chervil leaves often to enjoy the plant's best flavor. Pick leaves from the outside of the plant. To prolong the leaf harvest, pinch off flower stalks as soon as they begin to form. Use chervil fresh. Dried leaves have little flavor. Chervil retains its freshness up to a week when stored in a plastic bag in the refrigerator. Preserve chervil's flavor in white-wine vinegar.

Uses

Fines herbes Chervil is a key ingredient in the traditional French herb mix, fines herbes. Use the blend in preparing omelettes and salad dressings.

Chervil pesto Freeze chervil for later use in soups or sauces by making a flavorful paste that freezes well. Blend $1/3$ cup olive oil with 2 cups of the herb in a food processor until smooth. Press the pesto into ice cube tray compartments. When frozen, drop the pesto cubes into a freezer bag, label with the contents and date, seal well, and keep in the freezer for up to one year.

Parsley substitute Use chervil instead of parsley in spring salads, soups, and sauces. Chervil has a more complex flavor, with a hint of anise. Chervil is also rich in vitamin C, beta carotene, iron, and magnesium.

 YOU SHOULD KNOW Chervil is an annual herb, but it self-sows easily. Allow the flowers to form seedheads and you'll have lots of new plants.

Chicory
(*Cichorium intybus*)

Bearing pretty blue flowers, chicory is a common roadside flower. It has tough, twiglike stems and is known by other common names including blue sailors, succory, wild chicory, and coffeeweed. This European native has naturalized throughout the United States.

YOU SHOULD KNOW This plant is not to be confused with Belgian or French endive, which is also called chicory in Germany and the United Kingdom. Endive is a closely related species, *Cichorium endivia*.

Chicory has been cultivated for at least 5,000 years. It was used by the Egyptians, and was included in the gardens of Charlemagne and Thomas Jefferson. Chicory is valued as a dye plant and grown for animal fodder.

Best site
Plant chicory in full sun and well-draining soil. It will grow in poor soils and is not demanding. This is why you see chicory growing along roadsides and in ditches.

Planting
Sow seeds indoors in spring about six weeks before the last frost date. Or plant seeds directly in the garden once the soil has warmed. Chicory is not usually sold in plant form since it is commonly found in the wild.

Growing
Chicory is a biennial and blooms its second year in the garden. The plant has a long taproot that helps make it drought tolerant.

Harvest
Pick chicory leaves when they are young. Harvest the roots once the plant has matured—from midsummer into fall.

Uses

Salad greens Pick young tender chicory leaves to use fresh in salads as you would dandelion foliage. Blanching makes young chicory leaves less bitter.

Coffee enhancer or substitute Chicory earned the name coffeeweed because the long, white taproots can be harvested, dried, and used as an additive to substitute for coffee. This practice is common in Europe as well as New Orleans.

Chives
(*Allium schoenoprasum*)

This easy-to-grow perennial herb thrives in beds or pots. The grassy, hollow leaves can be harvested from early spring through autumn. This clump-forming member of the onion family also boasts edible, fragrant pink-purple flowers that appear in the spring.

Chives are native to Europe and Asia, where this herb grows wild. Medieval gardeners planted chives around the borders of gardens because of their decorative value and the belief that the herb deterred insects. It was also thought that chives warded off evil.

Best site
Plant chives in full sun and in average, well-drained soil. Although chives tolerate being planted in light shade, especially in regions with hot dry summers, they grow best in an area that receives six to eight hours of sun a day. Improve soil drainage by working in loads of organic matter such as chopped leaves before planting. Chives also grow well in containers; plant in a well-draining potting mix.

varieties:

❶ GARLIC CHIVES (*Allium tuberosum*) grow taller than common chives, producing flat leaves and white flowers. They can be invasive; remove the flowers before they develop seeds. As the common name suggests, the leaves have a mild garlic flavor. Zones 4–10.

Planting
Plant divided chunks of chives or new plants anytime during the growing season. Divisions and transplants usually produce flowers the first year (the foliage can be clipped for use anytime). Chives can also be planted successfully from seed; sow in early spring or, in mild-winter areas, in fall. Seed-grown plants may require a full year of growth before harvesting leaves and flowers.

Growing
Perennial chives grow for years, blooming in early spring. They are generally drought tolerant and do not require fertilizer. Deadhead faded flowers to prevent self-seeding and spreading throughout the garden. In warm climates, chives stay green all season; in cooler zones, plants die back to the ground over winter. Zones 3–10.

Harvest
When grown from seed, chives are ready to harvest in 75 to 85 days. Harvest the leaves as needed by cutting them just above soil level using scissors or a sharp knife. Chives can be dried but retain their color and flavor better when frozen.

Uses
Edible flowers Snip chive flowers and break them up into soups and salads.

Vegetable ties Use the long, strong leaves as simple-yet-decorative ties around wraps or bundles of vegetables.

Onion substitute Just before serving, sprinkle potato and egg dishes with freshly chopped chives for a subtle zip of onion flavor.

YOU SHOULD KNOW As chive plants mature, the clumps become overcrowded. Dig and divide them every couple years. Replant divisions in new locations or share them with friends.

Cilantro, Coriander
(*Coriandrum sativum*)

Cilantro is a two-for-one annual. The leafy part of the plant, called cilantro, is a favorite seasoning in Mexican and Asian foods. The seeds of a mature plant are called coriander and have a spicy, citrusy flavor.

YOU SHOULD KNOW
Newer varieties of cilantro are slower to bolt (when plants mature and set seeds). They can provide a longer harvest of leaves than earlier cilantro varieties.

Cilantro and coriander have been cultivated since 5000 BC and used commonly throughout the Middle East and Asia. The herb was introduced to Latin America, where it also became a staple ingredient in food preparation.

Best site
Plant cilantro in full sun to part shade and well-draining soil. Cilantro grows easily in containers too. Sow seeds in a pot and grow plants outside your door for quick and easy harvests.

Planting
Start from seeds or transplants. Sow seeds in early spring after the last frost. In regions with mild winters, sow seeds in the fall for winter harvests. Elsewhere, if you prefer, purchase and plant seedlings in spring after the threat of frost has passed.

varieties:

① **'DELFINO'** is an All-American Selections winner with ferny foliage. It tolerates warm weather well and is slow to bolt.

② **VIETNAMESE CORIANDER** (*Persicaria odorata*) is used in Southeast Asian cuisine. Hardy to Zone 10, it is grown elsewhere as an annual.

Growing
Water plants consistently during hot, dry weather to prevent them from bolting. To extend your cilantro crop, sow successive plantings two to four weeks apart. In colder climates, grow cilantro in a cold frame in early spring or fall for an extended growing season. Plants self-sow readily, so remove seedheads to keep cilantro from sprouting everywhere. If you like, keep a potted plant indoors over the winter on a sunny windowsill.

Harvest
Harvest leaves from the lower part of the plant once several stems have developed. The lower or outermost leaves have more spicy flavor than the upper foliage. The white or lavender flowers are also edible. But once the flowers appear, the flavor of the leaves becomes less palatable. To harvest the seeds, cut the stalks when the seedpods turn brown. Hang the dry stalks upside down in paper bags to catch the seeds.

Uses
Cilantro leaves Add cilantro leaves to cooked food just before serving; heat dissipates the flavor. Cilantro is best used fresh. It can be dried, but the flavor is milder.

Coriander seeds Grind coriander seeds with a mortar and pestle to release their bright flavor just before adding to a dish.

Dukka Coriander seeds play a big part of the North African nut, herb, and spice mix called dukka. The traditional way to eat dukka is to dip a piece of flatbread into olive oil, then dip into a bowl of powdery dukka. You get a burst of coriander flavor in every bite.

Citrus *(Citrus)*

Citrus—including lemons, oranges, and limes—produces juicy, sweet, or tart fruit. Planted in the landscape (in warm climates) or in containers (best for cold climates), these small trees add structure to a yard or patio and are true components of an edible landscape. Enjoy their flowers, fruit, and leaves.

Citrus fruit can be traced to Southeast Asia as far back as 4000 BC. It traveled the world with early explorers who introduced these sweet and tart fruits to the Americas in the 16th century.

Best site
Plant citrus in full sun. Plants grow best in well-drained soil. In hot, dry climates place citrus where it will receive light shade at the hottest time of the day. In cool climates, plant in the warmest spot in the yard, against a south-facing wall.

Planting
Where winters are mild and summers are hot, plant citrus in fall. Elsewhere, plant in early spring after frost. Dig a hole as deep as the nursery pot and slightly wider. For best results, plant with the graft (bulging area at the trunk's base) at least 2 inches above soil level.

Growing
Water regularly during dry periods. Trees need about 1 inch of water per week. Fertilize two or three times from February through September, and avoid overfertilizing. Protect the young frost-sensitive trees by wrapping them with an insulating material. In cold climates, grow citrus trees in pots and keep them indoors over the winter. Zones 9–11.

Harvest
Citrus fruits mature at various times of the year. To determine orange maturity, taste the fruit. Color doesn't indicate ripeness. Lemons, limes, and other acidic citrus can be picked whenever they reach acceptable size and juice content.

Uses
Patio planters Dwarf varieties of lemon, lime, and orange do well in roomy containers.

Asian bouquet garni Combine kaffir lime leaves with lemongrass and ginger.

Citrus zest To zest citrus, use a vegetable peeler, paring knife, or zesting tool (available at kitchen shops) to remove the outermost colored peel in long strips. Avoid the fruit's white membrane, or pith, which has a bitter flavor.

YOU SHOULD KNOW
Keep citrus trees in good health and well irrigated to minimize fruit drop. Well-watered and fertilized trees usually drop some fruit, but excessive fruit drop can indicate a problem.

varieties:

1. **KAFFIR LIME** *(Citrus hystrix, C. papedia)* is native to Indonesia. The peel, zest, and whole leaves are used in soups and curries, or cut into thin strips and added to salads and meat dishes.
2. **'IMPROVED MEYER LEMON'** is a favorite hybrid because of its excellent flowery flavor. The fruit is orange-yellow when mature and holds well on the tree. The small to medium tree is nearly thornless and well-suited to growing in a container.

Clary Sage
(Salvia sclarea)

Clary sage has been cultivated for centuries for use as a medicinal plant. In modern times, the herb is prized for its showy pink, white, and lilac flowers. It's a short-lived perenial or biennial. The plant self-sows easily so once you plant clary sage, you may not have to replant.

Clary sage is native to southern Europe. Historically it was used to flavor wine and as a substitute for hops in beer brewing.

Best site
Like many herbs, clary sage prefers a sunny site and well-draining, nutrient-rich soil.

Planting
Clary sage is easily grown from seed sown directly in the garden. Sow the seeds about ½ inch deep in a well-prepared seedbed. Once the seeds have sprouted, thin them to stand a foot apart.

Growing
Once established, clary sage requires very little care. Keep weeds at bay with seasonal cultivation and a 2-inch layer of mulch. Clary sage eventually grows about 2 feet tall and usually needs staking unless it is planted between stouter plants that will support it. At the end of the season, let some flowerheads mature to produce seeds for following years. Zones 4–9.

Harvest
The leaves and seeds can be harvested and used either fresh or dried. Harvest young leaves for use in fragrant blends of dried herbs and flowers, such as sachets, potpourris, and bath herbs (tub teas). Cut the flowers and add their fragrant beauty to bouquets.

(i) YOU SHOULD KNOW Stake this plant in early spring to prevent it from flopping over in the garden.

Uses

Aromatherapy Clary sage has a spicy haylike scent. The plant's essential oil (distilled essence) is a favored ingredient in massage oils and bath salts with its refreshing effect. It is also used to balance other scents when blending potpourris and sachets.

Flower gardens The colorful spires of clary sage stand out in a perennial garden. Catmint and fennel make handsome companion plants.

Comfrey
(*Symphytum officinale*)

Comfrey leaves are full of nutrients that make a natural fertilizer or addition to compost. This vigorous perennial sends down deep roots that pull nutrients into the plants' large, hairy leaves.

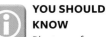

YOU SHOULD KNOW
Plant comfrey where you can control it. The plant spreads by its rootlike rhizomes and becomes invasive.

A native of Europe, comfrey was once used medicinally to help heal bone fractures (and had the common name knitbone). Now it is not recommended for internal use. This herb can cause liver damage in humans if consumed.

Best site
Comfrey is a heavy feeder requiring a rich, organic soil with a high moisture content. In its native Europe, this plant is often found growing wild along streams and waterways. Plant in full sun or partial shade.

Planting
Plant comfrey in the spring. Start with seedlings from a garden center or mail-order nursery, or root divisions from a fellow gardener. When dividing a plant, dig deeply to get as much of the roots as possible. Replant a division and water it every four or five days until it resumes growing.

varieties:

1 **'VARIEGATA'** is a variegated form of common comfrey with white-edge leaves.

Growing
Comfrey can grow up to 4 feet tall. To keep it looking good, shear it back once or twice a season to a few inches tall; it grows back quickly. Zones 4–9.

Harvest
Gather leaves anytime during the growing season. Wear gloves when harvesting and handling comfrey because the prickly leaves and stems can irritate skin.

Uses
Comfrey salve Make a soothing salve to help reduce swelling. Chop comfrey leaves, place in a jar, cover with warm olive oil, and allow to stand for 24 hours. Strain out the leaves and add melted beeswax to thicken.

Fertilizer Soak the leaves for a week or so in a bucket of water to make a nutrient-rich comfrey tea that you can use as a liquid fertilizer for plants. For a compost booster, cut plants to the ground and add the leaves and stems to the compost pile as a valuable source of nitrogen.

Dill (*Anethum graveolens*)

This tall annual herb reaches 2 to 4 feet tall and adds frilly foliage and flowers to the garden. It attracts butterflies and bees. The distinctive tangy leaves of dill add flavor to fish dishes and potato salads. The leaves and seeds provide the headline ingredient in dill pickles.

YOU SHOULD KNOW This easy-to-grow annual herb self-seeds with gusto. To keep it from growing all over the garden next year, snip off the seedheads before they mature in late summer and early fall.

Dill, native to the eastern Mediterranean and western Asia, is mentioned in Egyptian medical books dating to 3000 BC. It's a common herb in Scandinavian, Russian, and Greek cuisines.

Best site

Plant dill in full sun and moist, well-drained soil. Since dill grows tall, select a growing site that is protected from high winds—a back-of-the-border location is good. Dill thrives in rich soil: Dig in a 2-inch-thick layer of compost before planting.

Planting

Start dill from seeds or transplants. Plant seeds indoors a month before the usual spring planting time or directly in the garden in the spring. Sow seeds in the fall in warm-climate areas. Plant seeds ¼ inch deep and cover them with a fine layer of soilless seed-starting mix. Water gently. For a continuous supply of new plants, sow seeds once a month throughout the summer.

varieties:

1 **'FERNLEAF'** is a dwarf blue-green variety with high leaf yield that makes a superior addition to kitchen gardens and containers.

Growing

If planted from seed, thin dill plants when they are 6 to 8 inches tall. Use the thinned seedlings in cooking. Once established, dill tolerates short periods of drought. To help maintain consistent soil moisture, spread a 2-inch layer of mulch between plants. As flowers develop, snip them off to encourage foliage growth and prevent plants from self-sowing. Dill withstands cool weather, making it one of the year's first herbs sprouting in the spring garden and one of the last herbs standing in the fall.

Harvest

Fresh dill leaf has better flavor than dried. Harvest the foliage 30 to 55 days after seeding. Snip leaves for use in cooking or as garnishes. Air-dry leaves or freeze for long-term storage. Dill sets seed in 75 to 100 days and seeds turn brown when they are ready for harvest. To collect seeds, cut stems 6 inches below the mature seedheads. Hang the seedheads upside down inside a paper bag to catch the seeds as they dry and fall.

Uses

Tzatziki sauce Dill is a main flavor in Greek tzatziki sauce, which is made with yogurt, garlic, and cucumber.

Flower arrangements The plants are topped with umbels of yellow flowers in summer. Cut these blooms for lasting additions to bouquets.

Swallowtail host plant The striped (yellow, black, white, and green) caterpillar or larval form of the swallowtail butterfly feeds on dill.

Egyptian Onion
(*Allium cepa aggregatum*)

Called walking onions, these unusual members of the *Allium* genus have 2-foot-long stems topped with curly topknots of little onion bulblets. The weight of the bulbs causes the stem to fold over, allowing the onions to root in the ground and become ambulatory, hence the name.

Best site
Egyptian onion plants require a full-sun location and well-drained soil.

Planting
Plant the small bulbs in the fall in loose soil amended with loads of compost and rotted leaves. Or you can allow the bulblets to plant themselves and spread.

Growing
These hardy onions do well in cold climates. Zones 3–9.

Harvest
In the early spring, dig the onions to use the green stems while they are tender—before the bulbs form; use as you would green onions. After the bulblets form on the top of the plant, pick them off to use fresh.

Elderberry
(*Sambucus*)

A vigorous shrub that grows to 12 feet, elderberry or elder is prized for its pretty white flowers as well as its round, shiny blue-black fruit. In the wild, elderberry is often found along streambeds and at the edge of woodlands, where it thrives in sunny and moist conditions.

Best site
Elderberry thrives in a sunny or partially sunny location with rich, moist soil.

Planting
Start elderberry from seed or young plants found near mature specimens. Purchase native species as well as newer cultivars from local garden centers or mail-order sources.

Growing
Mulch the plant to maintain soil moisture and give it extra irrigation during periods of drought. Zones 3–9.

Harvest
Cut the flower clusters as soon as they open. When the large heads of fruit ripen, clip off the entire cluster, shake the berries into a bucket, and use them to make delectable syrup or jelly.

 YOU SHOULD KNOW The little bulblets that top Egyptian onions are extremely spicy—like garlic. They are excellent chopped and used fresh in dishes that benefit from onion flavor.

 YOU SHOULD KNOW *Sambucus nigra* 'Black Lace' is an easy-care ornamental shrub with dark, almost black foliage and edible berries. It makes a showy accent in contemporary gardens and attracts birds to feast on the berries.

Epazote
(*Dysphania ambrosioides*)

Also called Mexican tea, epazote is a pungent tender perennial most commonly used in Mexican cooking. It has a strong flavor that some people compare to gasoline or kerosene. Use the leaves fresh or dried in bean dishes and soups. Epazote blends well with oregano, cumin, and chiles.

Best site
Epazote isn't fussy about growing conditions, but prefers a sunny site and dry soil. This herb is highly invasive. Grow it in a container or in a place where you can easily control its spread.

Planting
Epazote grows readily from seed. You can also purchase seedlings. Space plants about 10 inches apart.

Growing
Mature plants reach 2 to 3 feet tall. By midsummer epazote develops pale greenish-yellow flowers. Zones 8–11.

Harvest
Epazote leaves can be harvested at any time.

Eucalyptus
(*Eucalyptus*)

The silvery leaves of eucalyptus trees are as beautiful as they are aromatic. Eucalyptus oil is a staple in spa treatments because of its sinus-clearing fragrance. The plants, native to Australia, are ideal for warm climates. In colder climates, grow eucalyptus in a patio container, then move it indoors for the winter.

Best site
Eucalyptus requires a sunny location and thrives in consistently moist, well-drained soil.

Planting
Varieties of the tree take years to grow from seed. Start with nursery-grown plants and transplant hardy young trees.

Growing
Grow aromatic eucalyptus in a sunny location, near a patio or a front entryway where you can enjoy the leaves' fragrance as it is released by the warmth of sunlight. Zones 8–10.

Harvest
The leaves and bark have a camphorous scent, comparable to a blend of menthol and sage. Cut stems and leaves for use in potpourri, sachets, long-lasting fragrant bouquets, and wreaths.

YOU SHOULD KNOW Often the biggest challenge with epazote is how to stop it from spreading throughout your garden. To prevent this from happening, remove flower stalks before the seeds mature.

YOU SHOULD KNOW Eucalyptus oil is flammable as well as poisonous. Take care when working with essential oils and avoid ingesting this herb.

Fennel
(*Foeniculum vulgare*)

If you appreciate the flavor of anise or licorice, you may already be a fan of fennel. The perennial green herb differs from the annual vegetable or Florence fennel (*F. vulgare azoricum*), which has a white, edible base. 'Purpureum', a cultivar of the herb, has bronze foliage and grows 4 feet tall.

Best site
Plant fennel in a sunny spot, in well-drained soil. Plants can take some light shade.

Planting
Sow seeds in early spring directly into the ground. Established plants transplant poorly.

Growing
Keep plants well watered. Avoid deadheading flowers because they attract beneficial and beautiful bugs including butterflies, ladybird beetles, and bees. Zones 5–9.

Harvest
Collect leaves all season. When seeds turn brown, clip flowerheads and suspend them, upside down, inside paper sacks, so dried seeds fall into the bags. To release their strong flavor, crush seeds in a mortar prior to using.

Feverfew
(*Tanacetum parthenium*)

The daisylike flowers of feverfew were once believed to be a fever reducer, but today this little perennial is enjoyed more for its ornamental and crafting value. Feverfew grows about 2 feet tall. The edges of the foliage are finely serrated and the leaves release a strong odor when cut or brushed.

Best site
Feverfew needs at least six to eight hours of sun a day. It will not thrive in partial shade. The plant is not picky about soil types.

Planting
Start feverfew from seed, nursery-grown transplants, or divisions in the spring.

Growing
The plants are a bit weedy in character and look more at home in an informal or wild garden. The blooms begin to appear in midsummer and continue until fall. Deadhead flowers as they fade to promote additional blooms. Zones 4–9.

Harvest
Clip the flowers when they are fully open. Hang stems to dry upside down in a dark, airy place. Store the dried flowers in an airtight container.

 YOU SHOULD KNOW Graceful, ferny fennel adds structure, texture, and airy beauty to any herb garden. It's also pretty enough to tuck the 2- to 4-foot tall plants into a perennial border.

 YOU SHOULD KNOW Although feverfew is thought to help reduce fever, headache, and arthritis, self-diagnosis and treatment are not recommended. Consult a physician instead.

Garlic (*Allium sativum*)

Sautéed, baked, or used fresh, this perennial bulb adds its unmistakable pungent flavor to stir-fries and sauces. Easy to grow, garlic is a big producer: One pound of cloves can yield 7 to 10 pounds of garlic the following year. Garlic is often listed among the top good-for-you foods.

YOU SHOULD KNOW
Three types of garlic are widely grown. Softneck varieties have strong garlic flavor and store well for up to nine months. Hardneck garlic varieties have a mild flavor and store for about six months. Elephant garlic is a leek, similar to garlic in flavor but less pungent. It stores for six months.

Garlic is native to Central Asia, and is a staple seasoning in the Mediterranean region, Asia, and Africa. Its use is traced back 6,000 years, when it was worshipped, used as currency, and thought to repel evil (including vampires).

Best site
Plant garlic in full sun and well-drained soil. Garlic thrives in slightly dry sites. Add a 2-inch thick layer of compost to the soil.

Planting
Plant garlic around the first frost date in fall. In mild-winter areas you can plant until January. Plants form deep roots and then mature the following summer. You can also plant garlic in the early spring, but plants will yield smaller bulbs. Garlic grows best during cool weather and stops growing at temperatures above 90°F. Plant

individual cloves (not the whole bulb) pointy side up 2 to 3 inches deep. Space cloves 6 inches apart in rows 1 to 2 feet apart. Plant elephant garlic 8 inches apart and 6 inches deep.

Growing
Water garlic well after planting in the fall to promote good root growth. In cold-winter areas, mulch after a few hard freezes with a 4- to 6-inch-thick layer of straw to prevent the bulbs from heaving out of the ground. In spring, weed around plants; weeds compete with bulb production. To boost your garlic harvest, add a high-nitrogen fertilizer in spring. Begin fertilizing once three leaves have formed, and continue monthly until bulbs begin to develop. Rotate crops and keep beds weed free to reduce troublesome insect populations. You can also grow garlic in containers. Zones 3–9.

Harvest
In summer, when about half of the garlic leaves begin to yellow and wilt, stop watering and knock over the tops. Allow the garlic to cure for one week in the garden, then harvest the bulbs. Remove excess soil and hang the garlic to dry in a cool, shady location with good air circulation. When the tops are dry, trim off to ½ inch above the bulb and trim the roots at the base of the bulb. Store the garlic in mesh bags in a cool room.

Uses
Bread spread Bake whole garlic bulbs with olive oil and salt and squeeze the warmed soft cloves over crusty bread.

Garlic scapes Cut immature flower stalks, called green garlic or scapes, to prompt bulb growth. Use them in stir-fries and pasta dishes.

varieties:

1. **'RUSSIAN RED'** is a hardneck garlic with purple stripes. Bulbs produce six to nine large cloves. This variety has good winter hardiness.
2. **'SPANISH ROJA'** is a hardneck type with medium-hot flavor. The brown-skinned cloves are excellent for roasting.
3. **'NEW YORK WHITE'** is also called 'Polish White'. This hardy, disease-resistant softneck variety is well-suited to gardens in cold-climate areas.

Germander
(*Teucrium chamaedrys*)

Easily sheared to form a low hedge, germander is an ideal choice for shapely knot or parterre gardens. Its shiny green leaves and mauve flowers make germander a great garden plant. Because germander only grows 12 to 18 inches tall, it makes a wonderful edging plant along pathways.

Best site
Germander requires a sunny location with well-draining soil.

Planting
Germander grows slowly from seed. Start with transplants instead. Space plants 6 inches apart for a knot garden; otherwise, space plants about 1 foot apart.

Growing
Trim plants in early spring to encourage new growth. The plants develop pretty mauve flowers in midsummer. Zones 5–9.

Harvest
Cut stems and use them fresh in crafts projects.

Uses
Container plants Germander grows well in pots, planters, and window boxes.

Crafts projects Fresh branches and leaves can be used as greenery in wreaths or floral crafts.

Bonsai Prune upright germander plants into bonsai forms.

Ginger
(*Zingiber officinale*)

This spicy herb is as healthful as it is flavorful. Ginger is a tropical plant that grows outdoors in frost-free regions or in containers in cold climates. Buy ginger roots from the grocery store (the same ones you cook with) and plant pieces of the tubers. Culinary ginger does not

Best site
Ginger requires a sheltered location out of direct sunlight. It needs warm, humid conditions. Plants must be overwintered indoors in cold climates.

Planting
Choose firm, fresh rhizomes. Soak the thick tubers overnight and break them into pieces, making sure each piece has at least two eyes or growing points. Plant pieces about 8 inches apart; cover with about 1 inch of potting soil.

Growing
Amend soil with compost or well-rotted manure. Keep the soil damp but not wet. Humidity is crucial for the plants, so mist them daily using the garden hose. In the garden, mulch ginger to maintain consistent soil moisture.

Harvest
In late summer, ginger foliage begins to die back. Dig up tubers. It takes about 10 months for ginger to reach harvestable size. In tropical regions, dig the tubers as you need them.

 YOU SHOULD KNOW Germander is a widely grown but little-recognized herb. You'll find this shrubby perennial in patterned knot or parterre gardens around the world. Yet, because it is neither showy nor edible, few people recognize it as an herb.

YOU SHOULD KNOW Culinary ginger is not as showy as its ornamental cousins, but you can reap a small harvest even from a container-grown plant.

Hops *(Humulus lupulus)*

Widely grown as a key ingredient in beer making, hops are actually the flowers and seedheads of a perennial vine. This hardy perennial vine is also beautiful, so it's an excellent option for use in the landscape—even for non-beer drinkers. Hops require 120 frost-free days to produce useable flowers.

YOU SHOULD KNOW When growing hops for their conelike flowers, start with female rootlike rhizomes. The plant can become invasive. Pull out excess plants including the rhizomes.

Cultivated since the 8th century, hops were used medicinally to treat nearly everything from fevers and fits to worms. In the 11th century, the herb became associated with beer production in Germany. Today, Germany is the largest producer of hops.

Best site
Hops requires a sunny location and well-drained soil. Because hops are rampant vines that can quickly grow up to 30 feet in length, you must be sure to plant them next to a sturdy trellis or arbor. Avoid planting near power poles.

Planting
You will need a female plant to produce flowers and a male plant to pollinate it. Start with rhizomes or container-grown vines from a local garden center or mail-order supplier. Keep the plants watered until they become established and mulch them to keep weeds at bay.

Growing
There's no secret to planting hops. Just put them in the ground and stand back. By the second year the female plant will develop yellowish conelike flowers. Prune the vines back to ground level every spring. Hops generally do not produce flowers their first year in the ground. Hops can be attacked by the hop aphid, which sucks the juices of young stems. To control, spray with an insecticidal soap. Hop vines can also become infected with downy mildew. Prevent mildew by keeping the plants' foliage dry. Use drip irrigation or hand-water to avoid wetting foliage. Remove the vine's lower leaves to ensure better air circulation. Zones 4–9.

Harvest
It is estimated that each hop vine can produce 1 to 2 pounds of dried flowers. Harvest hops when they feel dry and light to the touch. Spread them on a window screen to dry in an airy, shady place. Stir the hops every day until they feel crisp and completely dry. Store the hops in an airtight container and use them within six months.

Uses
Beer production Hop flowers impart a bitter, tangy flavor to beer. Different varieties offer varied flavors. Check with your county extension service for the best varieties for your region.

Landscape use Choose an ornamental hops variety for its interesting foliage, if you prefer.

Dream pillow Stuff a small pillow with the dried flowers and use it to inspire sweet dreams.

varieties:

❶ 'AUREUS' or golden hops vine is an ornamental vine with yellow-green lobed leaves. It bears small white flowers.

Horehound
(*Marrubium vulgare*)

Horehound is another hardy member of the mint family. It has fuzzy gray-green foliage and small white flowers. Like mint, this plant can become invasive. Horehound's longstanding claim to fame is its use as an ingredient in old-fashioned candies and cough medicines.

Championed as an ancient medicinal to treat coughs and upper respiratory illnesses, horehound is still used in this way. It tastes bitter, however, and lots of sugar or honey are used to make it more palatable.

Best site
Horehound is not fussy about growing conditions but it does prefer full sun. Almost any soil type will do as long as it is well drained. The plant grows to 2 to 3 feet tall. Horehound can spread aggressively, so be sure to plant where it can be controlled.

Planting
Horehound can be started from seed, division, or stem cutting. The plant is drought tolerant, but needs supplemental water if rain is scarce for an extended period. Young plants will need regular watering to become established. Cultivate around young plants to eliminate competition from weeds.

varieties:

❶ VARIEGATED BLACK HOREHOUND (*Ballota nigra*) Tiny purple flowers appear in summer on this white-variegated plant. It grows 2 to 3 feet tall, spreads aggressively, and has a strong odor. Zones 4–9.

Growing
There are few secrets to growing horehound. Basically, you can plant it and forget it. Trimming the plant periodically will encourage bushy growth. Horehound leaves have a minty fragrance when rubbed or brushed. The plant develops white flowers in mid- to late summer. Remove the seedheads before they mature to help keep horehound from spreading. Zones 3–9.

Harvest
Harvest leaves throughout the growing season by snipping off the stem tips and then use the leaves as needed. In mid- to late summer, harvest the plant: Cut the stems a few inches above ground level and hang them upside down in a cool, dry, airy location. Pull the dried leaves off the stems, compost the stems, and store the leaves in an airtight container.

Uses
Deer-resistant gardens Neither deer nor rabbits will eat horehound unless they are extremely hungry. Plant the herb to deter these pests if they are a problem in your neighborhood.

Cough suppressants Dried or fresh leaves can be boiled with water and honey to make homemade cough syrups and lozenges.

Sweets The boiled leaves of horehound can be used to make flavorful candy and syrup. Old-fashioned confectioners still stock horehound candy.

YOU SHOULD KNOW As a member of the mint family, horehound can easily grow out of control. Plant it in a pot or confine it within a bed to prevent it from becoming weedy.

Horseradish
(*Armoracia rusticana*)

This perennial herb has large green leaves, small white flowers, and large, tapered edible roots. Beware! Horseradish can become invasive. Plant it in a spot where you can control its spread. The sinus-clearing, pungent flavor of horseradish root adds zip to meat and potato dishes.

Best site
Plant in full sun and moist, well-drained soil.

Planting
Start horseradish plants in early spring from root cuttings. Plant the root cuttings horizontally, laying them in a 3-inch-deep trench. One or two plants will provide a generous harvest for horseradish lovers.

Growing
Water horseradish root cuttings well for about four weeks after planting. Once plants are established they will withstand dry periods. Root cuttings planted in spring produce roots in 180 to 240 days. Zones 3–9.

Harvest
Dig horseradish roots in the fall. You may also harvest them in the winter and spring. For best flavor, leave the roots in the ground until after a few frosts—this sweetens them.

Hyssop
(*Hyssopus officinalis*)

An evergreen, bushy perennial, hyssop produces upright stems with small white, lavender, or blue flowers. It grows to 2 feet and makes a good plant for garden edging and containers. This plant is not related to anise hyssop, but both plants attract bees, butterflies, and hummingbirds.

Best site
Hyssop requires a sunny location that receives at least six to eight hours of sun a day.

Planting
Grow hyssop from seed. Sow seeds about ¼ inch deep in soil. As the seedlings grow, thin them to 1 foot apart.

Growing
Hyssop blooms in midsummer. Remove the flower spikes as they fade to keep the plants looking good. After a few years, you may need to replace older plants. Zones 4–9.

Harvest
Fresh leaves can be harvested at any time. Use hyssop in sachets and potpourris. Snip flower stalks just before they open, then hang them upside down in a dark, airy place until dry.

YOU SHOULD KNOW
Harvested horseradish roots turn green quickly if exposed to light. To keep their white color, store them wrapped in black plastic in the refrigerator.

YOU SHOULD KNOW
At one time commonly used as both a medicinal and culinary herb, hyssop is not often seen in American gardens, but deserves much more appreciation.

Juniper
(*Juniperus communis*)

This large group of evergreen trees and shrubs bears round green fruits (small cones) that ripen to dark blue. Juniper berries are used as a flavoring similar to rosemary, with piney and citrus notes. As the primary flavoring in gin, juniper berries are sometimes called gin berries.

Best site
Plant juniper in full sun and well-drained soil. Plants tolerate a wide range of growing conditions and become drought tolerant once established.

Planting
Select container-grown, potted, or balled-and-burlapped nursery plants. Choose from upright, bushy, or low-growing junipers for versatile landscape plants.

Growing
Junipers fill space fast, adding color and texture, whether used as a groundcover, privacy screen, vertical punctuation in a border, or topiary. They vary in color from green to gray or blue. Sizes range from 6-inch groundcover varieties to 60-foot trees. Zones 3–9.

Harvest
Harvest berried branches in the fall and winter. Use them fresh in holiday wreaths and dried in fragrant potpourri.

Lady's Mantle
(*Alchemilla mollis*)

Lady's mantle gets its name from its pretty scalloped and folded leaves, once thought to resemble the cape of the Virgin Mary. Lady's mantle continues to be appreciated for its gray-green, fuzzy foliage. When it catches dew and other water droplets, the foliage appears to be sprinkled with sparkly diamonds.

Best site
Lady's mantle prefers a rich, moist soil in a partially shady location. It can also be grown in containers along with hostas, ferns, and other shade dwellers.

Planting
Plant in the early spring when the weather is still cool and damp. This herb can be grown from seed, but it is faster to start from transplants.

Growing
Lady's mantle makes a great addition to a herb or perennial border. It grows only 18 inches tall, so it's ideal at the edge of a border or along a garden path. Remove faded flower stalks to promote new growth and keep plants tidy. Zones 4–8.

Harvest
Snip the leaves and flowers throughout the summer and use them in bouquets.

YOU SHOULD KNOW Junipers require little care. Most varieties tolerate hot, dry conditions and thrive in poor soil, making them ideal evergreens for hard-to-plant locations.

YOU SHOULD KNOW The main role of lady's mantle in modern gardens is as an ornamental. Historically, this plant had many medicinal uses, and today it may be used to make hand lotion and facial cream.

Lavender *(Lavendula)*

One of the most beloved herbal fragrances, lavender evokes visions of neat rows of flower-packed fields in Provence. The shrubby Mediterranean herb is usually topped with purple flowers. Some varieties of the perennial have blue, pink, or white flowers. The flowers bloom for a month or more in summer. The leaves and flowers emit fragrance.

Lavender's scent is so distinctive that references to it appear in ancient texts from many different cultures. It has been associated with washing clothes and bathing—lavender makes things smell fresh and clean. Today the sweet and ever-popular fragrance of lavender enhances soaps, shampoos, bath products, linen sprays, sachets, and air fresheners.

Best site

Plant lavender in full sun and well-draining soil. Lavender thrives in sandy loam, but not in heavy clay or wet soils. It grows best in moderately fertile, slightly alkaline soil and flourishes with added drainage (gravel or perlite). This shrubby perennial is a must-have in an herb garden but also mixes well with perennials, annuals, and roses in beds or borders.

Planting

Start lavender from seedlings or cuttings in the spring, or in the fall where winters are mild. Water fall-planted transplants regularly to encourage root growth. Space transplants 2 to 3 feet apart, depending on the variety.

Growing

Lavender tolerates drought, heat, and wind. Choose a variety that is best suited to conditions where you live. Although lavender is considered drought tolerant, it requires regular watering during the first six weeks after transplanting to get a good start.

To promote dense plants and repeat blooms, shear plants by one-third after they bloom. In spring wait until the new growth has begun before cutting back plants. Trim them, removing dead stems, but do not cut them down to the ground. To prune, trim out about one-third of the stem length. In cold-climate areas, mulch around and over a plant to protect it over the winter.

Harvest

Lavender flowers are easy to harvest because they grow on long, stiff stems. Gather the flower stalks when about half of a plant's flowers open. Cut stems early in the morning when the oils are most concentrated. To dry flowers and stems, hang small bundles upside down in a dark, airy place.

Uses

Herbes de Provence Make the classic culinary blend using the following herbs in amounts that taste best to you: oregano, thyme, basil, sage, savory, lavender flowers, and rosemary.

Baking Lavender flowers have a distinctive flavor and can be used in baked goods such as shortbread, poundcake, or cookies.

Simple syrup Boil 1 cup water, 2 cups sugar, and 2 to 4 tablespoons fresh lavender to make a simple syrup to add to mixed drinks or lemonade.

Rosemary substitute The stems and leaves can be used in place of rosemary in many recipes.

Crafting Make sachets, wreaths, and bouquets with dried lavender flowers. Use them in your bedroom and closet. The scent helps you relax—and also repels insects.

 YOU SHOULD KNOW Lavender grows well in containers. Place it in a pot or window box of well-draining potting mix and a sunny location. Enjoy the plant's fragrance by growing it on a patio, deck, or entryway. In late summer, transplant lavender into the garden so it can establish a strong root system before winter arrives.

varieties:

① **'MUNSTEAD'** English lavender (*Lavandula angustifolia*) is a popular culinary variety with purple-blue flowers and green leaves. It reaches 2 to 3 feet tall. Zones 5–9.

② **'JEAN DAVIS'** (*L. angustifolia*) is a light-pink flowering form with a fruity flavor. It is hardy in Zones 6–11 and grows to 2 feet.

③ **SPANISH LAVENDER** (*L. stoechas*) has dark purple flowers on short stems and is very fragrant. It grows 2 to 3 feet tall. Zones 7–10.

④ **FRENCH LAVENDER** (*L. dentata*) offers finely serrated leaves on 2- to 3-foot-tall plants. Winter the plant indoors in cold climates. Zones 8–11.

⑤ **'HIDCOTE'** (*L. angustifolia*) is a popular lavender for hedging. It grows 12 to 16 inches tall and attracts pollinators. Zones 5–9.

⑥ **'PROVENCE'** (*L. ×intermedia*) is used for culinary purposes as well as for sachets. Its buds are easily stripped for simple harvests. The plant grows up to 2 feet tall. Zones 5–9.

Lemon Balm
(*Melissa officinalis*)

Where you cannot grow lemons, plant lemon balm. Use the pretty heart-shape leaves for their delicious mint-married-to-lemon scent and flavor. Use the fresh leaves in vegetable dishes, fruit salads, or drinks (iced or hot tea and lemonade).

YOU SHOULD KNOW
Lemon balm spreads easily and can take over. Plant it in a contained bed or a spot where it can self-seed without becoming an invasive pain.

Lemon balm was used as far back as the Middle Ages to reduce anxiety and promote sleep, and it still is today. The herbal liqueurs Chartreuse and Benedictine include lemon balm.

Best site
For the largest, most flavorful plants, grow lemon balm in part shade. If the soil is moist and rich, the herb can grow in full sun. Lemon balm self-seeds readily, making it a good candidate for a container garden. Plant it in a well-draining potting mix.

Planting
Lemon balm grows easily from seeds. Sow seeds in early spring or fall. The seeds are tiny, so cover them with a fine layer of soilless potting mix and water gently. Keep the seed-starting medium damp until the seeds germinate. Avoid overwatering. When starting with nursery-grown seedlings or divisions, plant in early spring. Space plants 2 feet apart. For the most flavorful foliage, improve the soil by working in a 2-inch layer of compost before you plant.

varieties:

1 **VARIEGATED** (*Melissa officinalis* 'Variegata') offers yellow-tinged leaves. It reaches 1 to 2 feet tall. Zones 4–9.

Growing
Plants grown from seed may be a bit small the first year but will fill out eventually and grow to 2 feet. When plants mature, remove the flowerheads before they form seeds to prevent plants from self-sowing and becoming weedy. In areas where the ground freezes in winter, mulch lemon balm plants with a 4- to 6-inch-thick layer of organic mulch. Zones 4–10.

Harvest
The best time to harvest lemon balm leaves is just before the plant blooms. Snip off the leaves to use them fresh or preserve by drying. Dried leaves lose much of their lemony scent. Keep the leaves from turning black by drying them quickly on a rack. Once they are dried, store them in an airtight container away from light and heat.

Uses
Lemon balm tisane Make a calming cup of tisane using lemon balm leaves: Cut fresh leaves, place them in a cup, add hot water, cover, and steep for 5 minutes. Sweeten with honey.

Mint substitute Use lemon balm any place you'd use mint. This member of the mint family imparts a lemony-minty flavor to beverages, such as iced tea, lemonade, and fruit juice.

Lemon balm pesto Grind together 2 cups fresh lemon balm leaves with ½ cup olive oil and 3 cloves garlic in a food processor. Use it on pasta or rice, or as a marinade for fish or chicken.

Pollinator attractor Lemon balm flowers attract bees and other pollinators.

Bath herb Use fresh or dried lemon balm to make a strong infusion, then add the tea to a bath for a relaxing effect.

Lemongrass
(*Cymbopogon citratus*)

An essential ingredient in Thai and Vietnamese cuisine, tropical lemongrass is a snap to grow in containers even in cold-climate gardens. Leaves of this tall, grassy, fast-growing plant can be harvested more than once a year where the climate allows.

A native of India, lemongrass was used throughout history as a medicinal and culinary herb. Prescribed as a digestive aid, lemongrass is still used in many countries as a folk remedy. It is also used in aromatherapy.

Best site
Lemongrass likes it hot. That's why it requires a sunny location, either in the ground or in a pot; and it thrives where summers are hot. It's not fussy about growing conditions, but does best in a rich, moist soil with a high nitrogen content.

Planting
It's easy to start lemongrass from young plants purchased at your local garden center or from an online source. Or take a division from an established clump. Lemongrass detests cold weather. Plant after any frost danger has passed and nighttime temperatures remain warm. If planting in a container, use a commercial potting mix that includes slow-release fertilizer. This 4- to 6-foot-tall plant requires a large pot.

Growing
Once planted, lemongrass needs little assistance. Just keep the plant well watered during dry spells. The hotter the temperatures, the more your lemongrass will grow. This fast grower can be pruned or sheared to maintain a more manageable size. Zones 9–11.

Harvest
Cut leaves as needed throughout the growing season, clipping them off at the base of the plant. You can also cut and dry the leaves for future use. Or you can freeze them for up to a year.

Uses
Marinade Lemongrass melds well with garlic and chiles. Place herbs in a food processor and make a paste. Use the paste to suit your taste on fish or poultry.

Lemongrass tisane Lemongrass requires liquids to disperse its essential oils. Steep leaves and stems in hot water, then flavor the tisane with honey.

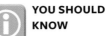

YOU SHOULD KNOW
In late summer, take a small division of lemongrass, pot it in soil, and bring it indoors to spend the winter on a sunny windowsill.

Lemon Verbena
(*Aloysia triphylla*)

This herb grows 3 to 4 feet tall as an annual in most gardens. Raised in a frost-free climate, the tropical shrub reaches 15 feet tall. The plant's intense lemon fragrance and flavor make it a favorite herbal ingredient in beverages and desserts.

YOU SHOULD KNOW
Finely chop lemon verbena leaves before using the fresh herb in recipes because the leaves are somewhat tough. Or use the leaves whole, as you would bay leaves, and remove them before serving.

A native of Chile and Argentina, lemon verbena has a fresh scent and flavor that made it a favorite among Victorian women, who tucked the herb into clothing. It remains a favorite for making various lemony drinks, from lemonade to alcohol-infused beverages. The citrusy scent is also used in perfumes and other fragrant products.

Best site
Plant in full sun. Easy-to-grow lemon verbena adapts to many soil types—from wet clay to sandy loam—but prefers rich soil. In warm climates, lemon verbena grows as a perennial, but elsewhere it is treated as an annual. Growing the plant in a container makes it easy to move it outdoors in the spring, and indoors to keep it going over the winter.

Planting
Start with cuttings or plant container-grown plants in the garden after the soil has warmed and the threat of frost has passed. Lemon verbena plants may be difficult to find. Look for them at specialty nurseries and mail-order sources. Lemon verbena also grows well in a container of well-draining potting mix.

Growing
Give lemon verbena plants about 1 inch of water per week for the first six weeks after spring planting. Trim the stem ends regularly to keep lemon verbena growing lush and bushy. This cold-sensitive plant drops its leaves if exposed to chilly weather. Protect your potted plant by moving it indoors in late summer and placing it in a bright, sunny window. If whiteflies become a problem, spray the plant with a blast of water from the garden hose. Zones 9–10.

Harvest
The lemony leaves can be harvested anytime by cutting the stems' tips. Harvest the entire plant at season's end and hang it upside down in a cool, well-ventilated place. Allow the leaves to dry thoroughly, then store them in a jar.

Uses
In the kitchen Get a lemony blast from lemon verbena by using the leaves to make salad dressings, marinades, jelly, cakes, or sorbet.

Fragrant blends Lemon verbena leaves hold their scent for months and provide a bright note in a sachet, dream pillow, or bath herb blend.

Lemon verbena simple syrup Add 1 cup sugar to 1 cup water in a pan; stir to dissolve. Add ½ cup whole lemon verbena leaves and bring to a boil. Remove the pan from heat; let the mixture cool. Strain the leaves; refrigerate.

Licorice Root
(Glycyrrhiza glabra)
This shrubby perennial is a member of the legume family. The plant has attractive leaves and develops an edible, sweet root. It is unrelated to the ornamental annual called licorice plant *(Helichrysum).*

The woody root of licorice has been used medicinally for a wide range of illness—from coughs to depression. On a sweeter note, it's also used to flavor candy. Glycyrrhizin, one of the compounds in the root, is 50 times sweeter than sugar and quenches thirst instead of increasing it.

Best site
Licorice requires a sunny spot with well-drained soil. Provide water during dry spells because this plant likes moist soil. You can also grow licorice in containers.

Planting
Start licorice by dividing the roots of established plants. You can also find licorice rhizomes available for sale from mail-order nurseries. Plants can occasionally be found at local garden centers.

Growing
Licorice is one of the taller herbs, often growing 3 to 6 feet tall. Plant it where it can reach mature height without getting in the way of other plants. Space the plants about 3 feet apart. Keep the planting area weeded to eliminate competition for nutrients and rooting space. Mulch plants heavily in the northern part of their range to help them survive the winter. If you grow licorice in a pot, use a high-quality potting mix. Bring the plant indoors in early fall before frost occurs. Zones 7–10.

Harvest
Most plants will not produce harvestable roots until they are at least several years old. When the roots are large enough to harvest, dig up the plant and cut off the foliage. Rinse any soil off the roots, then set them in an airy place to dry.

Uses
Candy Licorice candies get much of their flavor from the addition of anise; the licorice root is mainly used as the sweetener.

Perennial border This shrubby plant has a branching form. The small blue-violet flowers appear in midsummer. It's an ideal back-of-the-border plant in warmer climates.

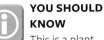 **YOU SHOULD KNOW** This is a plant for patient gardeners. Only when licorice is three or four years old will the roots be ready for harvest.

Lovage
(*Levisticum officinale*)

A relative of celery, lovage is a hardy perennial whose leaves can be used in soups or salads. The attractive leaves can even be used in bouquets as filler. Although its leaves and stems die back after frost, it will produce a flush of new growth the following spring.

YOU SHOULD KNOW
Lovage is a trouble-free herb. Give plants plenty of room to grow. Leaving 2 feet of space between plants will help prevent disease such as blight. Pull and destroy any rotted stems with yellow or reddish leaves.

A European native, lovage was included in apothecary gardens to treat stomach upsets and solve flatulence. It is similar in appearance to angelica.

Best site
Plant lovage in full sun and deep, compost-enriched, moist soil. Unlike most herbs, lovage thrives in wet soil. It also does well in clay and other slow-to-drain soils.

Planting
Start from seeds or division. Sow seeds directly in the garden in fall or early spring. If starting indoors, sow in late winter for transplanting in spring. Lovage can also be started by the division of established lovage plants in spring or fall. To give it a nutrient boost, mix a 2-inch layer of compost into the soil before planting. Water plants well after planting to help them establish strong root systems. This is necessary to keep plants over the winter.

Growing
Lovage grows up to 5 feet tall and 2 feet wide. Place this herb in an area where it can spread and not compete with other plants. Its small yellow-green flowers attract beneficial insects. After planting, lovage grows vigorously for about four years and then slows. Lovage is a self-seeder. Clip off flowers as soon as they appear unless you want more plants. Removing flowers also promotes more leafstalks. To help retain moist soil, mulch around lovage plants, adding a 4- to 6-inch-thick layer of organic mulch for overwintering in cold climates. Zones 3–9.

Harvest
Start harvesting a few leaves about three months after sowing seeds. After the plants are a year old, harvest leaves and stalks throughout the growing season. Although this plant self-seeds, allowing some flowers to develop is a good idea because they attract beneficial insects to the garden. Lovage seeds are edible and have a flavor reminiscent of anise and celery. Collect seeds by cutting off the nearly mature seedheads and hanging a bunch of them upside down in a paper bag. When dried or frozen, lovage leaves hold their flavor for about one year.

Uses
Salads Harvest young leaves, which have a celery flavor, and clip into spring salads.

Parsley substitute Cooks often use lovage in place of parsley or celery leaves, but in limited quantities because the flavor is stronger.

Perennial border Because of its shrubby habit and lush green leaves, lovage suits a mixed flower border as well as an herb bed.

Marigold
(*Tagetes*)

Among the most recognizable flowers in the world, marigolds have varied uses, from a colorful garden insect repellent to decorative flower garlands. These nonstop annual bloomers add cheery color to herb beds and flower gardens.

Marigolds were considered sacred flowers by the Aztecs. These long-blooming flowers are also used in Hindu ceremonies and can be made into beautiful wearable garlands.

Best site
Marigolds require a sunny location that receives at least six to eight hours of direct sun a day. They prefer a rich, well-drained soil and grow as well in containers as they do in a garden bed.

Planting
Start marigolds from seed or from seedlings purchased at your local garden center. If you use seeds, sow them ½ inch deep. Remember that marigolds are tender annuals; avoid planting

varieties:

1. **SIGNET MARIGOLD** (*Tagetes tenuifolia*) has finely divided lacy foliage topped with 1-inch-diameter bright flowers in orange, tangerine, or yellow. Signet marigolds grow 12 to 18 inches tall and are believed to be the most effective in repelling destructive nematodes that live in soil.
2. **FRENCH MARIGOLD** (*T. patula*) grows 8 to 12 inches tall and has frilly petals, often with a raised center.
3. **AFRICAN MARIGOLD** (*T. erecta*) is the giant of the family, growing up to 3 feet tall with large ball-like blooms in orange, yellow, or white.

them outdoors until all frost danger has passed. Eliminate weed competition by mulching marigolds after planting.

Growing
Marigolds are unfussy and once established they will flourish even if unattended. They prefer damp—not wet—soil. During dry periods, water them once or twice a week. To keep weeds from competing, mulch between plants. For potted plantings, water as needed when the soil begins to feel dry to the touch—daily during hot weather. Pinch off faded blooms. When frost comes, marigolds die. Remove the plants and consign them to the compost pile.

Harvest
Marigold flowers can be harvested at any time for use fresh or dried. If you want to save seeds, hang plants upside down and allow the seedheads to dry. Crumble the dried seedheads and sort out the needlelike seeds. Store the seeds in an airtight container to plant the following year.

Uses
Edging plants Dwarf varieties make a neat and colorful edging for beds and borders. Plant them around vegetable gardens to help deter insect pests from crops.

Dyes The flower petals can be used to make dye for fabric.

Kids' gardens Because marigolds are so easy to grow from seeds or seedlings, they are the perfect choice for children's gardens. If you have any budding gardeners at home, get them growing with bright marigolds.

YOU SHOULD KNOW Most insects avoid marigolds, but slugs and snails will dine on the stems and leaves. Use an organic slug and snail bait to keep these pests from destroying your plants.

Marjoram, Sweet Marjoram

(Origanum majorana)
This tender perennial, often called sweet marjoram, is related to oregano and a major player in Italian cuisine. The herb has a flavor that's milder and sweeter than oregano, offering fragrant notes of pine and citrus.

YOU SHOULD KNOW
Marjoram and oregano are both members of the mint family. Plants in the family have square stems and opposing sets of leaves. Marjoram is more tender than oregano.

Marjoram was the symbol of happiness in Greek and Roman cultures. Because of this association, it was often included in bridal bouquets.

Best site
Plant in full sun and well-drained soil. Marjoram does well in most soils but grows best in average, sandy soil.

Planting
Marjoram is slow to germinate and challenging to start from seed. A better bet for quicker harvests is to start with nursery-grown plants. In spring, wait to set out plants until after the danger of frost has passed. Space plants 12 inches apart and water them well after planting.

Growing
This tender perennial grows as an annual for most gardeners. Marjoram grows well in a container. Bring plants indoors over winter. The plants are low growing and form attractive clumps. The leaves and flowers are edible; varieties produce white, pink, or red flowers

in mid- to late summer. Because of its trailing habit, marjoram adds beautifully to hanging baskets. Cut off long, trailing stems to encourage bushier growth. Plantings dry out quickly. Water regularly to keep soil moist but not wet. When plants become woody, divide them. In mild regions where marjoram can overwinter in the garden, cover plants with a 4- to 6-inch blanket of mulch. Zones 8–10.

Harvest
Pick leaves and stems for use fresh or dried in cooking. Cut and bundle stems, and hang the bunch in a cool, dark, airy place. Strip the dried leaves from the stems and store them whole in airtight glass jars. Dried marjoram retains its flavor better than dried oregano, keeping well for about one year.

Uses
Oregano substitute Marjoram has a sweet, mild, slightly balsam flavor that complements basil, bay, garlic, onion, and thyme in culinary herb blends.

Za'atar Make this Arabic herb blend with marjoram, sumac, thyme, sesame seeds, oregano, and salt.

Vegetable seasoning Snip fresh leaves directly into salads or on top of cooked dishes just before serving to enjoy the herb's full flavor. Cooking diminishes marjoram's flavor.

Knot gardens Marjoram has a more compact growth habit than its cousin oregano, making it the herb of choice for edging many English knot gardens.

varieties:

1 **VARIEGATED** (*Origanum majorana* 'Variegata') has yellow-and-green leaves and a low-growing, prostrate habit. Zones 6–9.

Milk Thistle
(*Silybum marianum*)

Milk thistle is a striking member of the daisy family, but its thorny demeanor makes it feel more like a true thistle. When cut, the plant produces a white, milky liquid, which is how it got its name.

Native to the Mediterranean, milk thistle has been cultivated for centuries as a treatment for diseases of the liver and gallbladder, and an antidote to poisoning by deathcap mushrooms. The plants are grown primarily for their seeds. The leaves, flowers, and roots can be eaten.

Best site
Any sunny location is acceptable for this annual or biennial plant. It prefers rich, moist soil but will grow in almost any conditions and has escaped cultivation in the eastern United States and elsewhere to become a weed.

Planting
Milk thistle grows quickly from seeds sown 1 inch deep in the soil. Thin the seedlings to stand about 2 feet apart. Water your plant as needed during drought to sustain it.

Growing
Once planted, milk thistle requires no assistance from you. The plants will eventually grow 2 to 4 feet tall, producing shiny, pointed green leaves with white streaks. The plant develops a bold purple, prickly thistle blossom. Remove the blossoms to prolong the plant's interesting appearance. Keep an eye on your planting to ensure that it does not self-sow wildly and become a weed. Zones 5–9.

Harvest
Collect the seeds after the bright purple flowers have faded and begun to dry. Wear heavy-duty gloves to avoid being poked by the thistles, and carefully clip each blossom from the plant. Break open the thistle and remove the seeds. Set them in a protected place to air-dry thoroughly. Store the dried seeds in an airtight container.

Uses
Tea Thistle seeds can be ground and made into a tea made tastier with the addition of mint leaves.

Physic gardens Milk thistle is a traditional plant for medicinal herb gardens.

Salad greens Tender young milk thistle leaves can be added to salads or eaten as cooked greens.

Dried flowers Cut and dry the thistles for decorative use in wreaths and other crafts.

YOU SHOULD KNOW Check local regulations before you plant milk thistle. It may be considered a noxious weed in your region.

Mint (*Mentha*)

Fragrant and flavorful, mint is a vigorous perennial herb with a host of culinary and cosmetic uses. There are more than 600 varieties of mint, with luscious fragrances and flavors, ranging beyond peppermint's refreshing menthol and spearmint's surprising sweetness. This versatile herb is easy to grow. For some gardeners, it grows too easily, spreading wildly throughout the garden.

Native to the Mediterranean, mint is a symbol of hospitality. Reputedly, ancient Romans welcomed guests to banquets by littering the room with fragrant mint leaves.

Best site
Mint is adaptable to many soil types and light conditions. For best results, plant in full sun or part shade in rich, moist, well-drained soil. Amend soil with a 2-inch layer of compost before planting. Mint's hardiness depends on the variety. Use a creeping variety such as Corsican mint as a groundcover, tucking it between stepping-stones of a pathway. Other varieties grow more upright, reaching up to 2 feet, and work well in mixed beds.

Planting
Mint grows so easily that gardeners often look for ways to get rid of it. Start seeds in early spring. About six weeks before the last frost in your area, sow herb seeds indoors to get a head start on the outdoor growing season. Plant purchased plants in spring, after the threat of frost has passed. Or grow plants from root cuttings or divisions. Mint cross-pollinates easily. Separate different varieties to prevent this. To limit mint's spreading tendencies, plant it in a container that is sunk directly into the soil. See page 63 for details.

Growing
Cutting mint regularly keeps it looking lush, bushy, and attractive. Snip off the flowers as they appear. To provide mint with the maximum nutrients and moisture, remove competing weeds and grasses. To keep plants in top producing shape, divide mint every few years. Shear stems to the ground in late fall and then savor this end-of-the-summer mint crop.

Chase mites and aphids away by blasting them with a strong spray of water from a garden hose. If a soilborne disease such as verticillium wilt is a problem, plant mint in containers. When planting, leave room between plants to encourage air circulation. Zones 3–10.

Harvest
Mint leaves and flowers are edible. Freeze fresh leaves to retain their bright color. Cut the flowers when they begin to form to promote more leafy growth. Use the flowers and leaves fresh, or air-dry them. Cut stems, gather them into bundles, and hang in a cool, dry place. Strip the leaves and flowers from the stems and store them whole in airtight containers.

Uses
Drink flavoring The list of mint-inspired drinks is long. Start with mint julep, mojito, and iced tea.

Salad surprise Snip mint leaves into a green or fruit salad for a refreshing flavor blast.

Mint simple syrup Combine 1 cup sugar, 1 cup water, and ½ cup mint leaves in a pan. Bring to a boil, then allow to cool; strain.

Bath herb blend or tub tea Include your favorite mint in an herb blend for a relaxing and cooling bath. Try mixing equal parts dried mint, lavender, rose, lemon balm, and chamomile.

YOU SHOULD KNOW
Mint can be invasive. It grows fast and spreads rampantly. If you like the fresh flavor of its green leaves, grow mint in containers near your back door so you can clip leaves for recipes.

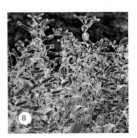

varieties:

1. **PEPPERMINT** (*Mentha ×piperita*) produces the strongest mint flavor. There are many varieties of peppermint. Zones 3–9.

2. **SPEARMINT** (*M. spicata*) packs a distinctive, sweet flavor. Zones 4–10.

3. **'HILLARY'S SWEET LEMON'** (*M. dulcia citreus*) produces large, flavorful leaves. Grows 1½ to 2 feet tall. Zones 4–10.

4. **PINEAPPLE MINT** (*M. suaveolens* 'Variegata') offers white-edged leaves and a fruity taste. Zones 5–10.

5. **CHOCOLATE MINT** (*M. ×piperita*) has a subtle chocolate fragrance and flavor. It has pretty dark stems and bright-green foliage. Plants grow 2 feet tall. Zones 4–9.

6. **ORANGE MINT** (*M. ×piperita citrata*) develops bright green leaves lightly tinged with red. Foliage bears a citrus fragrance and flavor. It grows 2 feet tall. Zones 4–9.

7. **APPLE MINT** (*M. suaveolens*) has a wintergreen flavor and fragrance. The fresh leaves can be used to make apple mint jelly or a stomach-soothing tea. It reaches 2 feet tall. Zones 4–9.

8. **'HIMALAYAN SILVER MINT'** (*M. spicata*) bears silver-green fuzzy leaves with pink flowers. This variety grows 12 to 18 inches tall. Zones 4–10.

Mugwort
(*Artemisia vulgaris*)

Mugwort is an herb that sounds like one of Harry Potter's alchemy ingredients. In fact, it was used by ancient herbalists for several purposes, but today its primary use is in aromatherapy. Mugwort has a sagelike scent with mint undertones and a bitter flavor.

YOU SHOULD KNOW
Mugwort has a reputation for being invasive. Plant it in a place where it can spread out, contain it a pot, or harvest before it goes to seed.

YOU SHOULD KNOW
Mullein is a good choice for cottage gardens because of its tall stature, wandlike blooms and soft, fuzzy leaves.

Best site
Plant mugwort in sun or partial shade. Once established, mugwort can grow in dry soil.

Planting
Sow seeds indoors in late spring and transplant into the garden once the threat of frost has passed. Or sow seeds directly on top of moist, sandy soil.

Growing
Mugwort grows 2 to 4 feet tall. It is a hardy perennial. Mugwort flowers from July through September. Plants can be reproduced by division. Zones 5–10.

Harvest
Harvest stems just after flowering in early summer and again in late fall. Bundle the stems and hang them in a cool, dry location to dry.

Mullein
(*Verbascum thapsus*)

Mullein is a biennial often found growing wild in fields and ditches. It was used medicinally to guard against asthma and cure respiratory illnesses. Plants grow up to 6 feet tall and the leaves are gray-green, fuzzy, large, and thick. Flowers are yellow and can be infused in olive oil to create a soothing oil for skin.

Best site
Plant mullein in full or partial sun. It does well in nearly any soil (hence its ability to grow wild).

Planting
Plant seeds indoors in early spring. Transplant plants into the garden after the threat of frost has passed. If growing outdoors from seed, sow directly in the garden in late spring or early fall. The plant also self-sows if allowed.

Growing
As a biennial, mullein will flower the second year. To protect plants over the winter, mulch in autumn. Zones 3–9.

Harvest
Pick flowers throughout the summer as they bloom or harvest the entire plant when it is flowering.

Mustard
(Brassica juncea, B. nigra)

Mustard is an annual, multipurpose plant: The greens are used for food and the seeds are used for spices and condiments. The seeds of different varieties yield the condiment's color, such as yellow or brown. Black mustard is a pungent herb used externally in warming poultices and baths.

Best site
Plant mustard in a sunny spot in well-draining, compost-enriched soil.

Planting
Mustard prefers cool weather. Sow mustard seeds directly in the ground in early spring about ¼ inch deep. Sow a second crop in the early fall.

Growing
Plant small crops in succession (about a week apart) to ensure a continuous supply of greens. Water plants during dry periods.

Harvest
Pick mustard greens as soon as they are tall enough to harvest. To harvest seeds, allow the plants to set seed. Then cut stalks below the branching stems. Bundle the stems and hang upside down to dry in a cool, dry place.

Myrtle
(Myrtus communis)

An evergreen shrub from the Mediterranean and Middle East, myrtle is used as an emblem of love. It can grow from 2 to 10 feet tall and has glossy, dark-green leaves and small, white blossoms. The leaves have a sweet fragrance when crushed. Avoid overwatering myrtle to prevent root rot.

Best site
Grow myrtle in full sun and well-drained soil.

Planting
In areas with mild winters, plant myrtle in the ground. In a cool-weather climate, plant myrtle in a container that can be moved indoors. Choose dwarf myrtle for hedges.

Growing
Lightly prune myrtle in the spring to help retain its shape. Lightly fertilize while the plant is in flower. Water when the soil begins to feel dry to the touch. Zones 8–11.

Harvest
Gather and dry the leaves for use in potpourris or sachets. Add fresh sprigs to bouquets. The purple-black berries can be used in cooking as you would use juniper berries.

YOU SHOULD KNOW The pungent greens of mustard grow knee-high within 35 to 45 days and provide a healthy source of calcium. If you allow the plants to develop seedheads, harvest the stalks and let them cure for one to two weeks before using the seeds.

YOU SHOULD KNOW The dwarf variety of myrtle (*M. communis* 'Compacta') is a slow-growing evergreen plant that reaches 2 to 3 feet tall.

Oregano
(Origanum vulgare hirtum)
This low-growing, sprawling perennial herb excels in gardens or containers. Clipped fresh into pasta sauces, sprinkled over stews, or used in a marinade for meat, oregano adds a warm, aromatic flavor. For lovers of Mediterranean cuisine, fresh or dried oregano is essential.

YOU SHOULD KNOW
Several different plants are sold as oregano. *Origanum vulgare*, or common marjoram, is sometimes sold as oregano. *O. majorana* is sweet marjoram. Sometimes summer savory (*Satureja hortensis*) is sold as oregano. If you are looking for the best oregano for culinary use, choose Greek oregano (*O. vulgare hirtum*).

Oregano has been used for medicinal and culinary purposes since ancient times. The pungent herb was associated with happiness, good luck, and health. For this reason, it was worn for weddings in ancient Greece and Rome.

Best site
Plant in full sun and well-drained soil. Like most herbs, oregano will not tolerate wet soil. If your soil is slow to drain, add organic matter (chopped leaves and compost) to your planting area. Otherwise, grow oregano in a raised bed or container.

Planting
Oregano is difficult to start from seed. Buy nursery-grown transplants instead and ensure that you are getting a true culinary variety. Set out plants in spring after frost danger has passed.

varieties:

1. **GREEK OREGANO** (*Origanum vulgare hirtum*) offers the best flavor for culinary use.
2. **'AUREUM'** (*O. vulgare*) is sometimes sold as creeping golden marjoram and has yellow-green leaves and white flowers. Zones 6–9.
3. **'HERRENHAUSEN'** (*O. laevigatum*) has purple-tinted leaves and showy pink flowers. It grows 18 inches tall. Zones 5–10.

Because of oregano's rangy growth habit, space plants 18 inches apart.

Growing
Water only during dry periods; too much moisture can result in root rot. Divide plants every few years when they become woody or begin to lose their compact habit. Plants grow to 18 inches tall. In cold climates mulch plants to provide protection. Zones 5–10.

Harvest
Oregano leaves are most flavorful when gathered just before the flowerbuds open. Cut stems as needed, using the fresh leaves and edible flowers for vegetable salads and other favorite recipes. To obtain two large harvests per season, shear back the entire plant to about 3 inches just before it flowers; after it regrows, shear it back again in late summer. Oregano has a somewhat strong flavor; use it sparingly. Oregano retains good flavor when dried. Clip stems, bundle them, and hang upside down to dry in a cool, dark location with good air circulation. When the stems are crisp-dry, pluck off the leaves and store them in an airtight jar. Fresh leaves can also be preserved by freezing.

Uses
Landscape use. Plant oregano as a low-grower in flower beds or between stones of a pathway or rock garden.

Pollinator attractor Allow your oregano to flower and it will attract bees and butterflies.

Rock gardens Dittany of Crete (*Origanum dictamnus*), a relative of oregano, is a beautiful choice for rock gardens because of its round, fuzzy gray leaves.

Parsley
(Petroselinum)

More than a tasty garnish, parsley is rich in vitamins and minerals. The green fronds of this herb are pretty enough to use in bouquets. Parsley's neat, mounding growth habit makes it an edible edging plant for ornamental and vegetable gardens. Choose from two types of parsley: curly- and flat-leaved.

Parsley was used by the Greeks to adorn the winners of athletic contests. It has been in cultivation for more than 2,000 years.

Best site
Plant in full sun and moist, well-drained soil.

Planting
Sow seeds or set out transplants in early spring. Parsley seeds are slow to germinate so, if planting directly in the ground, use a cold frame over the seeding site to warm the soil. Space plants 10 to 18 inches apart; parsley grows about as wide as it is tall—from 8 to 24 inches. If growing parsley from seed, thin plants to 10 inches apart. In warm climates you can sow seeds in spring and fall. To give newly planted parsley a boost, dig a 2-inch-thick layer of compost into the site before planting.

Growing
Spread a 2-inch-thick layer of mulch between plants to prevent soil from splashing onto the leaves when watering. Snap off flower stalks as they form. Although parsley is a biennial grown as an annual, it can overwinter in a cold frame or under a thick layer of straw in all but the coldest climates.

Harvest
Harvest parsley as soon as the plants are large enough—and as often as needed. Consistent harvests encourage new growth. Snip the full stem when harvesting. The entire plant may be harvested before winter or mulched heavily to protect it over the winter. Stand fresh-picked parsley stems in a glass of water and keep it on the kitchen counter or in the refrigerator for several days. Dry or freeze parsley for later use.

Uses
French herb blends Parsley is a key ingredient in bouquet garni and fines herbes.

Basil substitute for pesto Use parsley instead of basil to make a mild pesto.

Butterfly gardening Swallowtail butterflies use parsley as a host plant for their larvae (black-, green-, and yellow-striped caterpillars). Although these caterpillars will eat some parsley leaves, it won't be enough to damage the plant. Let them dine and enjoy the beautiful butterflies that ensue.

 **YOU SHOULD KNOW** Harvest fresh parsley in winter by growing it in a cold frame or on a sunny windowsill. The plant will continue to produce new leaves until spring.

varieties:

1. **FLAT-LEAF ITALIAN** (*Petroselinum neopolitanum*) makes an attractive garnish or addition to salads. Zones 5–9.
2. **CURLY LEAF** (*P. crispum*) contains vitamin C and iron, like other varieties. Nibbling on the leaves is an effective breath freshener.

Patchouli
(*Pogostemon cablin*)

The scent of patchouli is cryptic: Its spicy fragrance is used extensively in perfume production and is considered an aphrodisiac, yet it also repels insects. A member of the mint family, this tender perennial produces fragrant leaves that release their distinctive scent when rubbed.

YOU SHOULD KNOW

Patchouli requires moist soil. Keep the plant well watered, especially when growing it in a container. Mulch around the plant to help conserve soil moisture.

Used in China to cure headaches and in India to treat snakebites, patchouli is known to Western herb fans as a sweet woodsy scent in perfumes, lotions, soaps, and incenses.

Best site
Plant patchouli in partial shade in rich, moist soil.

Planting
Sow seeds indoors about six to eight weeks before the last frost date in your area. Transplant seedlings outdoors once the threat of frost has passed. Plant transplants 2 feet apart. Patchouli also grows well in containers and makes an interesting conversation piece.

Growing
Patchouli is a bushy plant that grows 2 to 3 feet tall, with subtley scented leaves and small white flowers. This native plant of India thrives and grows quickly in hot, humid weather. Bring your plant indoors before frost if you want to overwinter it. Frost will kill patchouli. Aphids and spider mites can be controlled with insecticidal soap. If you have slugs in your area, apply a layer of diatomaceous earth around plants. Patchouli is perennial in Zone 11; elsewhere it is considered an annual.

Harvest
Clip the flowers (which are small but more aromatic than the leaves). Harvest leaves throughout the summer. Bundle stems and hang in a warm, dry location. Remove dried leaves and store in an airtight container. You can keep a potted patchouli in your bedroom to scent your sleep. If the fragrance is overpowering, move the plant to a more shaded location.

Uses
Insect repellent Store clothing with sprigs of patchouli to repel moths. Or soak cotton balls with patchouli oil and place them in drawers and armoires to release its long-lasting scent.

Aromatherapy Add the flowers to potpourri. Release the seductive scent of patchouli in your home by simmering a few fresh leaves in water.

Pennyroyal
(*Mentha pulegium*)

This perennial grows 4 to 16 inches tall and features fluffy lavender flowers along the stems. The plant has a creeping habit and, as a member of the mint family, pennyroyal tends to spread and become invasive.

Pennyroyal is native to south and central Europe. Used in ancient times to repel pests, it is used today in natural insect repellents.

Best site
Grow pennyroyal in full sun to partial shade. It does best in moist, well-draining soil and is often found growing near streams.

Planting
Sow seeds directly in the garden approximately ¼ inch deep in early spring after the threat of frost has passed. In warm climates you can plant seeds in the fall.

Growing
To prevent it from spreading throughout the garden, plant pennyroyal in containers or a confined bed. This herb grows up to 16 inches tall and produces lavender, pink, or bluish-purple flowers in mid- to late summer. It can become weedy by spreading via underground runners or horizontal roots. When pulling gregarious plants, make sure you pull out the entire root to prevent the plants from regrowing. Zones 6–9.

Harvest
Pick leaves to use fresh when the plant is in full bloom—in early summer—when the leaves bear the strongest scent. To dry, bundle stems and hang upside down in a cool, dry place.

Uses

Insect repellent Use fresh leaves and stems to repel insects such as fleas. Rub leaves directly on skin; but first test for an allergic reaction by rubbing a leaf on a small area of skin. Keep from applying the essential oil to pets; do not ingest pennyroyal oil—it is toxic. Pregnant women should avoid any use of pennyroyal.

Groundcover This vigorous grower makes an ideal groundcover in areas that don't receive direct foot traffic. When brushed, it releases a pleasant minty fragrance.

YOU SHOULD KNOW
Like many members of the mint family, pennyroyal can be invasive. Plant it prudently in a place where it can spread without taking over.

Pepper *(Capsicum annuum)*

Chile, hot, or cultivated red peppers are famous throughout the world for their spice and heat. Chile peppers also play starring roles in herb and vegetable gardens. Ornamental varieties excel in containers and window boxes. Pepper plants produce fruits that ripen from green to gemlike colors of red, yellow, orange, purple, and brown.

YOU SHOULD KNOW
Chile heat ratings by the Scoville Heat Scale measure the amount of a chemical compound called capsaicin in the fruit and seeds of peppers. The scale starts with bell pepper at 0 and goes up to hot peppers, such as habanero, rated at more than 500,000 at the hot end. Some peppers are so hot that handling them can burn your skin.

Hot peppers define the cuisines of Mexico, India, Thailand, and Africa. Peppers are used as a seasoning and main ingredient. They also have been used medicinally in homeopathy.

Best site
Plant in full sun and well-drained soil. Good growth and fruit formation require at least eight hours of direct sunlight a day. Peppers are easy to grow in containers too. Choose a pot large enough to support the heavily-fruiting plants.

Planting
Peppers are easiest to grow from transplants. Peppers are hot-weather plants so hold off planting until the soil has warmed, about two weeks after the average last frost date. If you decide to start plants from seeds, start indoors six to eight weeks before the last frost date. Sow seeds ¼ inch deep. Place seedlings in a bright, sunny location. Lack of light will produce leggy, unproductive transplants. Peppers thrive in soil amended with lots of organic matter. Prior to planting, dig a 2-inch-thick layer of compost into the planting area.

Growing
Peppers like it hot and grow best between 70 and 80°F. Apply fertilizer after the first fruit is set. Keep the planting areas weeded and plants well watered. Apply organic mulch, such as chopped leaves or grass clippings, after the soil has warmed to help prevent weed growth and conserve soil moisture. Peppers are sensitive to frost, so if freezing weather is predicted, cover plants.

Harvest
Pick hot peppers at any stage. The fruits are hottest and most flavorful when allowed to fully ripen. Peppers turn fully colored when ripe. Plants suffering from water or nutrient stress produce fewer but hotter peppers. Cool, cloudy weather promotes milder peppers. Wear gloves when handling hot peppers to protect your hands and face from exposure to capsaicin, the chemical that makes peppers hot enough to burn skin and mucuous membranes.

Uses
Fresh or dried seasonings For salsas and sauces, hot peppers provide heat and flavor.

Ornamental plants Even if you don't consume hot peppers, compact varieties provide beautiful container garden plants or bed edgers.

Ristra A string of chile peppers is used as Southwestern-inspired decor.

varieties:

❶ **'PRETTY IN PURPLE'** bears attractive purple fruits, stems, and leaves. Fruits turn red when they mature in about 85 days.

❷ **'THAI HOT'** features pencil-thin fruits that are borne above the foliage. The extremely hot fruits are used in Thai cooking and mature in 42 days.

❸ **'HOLY MOLE'** is a mildly hot pasilla-type pepper that was developed especially for mole sauce. Look for fruits within about 85 days.

Perilla (*Perilla frutescens*)

Perilla is a multitalented plant. As a popular ornamental, it's an asset to flower and container gardens. Sometimes called beefsteak plant, this showy annual is also known as a culinary herb that resembles coleus. Red perilla, called shiso or Japanese basil, has leaves that add a delectable cinnamon-fennel-mint flavor to food and drinks.

Native to China, perilla came to Japan in the 8th century. It is used throughout Asia as a seasoning and garnish. Its anti-inflammatory properties give it medicinal value as well.

Best site
Plant perilla in a sunny to partially shaded location. A sunny location promotes more intense leaf color. The plant prefers fertile, moist, well-draining soil.

Planting
Start seeds indoors six to eight weeks prior to your region's last average frost date. Or sow seeds directly in garden soil after the threat of frost has passed and the soil has warmed. Seed germination is slow and requires patience. Plant perilla in a container to keep it handy for use in the kitchen.

varieties:

❶ RED PERILLA (*Perilla frutescens* var. *crispa*) Also called beefsteak plant, shiso, and purple mint, this variety has an anise flavor and is slightly less spicy than the green variety.

❷ VIETNAMESE PERILLA (*P. frutescens*) or tía tô is a culinary variety that grows 12 inches tall.

❸ 'MAGILLA' PERILLA (*P. frutescens*) is an easy-to-grow ornamental variety that resembles coleus.

Growing
Perilla grows up to 3 feet tall and 2 feet wide. You can grow it in containers for culinary use; or use the showy nonculinary varieties in containers, beds, and borders. Some types of red perilla will self-seed in the garden.

Harvest
Snip leaves to use them fresh throughout the summer. At the end of the summer, cut this annual off at its base, and hang it in a cool, dry place to dry. When the leaves are dry, pull them off the stems, and store in an airtight container. Dried leaves lose much of their flavor. Alternatively, you can preserve shiso leaves by marinating them in soy sauce to use with Japanese dishes.

Uses
Asian cuisine All parts of the plant, including the leaves, flowers, roots, seeds, and stems, are used in many Asian dishes. In Japan, fresh whole shiso leaves are served with sashimi and wrapped around sushi. Cut into thin strips, the leaves are tossed in salads, or meat or tofu dishes.

Container gardening Perilla excels in containers, where its colorful foliage and exotic demeanor make it a much-used option. It resembles coleus and grows in sun or part shade.

 YOU SHOULD KNOW Use ornamental foliage plants of perilla in sunny spots where you want a splash of color. Many new varieties offer bicolor leaves that are as beautiful as flowers.

Pineapple Sage
(Salvia elegans)

Savor the flavor of the tropics—even in cold climates—with pineapple sage. This fragrant salvia offers garnishes for fruity drinks, summer salads, and desserts. The scented leaves and the flavorful flowers are edible. Plants bloom in autumn, producing small scarlet tubular-shape flowers.

YOU SHOULD KNOW
A tender perennial, pineapple sage dies when exposed to frost. In cold climates, grow this tall, woody plant in a container and bring it indoors for the winter.

Pineapple sage is a native of Mexico where it is used medicinally to relieve anxiety.

Best site
Plant pineapple sage in a sunny spot with well-draining soil. In areas with extremely hot summers, plant it in a partly shaded spot.

Planting
This plant is at home in garden beds and pots. Give plants room to grow—they form large clumps and grow 3 to 5 feet tall. Since pineapple sage is an annual in all but the most temperate zones, many gardeners grow it in a pot so it can be moved indoors at the end of the season.

Growing
Keep plants well watered. Encourage branching by pinching off the tips off the main stem and side shoots. Although plants grow tall, their woody stems do not require staking. Pineapple sage is easy to propagate from stem cuttings. Clip a cutting and place it in a jar of water. When roots develop, plant the cutting in a pot of well-draining potting soil. Zones 8–11.

Harvest
Gather the flowers any time; they are edible as well as pretty. For the best flavor of flowers and leaves, snip stems early in the morning, just after the dew has dried. To dry the leaves, bundle several stems and hang them in a cool, ventilated place. Store the whole, dried leaves in an airtight container in a cool, dark location.

Uses
Butterfly and hummingbird gardening
The small flowers are rich in nectar and attract hummingbirds and butterflies.

Smoothies Chop fresh pineapple sage leaves and use them in yogurt smoothies for a pineapple flavor. The leaves add zing to salsa too.

Edible flower gardening The bright red blossoms of pineapple sage are fun to use fresh as garnishes for drinks or cakes.

varieties:

1. **'GOLDEN DELICIOUS'** offers showy yellow-green foliage on 15-inch tall plants. In autumn, it bears spikes of scarlet flowers that attract hummingbirds and butterflies. Annual except in Zones 8–11.
2. **PINEAPPLE SAGE** is a tender shrub that grows 3 to 4 feet tall with pineapple-scented foliage and bright-red flowers. A dwarf form is also available. Zones 8–11; elsewhere as an annual.

Plectranthus
(*Plectranthus*)

Common varieties of this leafy plant, commonly called Swedish ivy, are prized as ornamental annuals and often planted in containers. But here's a surprise: the thick succulent leaves of at least one other variety are used as a culinary herb with an oreganolike flavor and added to meat dishes.

Plectranthus species are warm-climate plants. Most are native to the Southern Hemisphere. In India, southeast Asia, and Africa a few varieties, including annuals and perennials, are raised for their edible leaves and roots. Most varieties are ornamental and not cultivated as edibles.

Best site
Plectranthus grows best in a semishaded location with well-draining soil. The plants grow beautifully in potted gardens.

Planting
Start with root cuttings or transplants in late spring, setting them outdoors after any possibility of frost has passed. In beds, space plants 15 inches apart. When planting plectranthus in a container, use a well-draining potting mix. Allow the plant to fill the pot with roots before transplanting it into larger pot.

Growing
Plants grow 12 to 18 inches tall and are sensitive to frost. Plectranthus does best in hot weather. In cooler climates, grow the plant in a pot and bring it indoors before frost. Keep plectranthus in medium-bright light indoors. Water it regularly when the soil begins to feel dry to the touch, but avoid overwatering. Known primarily for their foliage, plectranthus varieties also develop tiny flowers in rose, violet, or white in spring or summer. Propagate the plants easily from leaf or stem cuttings.

Harvest
Snip leaves from Cuban oregano year-round and use them fresh.

Uses
Oregano or sage substitute Use the fresh leaves of Cuban oregano in recipes that call for oregano or sage. Also called Spanish thyme, this herb adds its flavor to marinades for poultry and meat. Use it sparingly at first to determine whether you like this herb as a substitute flavor.

Flowerbeds Plectranthus offers pretty foliage for garden beds. Use it as an unusual landscape plant or in containers on a patio, deck, or porch. Some varieties of plectranthus offer delicate flowers as well as handsome foliage. Most are fragrant to some degree.

YOU SHOULD KNOW
Easy-to-grow plectranthus is a sturdy foliage plant that propagates easily. Root cuttings in water to make new plants to share with friends and family.

varieties:

1. **SWEDISH IVY** (*Plectranthus coleoides*) has trailing green foliage. It is a popular houseplant. A white-variegated variety is also popular.
2. **'MONA LAVENDER'** This hybrid shows off rich purple leaves topped by spikes of lavender-purple flowers. It grows 28 inches tall and wide.
3. **CUBAN OREGANO** (*P. amboinicus*) is a culinary variety that grows up to a foot tall. Use the young leaves for their bold flavor, similar to oregano.

Poppy
(*Papaver somniferum*)

Breadseed poppies' crepe-paperlike blooms are as welcome in the flower garden as they are in the herb garden. Poppies have another claim to fame: Opium can be extracted from the dried heads. However, you're more likely to encounter the talents of this plant on top of a bagel in the form of poppy seeds.

Poppies were commonly cultivated by ancient cultures, including Sumerians, Assyrians, Babylonians, Egyptians, Romans, and Greeks.

Best site
Plant poppies in full sun and rich, moist soil.

Planting
It's best to grow poppies from seeds planted directly in the ground, as plants do not transplant well. Sow seeds ¼ inch deep and water well.

Growing
These annuals are easy to grow and often self-seed, so they appear year after year. They grow about 3 feet tall. In late spring, plants bear gorgeous flowers in shades of pink, lilac, mauve, red, or white. The seedpods form in autumn. Zones 3–9.

Harvest
Allow the seedheads to dry on the plant. Cut the stems of the dried seedpods and use them in floral arrangements and wreaths. To harvest the seeds, place the seedheads in a paper bag and allow them to dry for several weeks. Break open the dried seedpods and shake the seeds into a bowl. Separate out any nonseed plant material. Store the seeds in an airtight container away from light and heat. Use them in recipes or for planting in next year's garden.

(i) YOU SHOULD KNOW
Because edible poppy seeds are from the same poppy used to make opium, they contain small amounts of opiate alkaloids which can be detected in drug tests.

Uses

Cottage gardens Poppy blooms are a cottage garden standard and look stunning scattered among late spring-blooming perennials.

Baking The common name for *Papaver somniferum* is breadseed poppy. The small, round bluish-black seeds get top billing in lots of recipes: poppy seed bagels, poppy seed sweet breads, and poppy seed rolls.

Dried arrangements The sculptural seedpods from poppy flowers are beautiful used in dried arrangements or tucked into wreaths.

Rose (*Rosa* selections)

One of the most revered blooms in the flower garden and landscape, roses are also an asset to herb gardens. They produce edible petals. And the hips, which are the fruit of the plant, are packed with vitamin C. They are consumed in a variety of ways, including in tea, jam, jelly, and syrup.

In ancient times, *Rosa* species were used to remedy a wide range of ailments from the common cold to problems of the skin, heart, and circulation.

Best site
Roses excel in a sunny spot where they will receive at least six hours of sun daily. Plant in well-draining soil enriched with compost and rotted manure.

Planting
Roses are sold in two forms: bare root and in containers. Bare-root roses are dormant. They come to life quickly once planted. Container roses are typically leafed out and may also be blooming. Plant roses 2 to 3 feet apart. Roses need plenty of air circulating around them to prevent fungal diseases.

varieties:

1 *ROSA RUGOSA* **'ALBA'** offers large hips, prickly thorns, and wavy leaves. Its white flowers open from pink-tinged buds and are sweetly tea-rose scented. It grows 8 feet tall and wide. Zones 2–9.

2 *ROSA GALLICA* **'VERSICOLOR'** is also called the Apothecary rose. Flowers are carmine-pink, cupped, and semidouble. They appear in spring to early summer and are followed by orange-red hips at the end of the season. Zones 3–9.

Growing
Roses need consistent watering. Water slowly at the base of a plant, allowing the soil to be thoroughly soaked. Avoid wetting the leaves, which can promote disease. Feed the shrubs with an organic fertilizer formulated for roses. Fertilize in spring when the bush leafs out. Feed again in midsummer when roses have finished their flush of bloom. Mulch around the base of the plants to help retain soil moisture and discourage weeds. Grow roses organically if you plan to use them in culinary or cosmetic recipes.

Harvest
To harvest rose petals, cut off the entire flower. Handle petals as little as possible, and store in the refrigerator until you are ready to use them. Pull the petal from the flower and remove the white end, which tastes bitter. To harvest rose hips, allow the summer's last flowers to remain on the plant. As the flowers fade, the fruits will form. Cut off the hips when they are plump and ripe. Use them fresh or dried. Freeze the hips to preserve them, if you prefer.

Uses
Rose-hip tea Crushed rose hips steeped in hot water are a good source of vitamin C. Chop fresh rose hips, cover them with water, and simmer for 15 minutes. Strain the liquid and refrigerate it.

Astringent Used in lotions and facial products, rose water is made from rose petals.

Edible flowers Mince rose petals and sprinkle them on salads or desserts just before serving for a colorful, delicately flavored touch. Rose petals can also be used to make jelly, jam, syrup, and other sweet treats.

 YOU SHOULD KNOW Roses benefit from growing near a structure for shelter and support. Plant tall or climbing varieties of the shrub against a sturdy trellis, arbor, wall, or fence.

Rosemary *(Rosmarinus officinalis)*

Fragrant and delicious, rosemary is also a beauty. Pruned into topiaries or allowed to grow into shrubby plants, rosemary is a favorite of gardeners and cooks alike. In warm climates this plant is an evergreen shrub that has scaly bark and multitudes of narrow dark-green leaves. The flavor of the leaves is distinctive; the scent is pungent and piney. It's a signature herb in Mediterranean dishes.

This Mediterranean native was reputed in ancient folklore to improve memory and provide a safeguard against witches. A necklace made of rosemary was said to keep people young—and attract elves. It was also used to flavor wine.

Best site

Plant in full sun and well-drained soil. Rosemary needs quick draining soil; it does not tolerate wet sites. If your soil is slow draining or clay, plant rosemary in a raised bed or grow it in a pot.

Planting

In spring after the danger of frost has passed, set out transplants or plants that spent the winter indoors. Start new plants from cuttings in spring or summer. Grow rosemary in a container indoors and outdoors. In warm climates, use plants as evergreen shrubs or groundcovers.

Growing

This herb comes in various forms, from stiff and upright (ideal for a hedge), to mounded and spreading (perfect for scrambling along a slope or wall). The secret to beautiful rosemary is to give plants warm, dry conditions. Grow plants in well-drained soil or a raised bed, and surround them with gravel mulch. In warm-winter areas protect rosemary from cold winter winds that may dry it out by wrapping the plant with burlap. In cold climates, grow rosemary in containers and bring plants indoors in late summer. To succeed indoors over the winter, rosemary needs consistent watering to keep the potted plant's soil damp. Zones 6–10; elsewhere an annual.

Harvest

Cut stems above the woody growth as needed throughout the growing season. Regular harvests encourage bushy growth. Strip off the resinous leaves from the stems and chop or grind them. To dry rosemary, bundle stems and hang them upside down in a cool, airy place. Dried rosemary leaves provide good flavor for culinary use, but fresh leaves pack more robust flavor and offer a softer, more edible texture.

Uses

Kabob skewers The woody stems provide flavorful skewers for kabobs or satay recipes. Strip off most of the leaves and put the the stems to work as you would bamboo skewers.

Topiary Rosemary's woody stems make the herb an ideal candidate for tree-form topiaries.

YOU SHOULD KNOW
The texture and flavor of rosemary's foliage vary throughout the season. The leaves are tender in spring, but have fewer aromatic oils. By late summer, the foliage packs a more potent flavor.

varieties:

1 TRAILING ROSEMARY (*Rosmarinus officinalis* 'Prostratus') has a low-growing, creeping habit that makes it excellent as an evergreen groundcover. It grows 3 feet tall and spreads 4 to 8 feet in Zones 8–10. In midsummer, this shrubby tender perennial is covered with light-blue flowers.

2 'BARBEQUE' is a selection of common rosemary developed for its excellent flavor and aroma. It can grow 4 feet tall and will develop beautiful blue blooms. Annual except in Zones 8–10.

3 'ROMAN BEAUTY' is a dwarf rosemary that grows about 2 feet tall and is topped with lavender blooms. It's an ideal choice for containers because of its compact and mounded growth habit. Annual except in Zones 8–10.

4 'TUSCAN BLUE' is one of the best rosemary varieties for topiaries. Plants develop dense, blue-green foliage that's easily sheared to any shape. It's also a highly fragrant variety that has many uses in the kitchen. It can grow 4 feet tall. Annual except in Zones 8–10.

5 VARIEGATED ROSEMARY features deep green leaves with yellow mottling. Variegated rosemaries include 'Gold Dust' and 'Aureus'. Plants have small blue flowers and an upright growth habit. Annual except in Zones 8–10.

Rue *(Ruta graveolens)*

This shrubby aromatic herb has been used for medicinal and culinary purposes for centuries. Although rarely eaten in this country (because it has a bitter flavor and not-so-pleasant scent), rue is used in small quantities to flavor cheese and egg dishes in some Mediterranean countries.

YOU SHOULD KNOW Rue has a bitter flavor and a strong scent, as indicated by its species name: *graveolens*, meaning heavy smell in Latin.

In ancient times rue was ingested to remedy a host of problems such as poor eyesight and gastrointestinal ills. Rue was also applied topically to ward off insect pests.

Best site
Grow rue in full sun or light shade. Although the plant can grow in poor soil, it must be well draining for rue to survive. Once established, this perennial herb grows well in hot, dry locations.

Planting
Sow seeds indoors four to six weeks before the last average spring frost date. Or you can sow seeds directly in garden soil once it has warmed in the spring. The seeds usually germinate easily. Keep the soil consistently damp until the seeds sprout and the seedlings develop. Set out transplants after the threat of frost has passed. Water regularly until the plants become well established—well into their first growing season. Rue can also be grown in container gardens. Lift the plant from a pot in early fall and transplant it into the garden, giving it time to root before winter arrives. You can enjoy the plant in next year's garden or transplant it again into a container.

Growing
In spring, clean up the plant by pruning away any of the prior year's spent foliage. Divide plants in spring. After summer flowering, cut the faded blooms to encourage new growth. Rue self-seeds, so remove flowerheads if you don't want more plants. In northern areas, mulch the plant in late fall to help protect it from damage due to winter's freeze-thaw cycles. Rue grows 1 to 2 feet tall. Zones 4–9.

Harvest
Wear gloves when harvesting rue leaves because its essential oil can cause a skin rash and blistering on hot days.

Uses
Knot gardens This woody shrub can be clipped into a neat hedge, making it an ideal herb for knot gardens.

Floral arrangements Use the attractive bluish gray-green leaves and yellow flowers in fresh flower arrangements.

Saffron *(Crocus sativus)*

Whether you call it an herb or a spice, saffron is the dried stigmas of one crocus species, *C. sativus*. If you love paella, curry, and other dishes that include saffron in their ingredients, you probably know about its costliness. This precious herb can be worth thousands of dollars per pound. Grow your own crop to gain significant savings.

Saffron has been in cultivation for more than 3,500 years. During the Renaissance, saffron was worth its weight in gold.

Best site
Plant in full sun to light shade in well-drained soil. If the soil is heavy with clay or drains poorly, the bulbs may rot. Improve the soil by digging in loads of organic amendments, such as compost and chopped leaves, before planting.

Planting
Plant *Crocus sativus* bulbs in early autumn. They will flower four to six weeks later. This perennial bulb will bloom year after year if planted in conducive conditions in Zones 6–8. Plant the bulbs 3 to 4 inches deep and about 2 inches apart. After planting, water well and spread a 2-inch-deep layer of mulch over the planting area.

Growing
Crocus sativus grows just 2 to 4 inches tall, so make sure it's planted in an area where you'll notice the flowers and gather their stigmas in time to use them. Water the plantings unless nature takes care of it for you.

Harvest
When the crocuses bloom, harvest the stigmas by carefully plucking each one, using your fingertips or small scissors. Each flower produces three stigmas. Harvest them on a sunny day when the flowers are fully open. Dry the stigmas in a warm, well-ventilated place. When dried, store them in an airtight jar. Many recipes call for saffron by the strand or thread, which amounts to one stigma.

Uses

Saffron recipes The fine stigmas are typically used sparingly in recipes. For example, most paella recipes call for a generous pinch of saffron. But those threads impart rich flavor and color to the classical Spanish dish.

YOU SHOULD KNOW
Plan a saffron crop if you like to use the herb in cooking. Each *Crocus sativus* flower produces only three stigmas. To grow 1 ounce of saffron, you need about 14,000 stigmas, or about 4,667 flowers.

Sage *(Salvia officinalis)*

For poultry-stuffing fans, sage is a traditional ingredient. This savory herb is also a favorite addition to breads, soups, and herb mixes used for vegetables (particularly squash and potatoes) and meat. But sage also has a sweeter and wilder side, showing up in cookies, sorbets, and even martinis. Besides sage's talents as a culinary herb, it's a popular fragrance used in perfumes, soaps, and hair products.

Native to the Mediterranean, sage was believed by ancient Romans and Greeks to impart wisdom. It has been used for centuries as a way to scent and purify the air.

Best site
Plant sage in full sun. The perennial grows best in rich soil that drains well, although the plant is adaptable to a range of soil conditions. Sage also grows well in containers—grouped with other herbs or mixed amid flowers. The ornamental varieties add color to the garden too. Once established, common sage blooms in late spring.

Planting
Seeds are difficult to germinate. Transplant container-grown plants or divisions in spring. Space plants 2 to 3 feet apart. Improve the soil by adding a 2-inch-thick layer of compost before planting. Sage grows 2 to 3 feet tall and wide.

Growing
Sage is a low-maintenance, drought-tolerant herb. Trim sage plants as needed to maintain their shape and to promote dense new growth. In autumn, protect sage by spreading a 4- to 6-inch-thick layer of mulch at the plant's base to prolong the harvest season. To enjoy fresh leaves through winter, dig up a garden plant in late summer or early fall and transplant it into a container of well-drained potting mix. Place the pot in a sunny window indoors. Zones 4–10.

Harvest
Cut 6- to 8-inch lengths of leafy growth above the woody stems in summer before the plant blooms. For the best flavor, snip stems in the morning after the dew has dried. Cut flowering stems for bouquets. Trim off spent flowers. To dry sage, bundle stems and hang them upside down in a dark, airy space, or strip leaves from the stems and spread the foliage on a screen to air-dry. When completely dried, remove leaves from stems and store them in a jar away from light and heat for up to one year.

Uses
Insect repellents Some naturalists swear by the insect-deterring qualities of sage leaves. To use, rub fresh leaves on skin. The distinctive scent also deters moths from damaging stored woolen clothing. Dried sage smells much better than mothballs.

Dry rubs Make your own dry rubs for preparing poultry or pork for cooking. Blend dried sage with oregano, thyme, and rosemary for a flavorful seasoning.

Smudge sticks Bundles of smoldering dessert or white sage stems and leaves played a part in Native American cultural traditions. To make a smudge stick, cut a handful of any variety of sage stems in 6- to 8-inch lengths and allow them to dry for about a week. Bundle the dried sage stems, add lavender or another fragrant herb if desired, and tightly wrap the bunch from top to bottom with heavy thread. To burn, light one end of the bundle, blow out the flame, and allow the herbs to smolder and smoke. The smudge stick will release the fragrance of the sage and any other herbs included in the bundle.

 YOU SHOULD KNOW Nonculinary varieties of sage make excellent ornamental edging plants in gardens. Colorful variegated types offer leaves striated with purple, chartreuse, and white.

varieties:

❶ COMMON SAGE produces textural oval gray-green leaves and purple flowers. The ornamental and edible plant grows 2 feet tall and should be replaced every five years or so. Zones 4–9.

❷ 'ICTERINA' or golden sage is a variegated green-and-gold variety and a colorful alternative to common sage. Plant it in beds, borders, and containers. It reaches 2 feet tall. Zones 5–11.

❸ 'TRICOLOR' SAGE leaves are variegated green, cream, and purple. Zones 6–9.

Salad Burnet
(*Sanguisorba minor*)

Cultivated in medieval gardens, salad burnet is a perennial herb native to western Asia and Europe. It was brought to North America by the Pilgrims and has naturalized here. Because it does well in poor soil, Thomas Jefferson used salad burnet to curb erosion. It was also used as food for livestock.

YOU SHOULD KNOW Salad burnet makes a lovely container planting for outdoor dining areas. The serrated leaves are pretty and can be snipped into salads, soups, and stews served al fresco.

Salad burnet was once erroneously thought to be a cure for the bubonic plague. The herb has been adapted in European cuisine. It is added to salads for its refreshing cucumberlike flavor.

Best site
Plant salad burnet in partial to full sun. The herb is adaptable and grows well in a variety of soil conditions. Although it grows best in a well-draining site, it will tolerate poor soil.

Planting
Start from seeds or transplants. If planting from seeds, sow indoors in early spring and transplant outdoors after the danger of frost is over. In areas with a long growing season, sow seeds directly in the garden after the threat of frost is past. Salad burnet makes a textural addition to kitchen gardens as well as containers.

Growing
Pretty salad burnet has small, serrated leaves; green-and-magenta flowers; and a mounded growth habit. Salad burnet does not need extra fertilizer. Average garden soil provides the plant's needed nutrients. Keep the soil free of weeds for best results when growing salad burnet. The plant does not need much water but it should have adequate drainage to prevent root rot. Cut back blossoms to encourage growth of new, tender leaves. Plants grow 1½ feet tall. Zones 4–10.

Harvest
Pick the leaves when they are young and tender; salad burnet gets bitter with age. Use this herb fresh or frozen; the leaves lose their flavor when dried. Pick the flowers for use as garnishes; they are pretty, but have only mild flavor.

Uses
Herb substitutes Use salad burnet leaves in recipes that call for dill, oregano, basil, or mint.

Herb blend The mild flavor of salad burnet blends well with other culinary herbs, including tarragon, thyme, and marjoram.

Spicy salad green Harvest whole leaves to sprinkle onto salads; they impart a fresh taste amid other greens.

Santolina
(Santolina)

Also called lavender cotton, santolina is grown mainly for its textural and aromatic foliage. It displays gray or green leaves and small yellowish flowers, which are pretty in passing but not the main event. It's all about the foliage, which mixes well in flowerbeds and borders—as well as in herb gardens.

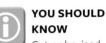

YOU SHOULD KNOW Cut or bruised santolina leaves can irritate skin or cause a rash.

Santolina is a popular plant used in knot gardens. There are two types—one that offers beautiful gray-blue foliage and one that is bright green. Both have woody stems and dense foliage.

Best site
Plant santolina in a sunny location and well-drained soil. Santolina is drought tolerant and can grow in poor, sandy soil. The plant does best in warm regions with low humidity.

Planting
Raise santolina from seeds or nursery-grown plants. Start seeds indoors in early spring. Transplant outdoors after the last frost date. To use this herb in a hedge or knot garden, start with transplants. Santolina grows 1 to 2 feet tall, depending on the variety. Space plants 1 to 2 feet apart and closer for a clippable hedge.

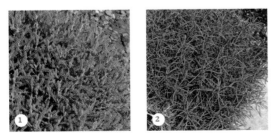

varieties:

1 GREY SANTOLINA (*Santolina chamaecyparissus*) is used for containers, topiary, edging, rock gardens, and knot gardens. Zones 6–9.

2 GREEN SANTOLINA (*S. virens*) is used for its lacy foliage in much the same way as the gray variety. Zones 7–9.

Growing
In cold climates, plant santolina in a container and bring it indoors over the winter. The plant blooms in mid- to late summer; the yellow flowers are small and can be removed to keep the neatness of the plant intact. Zones 6–9.

Harvest
Cut santolina flowers for fresh bouquets or dried flower arrangements. To dry the stems of flowers or foliage, cut and bundle them, and hang the bunch upside down in a cool, dry place.

Uses
Knot gardens Santolina's contrasting foliage and shrubby growth habit make it an ideal plant for a knot garden. Avoid heavy pruning when the plant is flowering; it may not recover.

Topiary Santolina makes lovely topiaries. The woody stem forms a trunk for a tree-form standard that can be shaped into a sphere or square, for instance.

Low hedge This textural plant makes an excellent low hedge or edging plant in flower or herb gardens.

Drought-tolerant gardens Santolina can star in a low-water-use garden. It requires little supplemental water to flourish.

Moth repellent Add dried santolina leaves to aromatic sachet blends, made to help repel moths from clothing and linens in closets and drawers.

Soup/sauce flavoring Although not well known in culinary circles, gray santolina leaves can be used in sauces and soups. Add a tiny amount at first to determine if you like the flavor; it may be an acquired taste.

Savory, Summer and Winter
(*Satureja*)

Aromatic and flavorful, savory imparts a spicy, fresh flavor with overtones of dill, thyme, and sweet marjoram. This Mediterranean native takes two common forms: annual summer savory and perennial winter savory.

YOU SHOULD KNOW For small-space gardens or containers, grow 'Nana' winter savory. This is an extremely cold-hardy dwarf variety that grows just 3 inches tall.

Savory has been used to enhance the flavor of food in various cultures for more than 2,000 years. Egyptians incorporated it in love potions. Summer savory (*S. hortensis*) offers a sweeter, more delicate flavor than winter savory. This upright annual has long gray-green leaves and is topped with small white or pink flowers. Winter savory (*S. montana*), a semi-evergreen perennial, has a trailing growth habit, white to lavender flowers, and a piney flavor.

Best site
Plant savory in full sun and well-draining, moist soil. Both varieties grow well in containers.

Planting
Start winter savory from transplants planted in the garden after the soil warms in spring. Winter savory can also be started from seeds, but they germinate slowly. Start seeds indoors four to six weeks before the last spring frost date. Summer savory seeds grow easily. Sow them directly in the garden after the last frost date in spring in northern climates or anytime during the growing season in mild-winter regions. Plant seeds ½ inch deep and 1 inch apart. You can also plant seedlings.

Growing
Savory enjoys consistent moisture. Keep soil around plants moist but not soggy. To encourage new growth, clip savory often (regular harvests accomplish this). Clip winter savory into a miniature hedge for a formal look. Both plants bloom in summer. Winter savory is hardy in Zones 6–9.

Harvest
Harvest stems of summer or winter savory when the flowers begin to form. To dry, spread stems on screens or tie them in small, loose bunches and hang them upside down in a dark, airy space. When the leaves are completely dry, strip them from the stems; remove the woody parts. Store herbs in airtight containers for up to two years. Use the leaves and flowers fresh or dried in meat or vegetable dishes.

Uses
Herbal enhancer Use fresh or dry summer savory leaves in vegetable, meat, and egg dishes.

Savory vinegar Add whole stems to a bottle of apple cider vinegar to flavor it. Let the herb steep in the vinegar for several days, then remove the stems. Use the vinegar to make a marinade or salad dressing.

varieties:

1 SUMMER SAVORY (*Satureja hortensis*) bears gray-green leaves and offers a peppery flavor.

2 WINTER SAVORY (*S. montana*) adds a strong, spicy flavor to meats. It's also occasionally used as a medicinal plant. Winter savory grows about 12 inches tall. Zones 6–9.

Scented Geranium
(*Pelargonium*)

With fragrances of fruits, flowers, spices, and even chocolate, scented geraniums delight the senses. Some of their scents are strong—and it takes just a jostle of the leaves to release the heady fragrances. The plants' tactile leaves—some fuzzy, some smooth—come in a wide range of shapes and hues.

Originally from Africa, scented geraniums made a big splash among Victorians. Since then, they have been favorites of herb gardeners as well as those who enjoy collecting scented geraniums and growing them as houseplants.

Best site
Situate plants in full sun and well-drained soil.

Planting
Scented geraniums are tender perennials. They have tiny, delicate flowers—unlike showy annual geraniums. Wait until late spring to plant them in the garden or outdoor containers. In cold climates, grow scented geraniums in pots and bring them indoors at summer's end. The plants grow well indoors in south-facing windows.

Growing
Although you can grow scented geraniums from seed, transplants and cuttings are a faster way to success. To propagate scented geraniums from cuttings, cut 3- to 4-inch-long stems and remove the lower leaves. Dip the stem ends in rooting hormone powder, then plant them in small pots of premoistened soilless potting mix. Place the cuttings in a partly shaded place and keep the mix damp until the plants develop. Transplant rooted cuttings into larger pots as needed. Pinch the stems' ends often to prompt bushier growth. Water when the soil feels dry. Zones 8–11.

Harvest
Pick leaves and flowers at any time. Snip off leaves and blooms with small scissors.

Uses
Edible flowers The flowers are small, beautiful—and edible. Snip blooms into salads; use on cakes or custards.

Potpourri Use dried scented geranium leaves in potpourris. Mix different scents such as citrus and rose.

Aromatherapy Rub or crush leaves to release a calming burst of scent. Rose-scented geraniums are used to heighten relaxation during meditation.

Flavored sugar Layer fresh leaves with sugar in a jar; allow to sit for four days, then remove the leaves. Use the scented geranium-flavor sugar in teas or baked goods.

 YOU SHOULD KNOW Scented geraniums provide natural room fresheners. Keep potted plants indoors and gently squeeze the leaves to release their scent. Add leaves to your vacuum's bag to impart a sweet, fresh fragrance.

varieties:

❶ PEPPERMINT (*Pelargonium tomentosa*) This variety has gray-green leaves and white flowers.

❷ VELVET ROSE (*P. graveolens*) produces fuzzy, rose-scented leaves and tiny pink flowers.

Soapwort
(Saponaria officinalis)

When boiled, the leaves and stems of soapwort, make a soapy liquid that's gentle and suitable for washing delicate fabrics. Also called bouncing bet, the sprawling perennial is appreciated for its cheerful spring flowers. A relative, *Saponaria oxymoides,* is a 6-inch groundcover that's popular for rock gardens.

Best site
Soapwort performs best in a sunny to partially sunny location with well-draining soil.

Planting
Start soapwort seeds six to eight weeks before planting in spring or fall. Or you can plant transplants. Space 8 to 10 inches apart.

Growing
Bouncing bet is a 2-foot-tall heirloom perennial. In late spring the plants are covered with sprays of small bright-pink or white blooms. Shear plants after flowers fade to enjoy a second bloom later in the spring. Zones 4–8.

Harvest
Pick stems and leaves anytime. The plant's roots can also be harvested; dig them using a garden fork. The roots have the highest concentration of saponin, the soapy component used for cleaning.

YOU SHOULD KNOW
Soapwort self-seeds readily but not invasively. Leave flowers on the plants so they produce seeds for next year's crop.

YOU SHOULD KNOW
Although its name suggests that it is part of the garlic family, society garlic belongs to the lily family.

Society Garlic
(Tulbaghia violacea)

At first glance, you may mistake society garlic for chives. But as you get closer, you'll smell the difference; it gives off a strong garlic fragrance. Plants grow 2 feet tall and develop attractive lavender-pink flowers from early summer until fall. In the North, grow plants in containers and move them indoors in early fall.

Best site
Society garlic requires a sunny spot in the garden that has quick-draining soil. This South African-native bulb will rot in wet or poorly draining soil.

Planting
Start society garlic from seeds or transplants. Water to establish young plants, then cut back on irrigation as they develop. In frost-free areas, society garlic makes an excellent groundcover for regions where water is scarce.

Growing
As it grows, society garlic requires very little maintenance. The flowers have a sweet fragrance and attract butterflies and pollinators. The plants are deer and rabbit resistant. Zones 7–9.

Harvest
Society garlic makes a better landscape plant than a culinary herb.

Sorrel
(*Rumex*)

In the early spring garden, when few other edibles are available, sorrel (*R. acetosa*) will be poking its bright green leaves out of the soil. The tart green is added to soups, salads, sauces, and egg dishese. Bloody dock (*R. sanguineus*) has bright green leaves with red veins. French sorrel (*R. scutatus*) is a less-acidic species.

Best site
Sorrel thrives in full sun or partial shade. It prefers a rich, slightly moist, well-drained soil.

Planting
Sorrel can be grown from seed or divisions. Sow in the early spring, planting about ¼ inch deep. Sorrel grows poorly during hot weather.

Growing
Sorrel grows 18 to 24 inches tall and develops a tall flower spike. Remove the flower spike as it develops to encourage the plant to put more energy into leaf production. If you want seeds, let the flower spike mature. Zones 3–8.

Harvest
Sorrel leaves can be harvested at any time. In fact, the more you cut the plant back, the more leaves it will produce. Young leaves have the best flavor. Older leaves contain more oxalic acid, making them more toxic.

Southernwood
(*Artemisia abrotanum*)

A member of the artemisia family, southernwood is an ornamental herb valued for its feathery gray-green foliage. It has a lemony fragrance. The leafy stems work well to make wreath bases or moth-chasing sachets for closets and dresser drawers. The plant is not attractive to rabbits and deer.

Best site
Southernwood requires at least six to eight hours of sun a day. It likes well-drained soil.

Planting
Start with transplants or divisions. The plant grows 3 to 5 feet tall and 2 feet wide. Place it at the back of a border or use it to make a hedge.

Growing
After plants leaf out in spring, pruning them to half their height encourages bushier growth. Mulch around plants to prevent weeds. In the late summer, plants develop small yellow flowers that attract butterflies and other pollinators. Zones 4–10.

Harvest
Gather stems at their peak of fragrance in late summer or early fall. Bend fresh stems into wreath bases. Dry stems by hanging them upside down in an airy, dark location.

YOU SHOULD KNOW
Sorrel can be eaten like any green, raw or cooked. It is used for its color and acidity.

YOU SHOULD KNOW
At one time considered an aphrodisiac, southernwood is an easy-care, woody perennial with fragrant lemony foliage.

St. johnswort
(*Hypericum perforatum*)

The cheery, bright yellow flowers of common st. johnswort are the big appeal of the woody perennial or small shrub. They stand out in the garden, blooming on 1- to 3-foot-tall plants. The herb has been used traditionally to quell depression and anxiety.

YOU SHOULD KNOW
Although st. johnswort is one of the most popular over-the-counter herbal supplement, it is not without its dangers. This herb is known to cause interaction with other drugs. Before you ingest any part of this plant, consult with your doctor.

Native to Europe, this herb was used by the ancient Greeks and Romans to ward off evil spirits. St. johnswort gets its name because it blooms around June 24, the birthday of John the Baptist. The word "wort" or wyrt is an Old English term for root.

Best site
Plant st. johnswort in a partially shaded location. Flower production diminishes as shade increases. St. johnswort does best in sandy, well-draining soil.

Planting
If planting in clay, heavy, or compacted soil, add organic matter, such as chopped leaves or compost, to improve soil fertility and drainability. Seeds are slow to germinate. Start seeds indoors about 12 weeks before spring planting time. Plant seedlings or transplants directly in the garden after the threat of frost has passed. Space plants about 1 foot apart.

Growing
This perennial herb is easy to grow. To grow new plants from cuttings, snip 4-inch stems, dip the cut end into rooting hormone powder, and insert the cuttings into a moist soilless potting medium. Zones 3–8.

Harvest
Clip about one-third of the flowering stems when flowers are fully open. Bundle the stems and hang them upside down to dry in a cool, dry location. When the flowers and leaves are dried, store them in an airtight container. Use them within one year.

Uses
Natural dyes The flowers produce a yellow dye; the stems produce a red dye.

Pollinator attractor The flowers of this herb attract bees. The leaves are a host plant for several varieties of butterflies.

Stevia *(Stevia rebaudiana)*

Stevia produces sweet-tasting leaves that are a pleasant alternative to sugar. Stevia is available commercially as a sugar substitute. But why not grow your own? Stevia goes by the common names sweet leaf and sugar leaf. Just pluck off a leaf and pop it into your mouth—you'll know why in one taste.

Also known as Paraguayan sweet herb, this native of South America, Central America, and Mexico has long been used as a sugar alternative. Stevia is relatively new in this country but has been used in Japan for decades as a replacement for artificial sweeteners.

Best site
Plant in full sun. This tropical plant thrives in moist, well-draining soil. It grows well in garden beds and containers. Stevia does not withstand drought well; keep it hydrated when rain is scarce.

Planting
Because stevia is a tropical plant, it's best to grow it as a container plant in most of the country. That way, you can move the plant indoors when frost threatens and keep it growing in a sunny window. You can grow stevia from seeds, transplants, or stem cuttings from mature plants.

Growing
Stevia is a snap to grow. Just give it plenty of sunshine and water whenever the soil begins to feel dry to the touch. The plant does not like to sit in wet soil, but it will wilt dramatically if the soil becomes too dry. Container plants typically require daily watering in the summer. Stevia grows about 30 inches tall and develops small white flowers late in the season. Zones 10–11.

Harvest
Stevia foliage can be harvested at any time, but it is most flavorful in the late summer or early fall. The leaves can be used fresh or dried. The amount of sweetness varies from plant to plant, so you might want to grow several if you have the space.

Uses

Natural liquid sweetener Steep crushed stevia leaves in hot water, let cool, and strain. Experiment to determine the correct amount of leaves to make the sweetener. Add it to coffee or tea to taste.

Diet aid Quell hunger cravings with stevia: Pluck off a leaf and suck on it for a zero-calorie treat.

Tea herb combo planter Combine dried herbs, such as stevia, spearmint, and chamomile, with a teacup or teapot for a pleasing gift.

Sugar substitute Finely mince stevia leaves and sprinkle them on strawberries or other fruit for a delicious dessert or snack. Stevia is 100 to 300 times sweeter than sucrose and has no calories. A large amount of the leaf may taste bitter.

YOU SHOULD KNOW
If you've never grown stevia before, you will be surprised at how sweet the leaves taste. The herb has been used for centuries, and current research reinforces its safe use as a sweetener.

Sumac
(*Rhus coriaria*)

Commonly called Sicilian sumac, this hardy shrub bears greenish-red flowers that become edible red berries. These berries are an ingredient in the Middle Eastern spice blend za'atar. This spicy condiment is sprinkled on vegetables or mixed with olive oil to make a delicious dip.

YOU SHOULD KNOW

Before you harvest and consume sumac, make sure you are using the right kind. Several species of sumac are toxic.

Best site
Plant sumac in a sunny location in well-drained soil. The large shrub makes a handsome accent plant on its own or a hedge in mass.

Planting
Plant sumac bushes in early spring.

Growing
Sumac grows about 9 feet tall and in midsummer bears flowers that turn into red berries. In the autumn, the leaves of sumac turn bright red. Zones 3–9.

Harvest
Collect sumac berries by clipping off the seedheads and hanging them up to dry in a cool, dry location. Store in airtight containers. Before using, grind seeds into a powder.

Sweet Cicely
(*Myrrhis odorata*)

All parts of sweet cicely are edible and impart a slight anise flavor to recipes. The leaves, either fresh or dried, can be used in salads or with fruit dishes. The roots can be peeled, boiled, and eaten as a vegetable. Use the seeds in salads, soups, or fruit pies.

YOU SHOULD KNOW

Sweet cicely is one of the few herbs that thrives in the shade.

Best site
Sweet cicely grows well in partial shade and nutrient-rich, moist soil.

Planting
Start from seeds sown in the fall or early spring. Seeds must undergo freezing and thawing temperatures to germinate.

Growing
Mulch to keep weeds at bay and to maintain consistent soil moisture. Feed plants with compost in spring. The plants can grow 3 feet tall and will self-sow. Zones 3–7.

Harvest
The leaves can be harvested at any time. Harvest the seeds when the flower stalks mature. Cut the whole stalk and hang it upside down to dry in an well-ventilated location. The roots can also be dug and harvested at any time.

Sweet Grass
(Hierochloe odorata)

Also called holy grass or bison grass, sweet grass is a native perennial grass prized for its fresh scent. In the wild, sweet grass grows naturally in meadows and along stream banks. Native American tribes have used sweet grass for medicinal purposes as well as for weaving baskets and making smudge sticks.

Best site
Sweet grass prefers full sun and moist soil, but will thrive in light shade. Confine the plant to an area to keep it from becoming weedy.

Planting
Sweet grass can be cultivated from seed, but it's much easier to buy started transplants or bare rootstock. Space plants about 3 feet apart.

Growing
Spreading by rhizomes, sweet grass eventually forms a thick mat of foliage. The grass grows about 2 feet tall, but has a tendency to flop over. Zones 3–7.

Harvest
After the first year, sweet grass can be cut and harvested in the summer by cutting the plant to 2 to 3 inches. Avoid harvesting late in the season, or the plants might not come back the next year.

Sweet Woodruff
(Galium odoratum)

This delightful perennial grows only up to a foot tall, but it makes a big statement in the shade garden. In spring, the plants are smothered with white flowers and the foliage when dried is said to have a sweet haylike fragrance. It makes a great groundcover for hard-to-plant dark places in your landscape.

Best site
Sweet woodruff grows best in full to partial shade. It likes a rich, well-drained soil.

Planting
You can grow sweet woodruff from seed, but it's faster to start it from transplants or divisions.

Growing
Sweet woodruff can become invasive if given the right conditions. Plant sweet woodruff where you can control it easily. Cut back old foliage in the early spring to promote new growth. It does not tolerate drought; water frequently during hot, dry spells to keep plants going. Zones 4–9.

Harvest
Pick leaves anytime. Dry them on a screen in a dark, well-ventilated location. Use the leaves in potpourri or sachet blends. Sweet woodruff is often used as a natural insect repellent.

 YOU SHOULD KNOW
Although sweet grass is mainly used in basketry and other crafts, it is occasionally used to flavor cheeses, beverages, and pastries.

YOU SHOULD KNOW
 Sweet woodruff makes a good companion for spring-flowering bulbs such as scilla, species tulips, or early narcissus. Plant your bulbs underneath a bed of sweet woodruff and in the spring you'll have a double dose of color.

Tansy *(Tanacetum vulgare)*

This hardy perennial mixes well in flower borders due to its cheery golden, buttonlike flowers. The plant's deep-green foliage stands out in cut-flower bouquets. Tansy is relatively rabbit and deer resistant but attractive to butterflies and other pollinators.

YOU SHOULD KNOW

Tansy is a vigorous, easy-to-grow perennial that develops beautiful foliage and flowers. It is also a natural insect repellent, but should not be eaten in any form.

Native to Europe, tansy was used medicinally to treat a variety of illnesses, including worms and flatulence, but most of its medicinal uses have been discredited. Today, enjoy it as a lovely garden flower.

Best site
Tansy is a vigorous perennial that thrives in full sun or partial shade. It tolerates almost any kind of soil, but prefers a rich, well-drained site.

Planting
You can start tansy from seeds or transplants. If you know anyone with a tansy patch, it's easy to dig a small clump and move it to a new location. Tansy can become invasive, so be sure to plant it where it will be easy to control. Plants grow to 3 or 4 feet tall.

Growing
After planting, there's little you need to do to keep tansy happy. In fact, your big challenge might be to keep it from spreading into its neighbors. Zones 3–9.

Harvest
Flowers can be harvested as they develop in summer. Hang the stems upside down in a dark, well-ventilated location to dry them. The blooms also make long-lasting cut flowers.

Uses

Insect repellent Dried tansy leaves can be mixed with dried artemisia and ground cloves to make a natural moth-repellent sachet blend for closets or dresser drawers.

Crafts Use dried tansy foliage and flowers in wreaths and floral arrangements. The flowers dry easily and keep their color for months.

Tarragon
(Artemisia dracunculus 'Sativa')

Tarragon is traditionally used to season fish, eggs, and poultry. It is also known as dragon's wort because the name tarragon is derived from the French word for little dragon. Tarragon is a member of the classical French culinary herb blend known as fines herbes, along with parsley, chives, and chervil.

Brought to North America in the 19th century, tarragon was once used to treat snakebites. Now it's value is mostly in the kitchen.

Best site
Tarragon prefers sunny locations with six to eight hours of direct sun daily, but it will tolerate partial shade. It likes rich, sandy, well-draining soil.

Planting
Plant tarragon from divisions or cuttings purchased at your local garden center. Plants are frequently mislabeled. Gently squeeze the plant and smell it before you choose the variety you desire. If you want to grow tarragon for culinary use, choose French tarragon, which is more flavorful than the Russian variety. Tarragon thrives in nutrient-rich soil. Dig a 2-inch-thick layer of compost into the soil before planting. Tarragon grows well in containers. Plant it in a pot filled with a well-draining potting mix. Then, in late summer, transplant French tarragon into the garden so it can establish a strong root system before winter.

Growing
Plant container-grown tarragon in the garden in spring; in areas with mild winters, you can also plant in fall. Space plants 18 to 24 inches apart. Snip the herb's stems regularly to encourage more branching and dense growth. In fall, cut back plants and mulch with a 4- to 6-inch layer of organic mulch for winter protection. Zones 5–9.

Harvest
Harvest stems and leaves as soon as the plant establishes a strong root system, about four weeks after planting. Remove the entire stem or simply snip leaves as needed from the tops. Fresh tarragon is more flavorful than dried; add fresh tarragon to cooked recipes just before serving to enjoy the most flavor. The leaves freeze well too.

Use
Herb blends Pair tarragon with lemon or other citrus because the bittersweet and slightly licorice overtones marry well. Want to spice up mayonnaise? Add lemon juice and fresh tarragon leaves to taste; blend them together with the mayonnaise in a food processor.

Tarragon vinegar Submerge leaves in vinegar, then use the tarragon-infused vinegar in salad dressings.

YOU SHOULD KNOW French tarragon rarely flowers so seeds are uncommon. Plants must be replaced every few years. To make fresh plants, divide existing plants in spring and replant the divisions.

varieties:

1 **FRENCH TARRAGON** (*Artemisia dracunculus* 'Sativa') is a versatile herb with a pronounced citrus and licorice flavor. The plant is sterile and does not produce seeds. Zones 5–9.

2 **RUSSIAN TARRAGON** (*A. dracunculoides*) is also called false tarragon. It is more vigorous than its French cousin and sometimes produces seeds. The leaves of this variety have little flavor or fragrance. Zones 3–7.

Thyme (*Thymus*)

Thyme is an aromatic groundcover or upright plant that excels in beds, borders, and containers. The woody-stemmed plants feature tiny, aromatic leaves and flowers that can be used fresh or dried. In midsummer, the plants' small blue-purple, pink, or white flowers attract bees. With dozens of different thyme varieties to choose from, you'll find lots of uses for the flavor variations.

A native of the Mediterranean, thyme was brought to Britain by the Romans and was considered both an aphrodisiac and an herb for embalming solutions.

Best site

Plant thyme in full sun and well-drained soil. Plants do not tolerate wet soil and grow best in moderately fertile soil.

Planting

Thyme can be started from seeds indoors or sown directly into the garden, but this is not the fastest way to grow it. Seed-grown plants start out slow and frequently need a year or more of growth before stems can be harvested. For more instant gratification, plant container-grown plants or divisions in the garden in spring. Space plants 8 to 12 inches apart.

Growing

Thyme doesn't like wet feet, so water plants only when needed to maintain soil moisture. Shear off the tiny, edible flowers after the plants finish blooming to keep energy concentrated on leaf and stem production. Thyme plants are long-lived but may lose vigor and need replacing after five to seven years. To keep plants in top shape, divide thyme in midspring. Dig up the entire clump and use a sharp spade or trowel to slice through the plant from the top down. Cut the plant into three or four divisions, alloting roots and foliage to each new clump. Plant the new, smaller plants, leaving growing room in between them. Zones 5–9.

Harvest

Harvesting stems throughout the growing season encourages new, lush growth. To harvest the entire plant, cut it back to 2 inches above ground in midseason. Strip the leaves from the stems and use them fresh. Add them to recipes just before serving to preserve their fresh flavor. To dry thyme, harvest stems and tie them into small bundles; hang them upside down in a cool, airy room. When the leaves are completely dry, slide them off the stems and store in an airtight glass jar for up to one year.

Uses

Groundcover Use creeping varieties of thyme as groundcovers that can handle moderate foot traffic. Tuck the plants in between the stepping-stones of a garden path.

Containers Thyme grows well in containers including window boxes, where its trailing fronds make an edible edger. If planting in a container, use a well-draining potting mix to ensure the roots receive the drainage they require.

Bouquet garni Thyme is an essential ingredient in bouquet garni as well as a prime ingredient in Benedictine liqueur.

Cold treatment Thyme tea is frequently recommended for cold treatments—both the steam from a hot cup of the steeped leaf and the liquid are soothing.

Insect deterrent Any dried thyme variety adds its moth-chasing fragrance to sachets. In the garden, plant thyme to deter cabbageworms and whiteflies.

 **YOU SHOULD KNOW** Thyme can participate in every course of a meal—it blends easily in savory to sweet dishes. It enhances almost any beef, pork, poultry, or seafood dish. It also has a sweet side and is used in cookies, scones, and jellies. Thyme marries especially well with lemon.

varieties:

1 **'AUREUS'** (*Thymus ×citriodorus*) is a variegated form of lemon thyme, growing 6 to 12 inches tall. The leaves' green-and-yellow coloration is most pronounced when growing in cool regions. Zones 5–9.

2 **ENGLISH THYME** (*T. vulgaris*) is also called common thyme. The hardworking little plant has almost as many uses in the kitchen as it does in the garden. It has small aromatic leaves and white flowers that bloom in the summer. This upright variety reaches 12 inches tall. Zones 5–9.

3 **'VARIAGATUS'** (*T. ×citriodorus*) is a beautiful edible ornamental. The lemon-scented foliage is versatile in the kitchen, and the plant itself makes a striking groundcover for sunny spots. The plant grows 15 inches tall. Zones 5–9.

4 **LEMON THYME** (*T. ×citriodorus*) produces dark-green leaves with an intoxicating lemon fragrance. Like its variegated cousin, lemon thyme looks as good in an edible garden as it does in a flowering border. A good container plant, lemon thyme grows up to 15 inches. Zones 5–9.

Valerian
(*Valeriana officinalis*)

This upright, hardy perennial is topped with pink or white flowers in midsummer. It's also called garden heliotrope and was once used in perfume production. However, some people find the odor of valerian to be offensive, so avoid planting it near pathways or walks.

YOU SHOULD KNOW For medicinal use it's best to buy commercially prepared valerian. But you can still enjoy this plant as a fragrant ornamental.

For centuries, valerian has been grown as a medicinal plant to cure a variety of ailments including sleep disorders and migraines.

Best site
Valerian isn't fussy about where it grows, but it prefers a sunny location with rich, moist soil. It is a heavy feeder, so be sure to amend the soil with compost, rotted manure, or another nitrogen-rich fertilizer.

Planting
This vigorous perennial can be grown from seed, but is best started from a division or transplant. Valerian grows from 3 to 5 feet tall. Plant it at the back of a border or bed; space the plants at least 18 inches apart.

Growing
Once established, valerian has very few needs. Water as needed to maintain soil moisture, especially during dry spells. Mulch to minimize watering and weeding. The plant develops pretty serrated, bright-green foliage. Stalks of fragrant blooms appear in midsummer. The plant self-sows if the seeds are allowed to mature. Zones 4–9.

Harvest
Valerian roots can be harvested in the spring or fall. Dig the plants, remove the roots, and wash away all the soil. Then slowly dry the roots in an oven set on low heat; check them often to determine when they are dry. Cool and store the dried roots in an airtight container.

Uses

Butterfly gardening Valerian is a host plant for several butterfly and moth species.

Catnip substitute The foliage of valerian is as attractive to cats as catnip. Felines can damage plants by rubbing against them.

Yarrow
(*Achillea*)

A tough-as-nails, sun-loving perennial, yarrow makes a colorful addition to any herb or flower border. It's a native plant that is naturally resistant to pests, drought, and disease. Most yarrows bloom in mid- to late summer. They are deer resistant and popular with butterflies and other pollinators.

Another common name for yarrow is bloodwort, which may be derived from one of its ancient uses as a topical wound application.

Best site
Yarrow grows best in a site that gets at least six to eight hours of sun a day. It tolerates a range of soils, but succeeds best in a rich, organic, well-drained soil.

Planting
Although yarrow can be grown from seed, it's a lot easier to buy started transplants from your local nursery or garden center. Yarrow varieties vary in height, so read the plant tag before you set your plants in the border. Plant taller varieties (3 feet tall) in the middle to back of the border. More compact forms should be planted up front where they won't be hidden by larger plants. Water new plants until established, but keep in mind that yarrow will not thrive in muddy soil.

Growing
Once planted, yarrow requires very little assistance. Some taller varieties can grow top-heavy when in bloom and flop over. Stake the plants in spring to keep them growing upright. Dig and divide clumps of yarrow every few years to keep the plants growing vigorously. Also, if you deadhead faded flowers you may enjoy a second flush of bloom later in the season. Zones 3–10.

Harvest
Yarrow flowers can be cut for fresh or dried bouquets at any time. To dry, clip stems at the base of the plant and bundle together tightly with a rubber band (it will hold the stems as they dry and shrink). Hang the bunch in a cool, dry location. Keep the dried blossoms away from bright light to preserve their color longer.

Uses
Everlasting flowers For dried arrangements or wreaths, yarrow with golden or other-color flowers adds long-lasting appeal.

Dyes Yarrow flowers are also used to create a light green to yellow dye.

 YOU SHOULD KNOW Yarrow can be affected by powdery mildew. To prevent it, space plants at least 2 feet apart to promote good air circulation.

varieties:

1. **COMMON YARROW** (*Achillea millefolium*) This 2-foot-tall, fast-spreading species has fine foliage and creamy white flower clusters in early summer. Zones 3–10.
2. **FERNLEAF YARROW** (*A. filipendulina*) has fernlike foliage, grows 3 feet tall, and develops quantities of golden flowers. Zones 3–9.
3. **'LEMON' DWARF WOOLLY YARROW** (*A. tomentosa*) is a 6-inch-tall, ground-hugging type with gray fuzzy leaves. It's a good choice for rock gardens or cracks in pathways. Zones 4–8.

USDA Plant Hardiness Zone Map

Each plant has an ability to withstand cold temperatures. This range of temperatures is expressed as a zone—and a zone map shows where you can grow a plant.

Planting for your zone

There are 11 zones from Canada to Mexico, and each zone represents the lowest expected winter temperature in that area. Each zone is based on a 10-degree F. difference in minimum temperatures. Once you know your hardiness zone, you can choose plants for your garden that will flourish. Look for the hardiness zone on the plant tags of the perennials, trees, and shrubs you buy.

Microclimates in your yard

Not all areas in your yard are the same. Depending on your geography, trees, and structures, some spots may receive different sunlight and wind and consequently experience temperature differences. Take a look around your yard and you may notice that the same plant comes up sooner in one place than another. This is the microclimate concept in action. A microclimate is an area in your yard that is slightly different (cooler or hotter) than the other areas of your yard.

Create a microclimate

Once you're aware of your yard's microclimates, use them to your advantage. For example, you may be able to grow plants in a sheltered, south-facing garden bed that you can't grow elsewhere in your yard. You can create a microclimate by planting evergreens on the north side of a property to block prevailing winds. Or plant deciduous trees on the south side to provide shade in summer.

Some perennial varieties such as lavender come in a range of zones. Check plant tags to verify that the zone is appropriate before you plant.

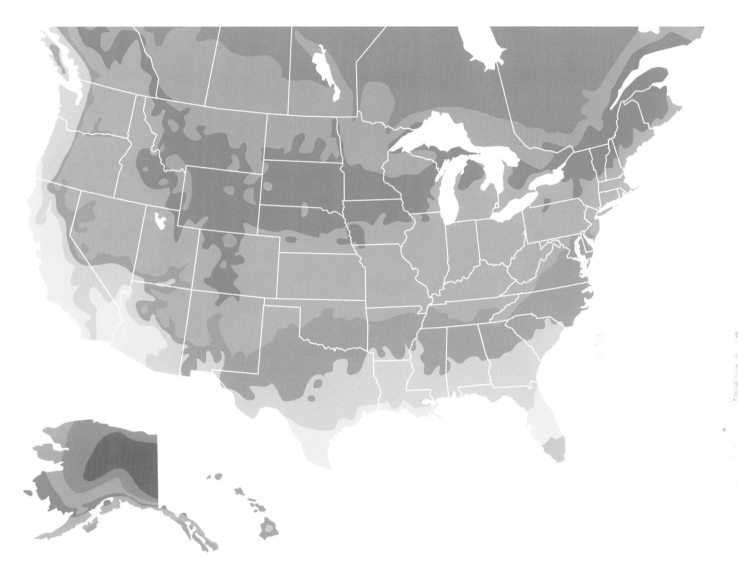

Range of Average Annual Minimum Temperatures for Each Zone

- Zone 1: below -50°F (below -45.6°C)
- Zone 2: -50 to -40°F (-45 to -40°C)
- Zone 3: -40 to -30°F (-40 to -35°C)
- Zone 4: -30 to -20°F (-34 to -29°C)

- Zone 5: -20 to -10°F (-29 to -23°C)
- Zone 6: -10 to 0°F (-23 to -18°C)
- Zone 7: 0 to 10°F (-18 to -12°C)
- Zone 8: 10 to 20°F (-12 to -7°C)

- Zone 9: 20 to 30°F (-7 to -1°C)
- Zone 10: 30 to 40°F (-1 to 4°C)
- Zone 11: 40°F and above (4.5°C and above)

Garden Profiles

BALLYKNOCKEN COOKERY SCHOOL
Catherine Fulvio
www.thecookeryschool.ie

**HAPPY VALLEY LAVENDER
& HERB FARM**
Lynda and Michael Dowling
250/474-5767
www.happyvalleylavender.com

LONG CREEK HERBS
Jim Long and Joshua Young
417/ 779-5450
www.longcreekherbs.com
www.jimlongsgarden.blogspot.com

MARTHA'S HERBARY
Michelle King
860/928-0009
www.marthasherbary.com

PAMELA CRAWFORD
www.sideplanting.com

SHADY ACRES HERB FARM
Theresa and Jim Mieseler
952/466-3391
www.shadyacres.com

TANGLED GARDEN
Beverly McClare
902/ 542-9811
www.tangledgarden.ns.ca

WALKER CREEK GARDEN DESIGN
Hilarie Holdsworth
978/281-2009
www.walkercreekdesign.com

Plants and Seeds

BONNIE PLANTS
Bonnie Plant Farm
1727 Highway 223
Union Springs, AL 36089
334/738-3104
www.bonnieplants.com

NICHOLS GARDEN NURSERY
1190 Old Salem Road NE
Albany, OR 97321-4580
800/422-3985
www.nicholsgardennursery.com

RENEE'S GARDEN SEEDS
6060A Graham Hill Road
Felton, CA 95018
888/880-7228
www.reneesgarden.com

RICHTERS HERBS
357 Highway 47
Goodwood, ON
LoC 1Ao Canada
800/668-4372
www.richters.com

SANDY MUSH HERB NURSERY
316 Surrett Cove Road
Leicester, NC 28748
828/683-2014
www.sandymushherbs.com

Specialty Supplies

ALLSOP HOME & GARDEN
660 North Main Street, Suite #220
Ketchum, ID 83340
866/425-5767
www.allsopgarden.com

CRESCENT GARDEN
877/477-0027
www.crescentgarden.com

GARDENER'S SUPPLY CO.
128 Intervale Road
Burlington, VT 05401
888/833-1412
www.gardeners.com

GEOHUMUS INTERNATIONAL
www.geohumus.com

INGENUITEA TEAPOT
www.adagio.com

**JAMALI FLORAL AND GARDEN
SUPPLIES**
149 West 28th Street
New York, NY 10001
212/996-5534
www.jamaligarden.com

KINSMAN CO.
P.O. Box 428
Pipersville, PA 18947
800/733-4146
www.kinsmangarden.com

LEE VALLEY TOOLS
P.O. Box 1780
Ogdensburg, NY 13669-6780
800/267-8735
www.leevalley.com

MUD GLOVES
26 Computer Drive East
Albany, NY 12205
866/916-1563
www.mudglove.com

**SIMPLE GARDEN JR.
FERTILE EARTH**
877/883-2784
www.fertileearth.com

index